most diligent of scholars. The attentive reader will especially value the rich body of primary materials that document this lively account of Funston's part in the fight for *Cuba Libre*. The scholarship is matched by the exceptional prose quality of the work, at once testament to the author's decades of success as a lawyer and his commitment of making history accessible to all."

—**William J. Crowe**, emeritus Dean of Libraries of the University of Kansas

---

"Frederick Funston, one of America's greatest and most romantic soldiers, has been all but forgotten by history. Clyde Toland's definitive trilogy on the Kansas hero has rescued Funston from this ill-deserved obscurity. This third volume in Toland's biography combines the author's graceful prose and insightful interpretation with a treasure trove of original letters and newspaper stories. The author has spent a lifetime on Funston's trail and the depth of his research is simply breathtaking. This is not only an invaluable biography of Funston but also a fascinating history of the important role a handful of American adventurers played in the Cuban Revolution. Their actions, and especially those of Funston, helped to bring the United States into the conflict and secure the liberation of Cuba. Of course, this was but the beginning of a remarkable military career that would see Funston's meteoric rise to high command. This is both solid history and a rousing adventure story that will captivate all readers of military history."

—**Paul Andrew Hutton**, Distinguished Professor of History, University of New Mexico

---

"'*Yankee Hero*' reminds us what a remarkable man Fred Funston was: remarkably brave, a thrill seeker, on the make, and a man who played a crucial role in the fight for Cuban independence as a commander of artillery in the Cuban Liberation Army. For me, the best part is that Clyde Toland mostly allows Funston to speak for himself. This makes parts of the book almost a collection of documents, which readers can use to draw their own conclusions about Funston and his times."

—**Dr. John Lawrence Tone**, Professor of History, The Georgia Institute of Technology and author of *War and Genocide in Cuba, 1895-1898*

"Yankee Hero":
Frederick Funston, Expedicionario in the Cuban Liberation Army,
1896-1897

Volume Three

of

Becoming Frederick Funston Trilogy:
A Tale of "cool courage, iron endurance,
and gallant daring"

Clyde W. Toland

Flint Hills Publishing

"Yankee Hero": Frederick Funston, Expedicionario in the Cuban Liberation Army, 1896-1897

Volume Three of *Becoming Frederick Funston Trilogy: A Tale of "cool courage, iron endurance, and gallant daring"*

Book Design by Carol Yoho

Cover Design by Amy Albright

Editorial Oversight, Thomas Fox Averill

This book was made possible by the Thomas Fox Averill Kansas Studies Collection, and through the generous support of the Washburn University Center for Kansas Studies.

Flint Hills Publishing
www.flinthillspublishing.com
Topeka, Kansas

Printed in the U.S.A.

ISBN: 978-1-953583-39-0
Library of Congress Control Number: 2022917014

Cover photo: Frederick Funston in the uniform of the Cuban Liberation Army. His blue baldric bears the two gold stars of a lieutenant colonel. Photograph taken on February 10, 1898, in Iola, Kansas.

Becoming Frederick Funston Trilogy
A Tale of "cool courage, iron endurance, and gallant daring"

This trilogy tells the story of the coming of age of Frederick Funston, the future famous United States Army Major General and American hero at his death in 1917. At age thirty-two, he discovered who he was, and the course of the balance of his life was set. In the process of self-discovery, he lived a fascinating life of adventure, and that life, and certain of the times in which he lived it, are told in this trilogy.

Volume One: *American Hero, Kansas Heritage: Frederick Funston's Early Years, 1865-1890*

Volume Two: *Heat and Ice: Frederick Funston's Exploration of Death Valley, Alaska, and the British Northwest Territory, 1891-1894*

Volume Three: *"Yankee Hero": Frederick Funston, Expedicionario in the Cuban Liberation Army, 1896-1897*

The **Becoming Frederick Funston Trilogy** has forty chapters. The biblical number forty generally symbolizes a period of testing, and these chapters tell, in part, the testing of Frederick Funston in the formative years of his life.

The research and writing of this trilogy were done over a period of twenty-four years (1995-2019). The available time to research and write was the controlling factor. If there are any inconsistencies or errors in style throughout this trilogy, they have persisted despite my best efforts to eradicate them. My apologies for any such inconsistencies or errors.

About the Author

Clyde W. Toland received a BA in history in 1969 from the University of Kansas, and in 1971 a MA in history from the University of Wisconsin-Madison. He received his JD from the University of Kansas in 1975. He is a member of Phi Beta Kappa and the Order of the Coif. Mr. Toland is a semi-retired lawyer in Iola, Kansas.

As a grade school student, he became fascinated by his local Allen County, Kansas, history and by Frederick Funston's early adventurous life in Death Valley, Alaska, the British Northwest Territory, and Cuba. For more than thirty-five years, he has been a student of Funston's life. As president of the Allen County Historical Society, Inc., in Iola, Kansas, he was the driving force in the successful move in 1994 of Frederick Funston's rural childhood home to the Iola town square and in its subsequent restoration and opening as a museum in 1995. He did the research and writing for most of the eleven exhibits in the Funston Museum and Visitors' Center, which opened in 1997 next door to the Funston Home Museum.

Mr. Toland founded the Buster Keaton Celebration, a nationally known humanities event held annually in Iola, Kansas, from 1993 through 2017. He served as co-chair of the Keaton Celebration Committee for the first five celebrations, and continued as a committee member through the 2005 celebration. He was a member of the committee which revived the Buster Keaton Celebration on September 24 and 25, 2021.

At age fifteen he became a Life Member of both the Allen County Historical Society, Inc., and the Kansas State Historical Society. Mr. Toland and United States Senator Nancy Kassebaum Baker in 1996 were the two first recipients of the Alumni Distinguished Achievement Award from the College of Liberal Arts and Sciences of the University of Kansas.

For
Nancy, my wife

Our children and their spouses:
David and Beth
Andrew and Anna
Elizabeth and Bart

Our grandchildren:
Caroline
William
Charlotte
Isaac

Institutional, Book, and Article Credits for Illustrations:

Institutions:
Allen County Historical Society, Inc., Iola, Kansas
Cover photo and pages 18, 188, 189

Kansas State Historical Society, Topeka, Kansas
Pages 19, 38, 166, 190, 191

Library of Congress
Pages 94-97

Books:
Frederick Funston, *Memories of Two Wars*
(Scribner's Edition)
Pages 37, 41, 61 (bottom), 91, 92 (top), 93, 125, 165

Frederick Funston, *Memories of Two Wars*
(Constable Edition)
Pages 40, 92 (bottom), 126 (bottom)

Gonzalo de Quesada, *The War in Cuba* (1896)
Pages B, 57, 58, 59, 60, 89

Horatio S. Rubens, *Liberty: The Story of Cuba*
Page 39

Marcus F. Wright, *The Official and Pictorial Record of the Story of American Expansion* (1904)
Pages 17 (bottom), 61 (top), 90, 126 (top), 127

Articles:
Frederick Funston, "Desmayo – The Cuban Balaklava"
Page 75

Charles S. Gleed, "Romance And Reality In A Single Life. Gen. Frederick Funston"
Page 17 (top)

"History is the essence of innumerable biographies."

—**Thomas Carlyle** (1795-1881)

* * *

"War makes rattling good history..."

—**Thomas Hardy** (1840-1928)

* * *

"There are men ready to lead without reward, to suffer for others, and to burn so they may shed the light."

—*José Marti* (1853-1895)
Writer, orator, poet and martyr who inspired and organized the Cuban Revolution of 1895 in which he was killed in battle

* * *

"[B]efore entering the service of the United States I was already the seasoned veteran of a terribly bloody and destructive war."

—**Frederick Funston** (1912)

* * *

"Funston and myself we were <u>very</u> <u>good</u> <u>friends</u>. We fought many times together, and heard the same bullets.... He was a good, honest and brave man."

—**Luis R. Miranda** (1932)
Formerly of the Cuban Liberation Army

* * *

"If there ever was a hero in this country it is Fred Funston.... He is brave, gentle and generous and he deserves every kindness that has come to him."

—**William Allen White** (1898)

* * *

"What a man [Funston] is! He is my ideal of the American volunteer.... I saw [in 1898] that he was every inch a man. I admire him greatly. He is a corker... My, what a fighter he is! What a dare-devil! How I would like to be with him with a troop of rough riders. The [Twentieth] Kansas boys and my boys would be invincible."

—**Theodore Roosevelt** (1899)

* * *

"Fred Funston is my ideal of a commander."

—**Wilder S. Metcalf**
Funston's fellow officer in the
Twentieth Kansas

* * *

"Funston was a first-class fighting man who served his country loyally and ably."

—**General John J. Pershing**

* * *

"[Frederick Funston] was a man of deeds, not words, and to say more would be displeasing to his soul. We know his worth and service, and he will not soon be forgotten among us."

—**Rev. William Kirk Guthrie**
Sermon at Funston's funeral

* * *

"Frederick Funston was a national hero and the object of great national affection."

—***The Miami Herald***
Editorial on Funston's death

* * *

Table of Contents

Table of Contents, *continued*

For Cuba.

By Maurice Thompson

Have you heard the call from Cuba
   Coming northward on the breeze?
Have you seen the dark cloud hanging
   To the southward o'er the seas?

It is a gasp for liberty,
   That shudders on the air;
Spain has relit her torture-fire,
   And men are writhing there.

Oppression's tempest gathers force,
   Its tidal wave rolls high;
Old Europe's shadow dims the stars
   We kindled in the sky.

The time is come for action,
   Now let the right prevail;
Shall all our boasted sympathy
   With slaves downtrodden fail?

Shall we be mockers of the faith
   By which our course was set?
Shall we deny what we received
   From men like Lafayette?

Help! help! the swarthy patriots cry,
   While Spaniards beat them down,
Because they will not bend the knee
   To one who wears a crown.

The hoary, mediaeval lie,
   That robes the power of kings,
And rivets chains on bleeding hands,
   Once more its logic brings.

At subtle diplomatic pleas
   Let free-born statesmen scoff;
Poor, drowning Cuba grips our skirt,
   Shall Freedom shake her off?

Oh no! fling out the fleet and flag,
   To shield her from the storm,
And let that splendid Island feel
   The clasp of Freedom's arm.

The poem *For Cuba* "aptly voices the feeling of the American people" and was published in *The War in Cuba* by Señor Gonzalo de Quesada, Chargé d'Affaires of the Republic of Cuba, at Washington, D.C. and Henry Davenport Northrop (Chicago: Monarch Book Company, 1896). The famous American novelist and poet Maurice Thompson (1844-1901) is probably the Maurice Thompson to whom this poem is attributed in *The War in Cuba.*

A

The Provinces of Cuba in 1896

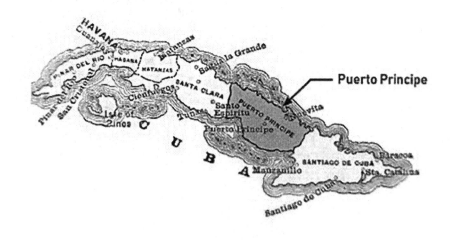

INTRODUCTION

In 1895, the people of Cuba launched a new revolution against their oppressor, Spain. Young men living elsewhere not only read news accounts of the fighting but some of them chose to join it on behalf of the revolutionists, who were also known as insurgents. Horace Walinski, who was of Polish descent, came from England. A former English marine soldier, Arthur Potter, who had lived in the United States for several years, joined. Canadian Charles Huntington, who had served in the Northwest Mounted Police and who also had lived in the United States for a few years, was attracted to the cause of *Cuba Libre* (Free Cuba).

From the United States came most of the *expedicionarios*, as these volunteer fighters were called. They were primarily from the East and Midwest, and some were from middle to upper-middle class families. Arthur Royal Joyce and W. R. Welsford were from Connecticut and New Jersey, respectively. James Pennie of Washington, D. C., was a St. John's College, Annapolis, graduate. Walter Moses Jones, a New York State native, did not have to travel far to join the *Ejercito Libertador de Cuba* (Cuban Liberation Army), since he had lived in Cuba for ten years. William Smith had served in the United States cavalry, and James Devine was a former Texas Ranger.

Other young men who made the sea journey to the war-torn "Queen of the Antilles" included Charles Gordon, Joseph Napoleon Chapleau—a volatile and dashing figure who was to acquire a reputation for daredevil exploits, Emory W. Fenn, Joseph "Pepe" D'Estrampas of New Orleans, and William Cox, who hailed from Philadelphia. Dr. Harry Danforth, a surgeon from Milwaukee, did not go to Cuba to fight but to be a medical officer. He survived this war but was killed by a Spanish sharpshooter's bullet to the head while tending the wounded after an 1898 Cuban battle during the Spanish-American War. From St. Louis came T. Rosser Roemer and Harry Hillegass. Other gallant Americans included Flood, McBride, and Frederic, who all gave their lives for *Cuba Libre*.

A University of Pennsylvania sophomore, whose name is now unknown, was killed in battle in 1896. His fellow Penn student, Osmun Latrobe, a great-grandson of the architect who designed the United States Capitol, and Johns Hopkins graduate Stuart Janney were close friends and scions of prominent Baltimore families. To join the fight, they slipped out of the city without telling their parents. Twenty-one-year-old Latrobe wrote to his "dear Papa": "It grieves me more

1

than I can tell you to leave you in this manner, but I think you can see why it was necessary for me to do so. So please do not think badly of me for I am now on the water on my way to join the insurgents in Cuba. Surely there can be no disgrace in fighting with them for their good cause against unjust Spain."

The most famous of the *expedicionarios* at that time was 25-year-old Winchester Dana Osgood, an outstanding amateur athlete. The son of an army officer, "Win" Osgood was a student at Cornell University first, and then at the University of Pennsylvania where he received bachelor's and master's degrees in civil engineering. He was "also a good French and Spanish scholar and was well-versed in English literature." Osgood was a star football player, oarsman, bicyclist, tennis player, boxer, wrestler, and all-round gymnast. Known as the "American Firebrand," Osgood was the object of devotion by the Pennsylvania student body, whose cheer was "Who's good, Osgood, the whole damn team's good." This was shouted by the students even in the Chapel "under the Provost's nose." He belonged to a church and was greatly interested in the work of the Young Men's Christian Association.

Built like an Achilles, when Osgood stripped he revealed almost perfect muscular development that rivaled that of his slightly older contemporary, Eugen Sandow, the famous German bodybuilder and showman, who today is considered the father of modern bodybuilding. Although Osgood possessed tremendous physical strength, he was a gentle and bashful soul. He neither smoked nor drank nor swore. He joined the Cuban Liberation Army primarily from a sense of fairness, a desire for adventure, and a liking for army life. He may also have sought to forget a failed romance. In joining the Cuban Liberation Army, football-great Osgood stated that he wanted to "get into the game."

At five feet, eight inches and 160 pounds, Osgood was four inches taller and forty pounds heavier than a fellow American who was later to become even more famous than the athletic Osgood—five feet, four inch, 120-pound Frederick Funston. A nationally unknown figure at age thirty when he joined the Cuban Liberation Army, Funston, at his death in 1917, was a Major General in the United States Army, and, as *The Miami Herald* editorialized, was "a national hero and the object of great national affection." President Woodrow Wilson personally wrote a letter of condolence to Funston's widow.

Funston, who was known as Fred Funston, was born on November 9, 1865, in an upstairs room of the Mitchell House, the hotel owned by his maternal grandmother in New Carlisle, Ohio. His parents, Edward Funston, known as Ed, and his mother, Ann Eliza Funston, who went by Lida, were physical opposites of each other. He was six feet, two inches in height, while she was either four feet, eleven inches or five feet, two inches (the sources disagree). He weighed about 225 pounds; she weighed ninety pounds; had a nineteen-inch waist; and wore a size-one shoe. Ed had a booming voice, and in his political career was known as "Foghorn" Funston. He served as speaker of the Kansas House of Representatives and as president of the Kansas Senate before being elected to Congress in 1884, where he served until 1894.

Even though Ed had a large personality, that fact and the ten inch, approximately 100 pound difference in physical size of father and son did not prevent their having a close relationship. Fred was the only one of his father's six children not in awe of him. Fred respected his father and confided in him. His droll observations as a youth precipitated roaring laughter from the elder Funston. Fred was devoted throughout his life to his mother; perhaps this was, in part, because they shared short physical stature.

In January of 1868, Civil War Union Army veteran Ed purchased a 162-acre upland prairie farm in Allen County, Kansas. That spring, Lida, with their first-born, Fred, and baby Burt, traveled from Ohio, first by train and then by stagecoach, to join Ed. As they traveled on the train, two-year-old Fred picked out the ABCs on station signs. This farm was to be Ed and Lida's home for the balance of their lives, and Fred's until his marriage in 1898.

Fred had a typical upbringing as a farm boy. When he and Burt were small children, their father stationed them at opposite ends of his fields so that he could plow his furrows straight. As older boys, they helped with the plowing, harvest, and other farm chores. This hard work benefited Fred physically. An 1899 description noted: "Although small in stature, he has a magnificent physique. He can withstand hardships and exertions under which many a larger man would succumb."

When he was not working, Fred loved to fish and to swim in nearby Deer Creek, to hunt, and to read. Ed's library, stocked with the classics, was one of the finest in the county. Fred read all of these books as well as borrowing others from neighbors. He read history, adventure, and everything he could obtain of a military nature. From the age of sixteen, he subscribed to a humorous publication. He loved jokes but seldom made one. He was constantly whistling.

Fred attended nearby Maple Grove School, a typical wooden, one-room rural schoolhouse, where one year about seventy students of all ages were taught. "Fred was recognized as a thorough student bubbling over with fun and full of all sorts of practical jokes. He always saw the funny side of any situation and was quick to analyze the situation." Fred also occasionally engaged in fist fights. Although he was small, he was wiry and fearless. He worshipped with his family at the Presbyterian Church near the tiny community of Carlyle located northeast of the Funston farm.

Finishing his studies at Maple Grove School about 1882, Fred, at age eighteen, attended briefly in the spring of 1884 a business college in Lawrence, Kansas. Ed Funston had been a lieutenant in the Union artillery during the Civil War, and Fred was an avid listener to his father's war stories. Not surprisingly, Fred competed that spring for an appointment to West Point. Although his five-feet, four-inch height exceeded the minimum height requirement, he came up short in the competitive examination, placing third. His score was impressive, however, since it was only slightly more than two points below that of the successful older candidate. Military fame and glory would have to wait fifteen years.

Fred struck out on his own in the fall of 1884. Boarding at a nearby farmer's home, he taught at a rural stone schoolhouse about ten miles from the Funston home. The school was popularly known as "Stoney Lonesome" because of its composition and location. During his one term as a pedagogue, Fred's most notable experience was successfully disarming the school bully who brought a gun to school. This was accomplished only after a violent fist fight and struggle between teacher and pupil. The rest of the class was so scared by this that they fled by jumping through the building's open windows.

In the fall of 1885, Fred entered the Iola High School, where he was classified as a senior. The town of Iola is located five miles from the Funston farm, and Fred daily made the ten-mile round trip by riding a horse of a volcanic disposition which had the desire to throw his rider. Fred was not deterred. He so enjoyed such physical challenges that he would occasionally mount a wild calf while a friend held the calf in place, and then holding the calf's tail and after it was let loose, he would ride it as it tried to throw him.

Fred was of a restless and adventurous disposition and uncertain what he wanted to do with his life. After graduating from high school in May of 1886, he attended the State University of Kansas in Lawrence for one year before leaving to work. This one year was an important one for him, however. He pledged the social fraternity Phi Delta Theta, where he became close friends with several young men who, like himself, were to become nationally famous. One was William Allen White, the future Pulitzer-prize-winning editor of the *Emporia* (Kansas) *Gazette* newspaper. His nickname was Billy and Fred's was Timmy. By those names, Billy and Timmy enjoyed a friendship severed only by Fred's death thirty years later.

After leaving the university, Fred first spent the summer working as the rodman for a railroad survey crew. Then, briefly, he was a newspaper reporter in Kansas City, before fulfilling the same role in Fort Smith, Arkansas. There he became acquainted with the notorious hanging judge, Isaac Parker. Working for a Democratic newspaper did not suit Republican Fred. When the newspaper's owner was out-of-town one day, Fred was left in charge, and editorially condemned the Democratic Party. He soon left town. "I thought likely it might come out that way," Fred explained to his Kansas friends when he came back, "but I didn't like the town and I didn't like my boarding house, and I didn't like the job and I thought I might as well let them know I had been there before I quit." The newspaper never recovered from the uproar he had created. It failed.

Fred's next job had more permanence to it. For the year of 1888, he was a ticket collector for the Santa Fe Railway. He also bounced from the train cowboys who did not have the required fare. In response to Fred's request for his ticket, one cowboy pulled his revolver and responded, "I ride on this." Fred's response was laconic: "That's good, that's good." Later, he returned with a large-bore rifle and announced that he had come to "punch that ticket." Presumably, the cowboy complied. Fred returned to the university for the spring 1889 semester and the year 1889-1890. It had become obvious to him that it was time to move on. One legacy of his college education was a tremendous desire to be independent. Although he did not know what he wanted to do, he knew that the academic world was no longer for him.

Fred and his good friend, the future noted entomologist Vernon Kellogg, spent the beginning of the summer of 1890 in Colorado collecting natural history specimens for the university. They had a nearly fatal experience when a blizzard developed while they were scaling a mountain. Fred turned this experience into his first published article, the thrilling "Storm Bound above the Clouds."

Fred's restlessness and love of adventure showed clearly in his next employment, which was for the United States Department of Agriculture. In 1891, he was a botanist and explorer in Death Valley as a member of the first scientific expedition to venture into the valley's hellish heat. Next, for nearly three years, 1892-1894, botanist Funston, usually alone, explored Alaska and the British Northwest Territory as far north as the Arctic Ocean, where whalers played baseball in 47° below zero weather. Fred's explorations and extraordinary adventures as a botanist are the subject of volume two of this trilogy of the early life of Frederick Funston.

Leaving government service at the end of 1894, Fred set out on a course which ultimately led to his departure for Cuba. He had not yet figured out who he was. Although his short height did not affect his close relationship with his father, Fred was still self-conscious about his stature. Also, he had exhibited since childhood an "illimitable clumsiness," "a great natural awkwardness." He stumbled over any obstacle that another person would simply step over. On the Death Valley Expedition, he had several clumsy incidents where he fell into small bodies of water. Additionally, he had been unsuccessful in love. His most recent love had dumped him in early 1893. He subsequently described himself as always "damned small potatoes" with the girls. The crucible of the Cuban war was to change all of this.

Fred left for Cuba in August of 1896. He was not to return until January of 1898. He memorialized his military adventures in the Cuban war of independence in *Memories of Two Wars: Cuban and Philippine Experiences*. First published in 1911, after being serialized, in part, in 1910 in *Scribner's Magazine*, this book is exactly what one would expect from Fred Funston. Well-written with crisp prose, vivid language and descriptions, and typically self-deprecating, this work provides a highly detailed account of his experiences in the Cuban revolution and in the subsequent war in the Philippines. It is a delight to read, and I heartily recommend it, both for reading pleasure and for learning, in addition to what I present in the following chapters, further details about his military experiences in the Cuban Liberation Army.

Like any memoir written a number of years after an event or series of events, *Memories* represents what Fred recalled and felt in 1910, and thus, as a record, lacks contemporariness with his experiences. Fortunately, twenty of his letters have survived in whole or in part. Written while he was in Cuba and in New York City before and after his Cuban adventures, they are invaluable, since they are unfiltered by hindsight and since even the best of memories can fade over time and facts and feelings can be incorrectly remembered or even forgotten. Fred also wrote an article about the battle of Desmayo, which has the concreteness of the recently-lived account. Using his letters and the battle of Desmayo article in their entirety surpasses paraphrasing them no matter how well that might be done.

Fred's letters provide the framework in this book for his final story of adventure before he began his career as a soldier for Uncle Sam. Necessary detail to connect and explain events described in these letters comes largely from *Memories of Two Wars,* thus allowing Fred to tell his adventurous story in his own graphic prose.

The letters of Fred Funston are a rich contribution to the literature of war as the story of one soldier. They show his evolution from the impassioned idealist, determined to help boot Spain from that war-torn island, to the seasoned, battle-scarred, war-weary veteran. The Cuban war was also a crucible out of which Fred emerged knowing, at last, at age thirty-two, who he was. He had come of age.

Before telling Fred's story, how many Americans were *expedicionarios*? In an 1898 interview soon after his return from Cuba, Fred provided this assessment: "I don't think there are more than 20 who are [now] actively engaged in the war. At one time the number was much larger, but one by one they have been killed or have returned to the United States.... There is no fun in it, and very little romance. Of course, it is exciting, but that is an inducement which, by itself, seldom keeps men in such a position of danger and hardship as Cuban soldiers occupy."

Asked to describe the "class of Americans" remaining in Cuba, Fred responded: "Mostly adventurers, men who fight for fame or glory, and some few for possible gain. Then there are a few sentimental chaps, some prodigal sons and a few fugitives." Fred subsequently claimed that eighty-two Americans had been *expedicionarios* and that only twenty-three "survive today." Those who did not survive rested in forgotten graves, having, in Fred's words in 1910, "assisted the Cubans in their struggle for independence, but whose very names are not known by the people for whom they gave their lives."

Although this book tells the story of soldier Fred Funston in the Cuban Liberation Army, through his experiences it is also the story of all of the courageous young men who chose to leave the comfort of their homes, and, in the words of Fred Funston, to fight in "a strange land for a cause not their own." My admiration for them knows no bounds, and it is to their memory that I dedicate this book.

CHAPTER ONE

A "Highly Moral Lecture," a Coffee Plantation, and the Cuban Fair

January 4, 1895 – May 27, 1896

A Mexican coffee bean was Gen. Frederick Funston's lucky stone.

Twenty years ago he, an obscure young Kansan, gambled with Fate's dice in the form of coffee beans—and lost. But Fate, unknown to him, had "coppered" his bet for him, so that in losing the hazard of ephemeral dollars he won the stake of eternal fame.

—Frank Lundy Webster,
investor in the Rio Coachapa Plantation Company

Fred Funston began the year of 1895 with his first public lecture about his Alaskan and Yukon experiences. Given on January 4, his presentation was, appropriately, in the Opera House at Iola and in appreciation of the "kind reception" that the people of Iola had so recently given him on his return home, Fred charged no fee for his services. The admission fee of twenty-five cents benefited the Young Men's Guild.[1] "The house was crowded and the people showed by their hearty cheering that they were well pleased."[2]

The next evening, Saturday, January 5, Fred lectured at no charge at his church, the Presbyterian Church in Carlyle. His talk was "very interesting and instructive, and was well received by a crowded house."[3] Two evenings later he lectured, again at no charge, at the nearby community of Geneva. The sum of fifteen cents per couple was charged for the benefit of the Congregational Church.[4]

According to Fred's father, Fred initially made no charge for his services, since "he wanted to see how the people liked it before he charged to hear him." Ed Funston also recollected his impression of Fred's talk at the Carlyle Church: "I went and I want to say it was one of the most interesting lectures I ever heard. I was surprised to hear the boy do so well. He used to be one of the best in reciting pieces at the literary when he attended the Maple Grove School, but I never expected him to deliver such a good lecture."[5]

Having shared first with the people of Allen County, at the end of the week Fred told of his far north experiences at Lawrence. A benefit for the university's Athletic Association,[6] the presentation was given on January 11 at the Opera House with the "stage title" of "Beyond the Yukon." "When dressed in his Esquimaux suit," observed one reporter, "he looks very much like the tallow eating inhabitants of the far north."[7] "[F]or over two hours Fred Funston delightfully entertained his audience with vivid word pictures of the trials and hardships through which he passed. These were illustrated with scenes reproduced on the canvas from kodak pictures taken by him in that country, many of them showing sights never before pictured for the purpose."[8] In the audience were Fred's longtime friends, Professor Will Franklin from Ames, Iowa, and Will's sister, Nellie (Franklin) Troutman, of Kansas City.[9]

For subsequent lectures Fred at times broadened his talk's title to "In the Yukon Land and Beyond."[10] For his lecture in Chanute, eighteen miles south of Iola, he purchased a large newspaper advertisement, which described him as "The Great Alaskan Explorer," in which he noted that he would show 150 views "on Canvas by Electricity." His talk was described as "The Greatest Moral and Instructive Lecture of the Season."[11] And so the lecture tour continued for some weeks.

Frank Lundy Webster, the editor in the 1890s of *The Lawrence Daily Gazette* in Lawrence, was one of Fred's friends. Many years later he succinctly described Fred and his state of mind: "In the spring of 1895 Funston had been out thru Kansas with what he was pleased to term his 'highly moral lecture' on his Alaskan experiences. It was an interesting entertainment and successful in a small way, but distasteful to him. Then, as always, he preferred doing things to talking about them."[12]

At that time, there was significant interest in Kansas concerning the possibility of establishing a coffee bean operation in Mexico. Several companies were formed in Kansas City for the purpose of developing lands on the Isthmus of Tehuantepec. The plan was to sell to various investors a few acres each of raw land out of a large tract. The company's responsibility would be to clear the land; plant the coffee bushes; cultivate the plants; and, hopefully, produce a crop of coffee beans.

Fred and Frank Webster were "quite excited over the opportunities," but decided on a grander plan—rather than selling land, they would organize a company that would actually operate a big coffee plantation. Fred ended his lecture tour and attended in April at least one more party with his Lawrence friends. A reporter described this social event: "The closing ball of the Chesterfield Club was given at Fraternal Aid hall last evening and the party was decidedly the most elegant of the many they have given. Drawing room decorations were disposed with pleasing effect and flowers added to make the interior attractive to the dancers. Bell's orchestra music was furnished for the dancing." A large number of couples and single persons attended, including Frank Webster and his wife and Fred Funston and his close friend, Buck Franklin.[13]

A week later, on May 1, Fred visited friends in Iola to tell them good-bye. His good friend, Charlie Scott, wrote in his newspaper, *The Iola Register*, that Fred "has got an idea that there is some money in the coffee business in the Tehuantepec country in southern Mexico and he is going down there to look into it." Fred expected to be gone about six weeks.[14] *The Emporia Gazette* noted that Fred was "going down to see if he can't get thawed out after his walk across Alaska."[15] When Fred left Lawrence for his trip to Mexico on May 18, he took with him "a fine photography outfit."[16]

For unknown reasons, the *Garnett Republican-Plaindealer,* located in the town of Garnett, thirty miles north of Iola, sniped at Fred's latest venture: "Fred Funston, son of the ex-Congressman Funston, has discovered that he wasn't a success in the lecture field or else the people were not interested in his trip through Alaska and has quit and will now try coffee raising in Mexico. He is likely to find something out in that country, and possibly coffee raising will not be so much in his line as corn and hogs in Kansas."[17] The newspaper's editor clearly had no conception of what motivated Fred. Charlie Scott editorially responded to the charges of the *Plaindealer*: "Fred Funston cleared $1200 during the three months he was in the lecture field. That was fairly good success, was it not Bro. *Plaindealer*? Fred Funston never made a failure at anything yet."[18] In 2022 dollars, $1200 is approximately $41,000. Not bad for three months work at a job one does not like. Making large sums of money clearly was not the driving force in Fred's life. Opportunities for adventure and action were another matter.

In Mexico City, Fred visited the British Consul General, Sir Lionel Carden, the executor of an estate that owned vast tracts of land in the Isthmus of Tehuantepec. These lands were located in the State of Vera Cruz on the Coachapa River, a navigable tributary of the Coatsacoalous River, which flows into the Gulf of Mexico. After selecting the lands that he wanted, Fred returned to Mexico City where he secured from Carden a purchase option on 5,000 acres of land at $2.50 per acre. Fred would not see Sir Lionel Carden again until 1914, when Fred was commanding the United States Army troops occupying the city of Vera Cruz and Sir Lionel was the "British Ambassador" to Mexico.[19]

In all his campaign General Funston carried a 45-calibre pistol that extended from his waist to his knee—not a long way, at that. When he came ashore at Vera Cruz to take command of the city, Admirals Fletcher and Badger, with their staffs, were drawn up in line to greet him. They were in white, with shining swords and accoutrements. The General was in his olive drab uniform, without a blouse, and had his enormous pistol strapped to his waist.

The British Consul was there with his staff, too, and failing to see any resplendent officer with gold and lace, he asked: "Where is the General? Is he the little Chinaman at the head of the column, or is that just an American artillery regiment?" General Funston often told the story himself.[20]

By early July 1895, Fred was back home in Kansas. Charlie Scott reported the latest news about Fred: "He thinks it is a great country to make money, but a mighty tough one to live in."[21] Fred's close friend, Charlie Gleed, who became an investor in this coffee plantation scheme, recalled several years later the difficulties of the venture: "Land considered suitable for raising coffee, ordinarily has on it a very dense vegetable growth. This has to be cleared away so that the coffee may have room. The business is as profitable as it is unattractive on other accounts, and Funston felt certain that in a reasonable time he could make competency, and he went at the enterprise with his usual vigor."[22]

Charlie Scott noted with pleasure in the September 6 issue of *The Iola Register* that "Fred Funston's fame is not confined to his home county or State." A friend had sent Charlie an item from a South Dakota newspaper, which incorrectly noted that Fred had "slept out of doors in every State, Province and Territory west of the Mississippi between the Arctic circle and the Rio Grande river, with the exception of two. Mr. Funston is yet well on the sunny side of 30, and if he keeps up his present luck until he is ready to retire, he will see about all the world that is worth looking at."[23]

Fred's next step was to raise $100,000 (approximately $3,400,000 in 2022 dollars) to finance the corporation. During at least part of the summer Fred lived in Lawrence, but, as he wrote his mother on August 20, he occasionally went to "Kansas City Leavenworth and

Topeka on business connected with the company that I am getting up to start a plantation in Mexico. I do not know yet when I shall come down home."[24] Charlie Scott reported on September 20 that Fred had been in Iola that week concerning his Mexican coffee enterprise. "He has been busy this summer organizing a company with a capital of $100,000 to take hold of the business, and the stock is now nearly all taken."[25] What Charlie Scott did not tell his readers was that he was personally involved in Fred's new company.

On October 20, both *The Topeka Daily Capital* and *The Kansas City Daily Journal* announced the filing the day before with the Kansas Secretary of State of articles of incorporation for Fred's new corporation, The Rio Coachapa Plantation Company.[26] The charter of the corporation designated its places of business as Lawrence, Kansas, and in the Canton of Minatitlan, State of Vera Cruz, Mexico. The incorporators adopted broad purposes for which the corporation was formed:

(1) To transact a manufacturing, mining, mechanical, chemical, mercantile and agricultural and produce business;
(2) To encourage agriculture and horticulture;
(3) To build and navigate steamboats and carry persons and property thereon; and
(4) The conversion and disposal of agricultural products.[27]

There were five incorporators: the Lawrence newspaperman Frank L. Webster, Frederick Funston, C. S. Gleed, D. E. Palmer, and Clad Hamilton. C.S. Gleed was Fred's Topeka attorney friend, Charles "Charlie" Gleed. D.E. Palmer may have been David E. Palmer, a Topeka businessman, and Clad Hamilton was a Topeka attorney.

Seven directors were named in the charter: Charles S. Gleed, W. J. Patterson of New York City, Charles F. Scott of Iola, Frederick Funston of Minatitlan, Mexico, Frank L. Webster, Wilder S. Metcalf, and A. Henley, the last three of Lawrence, Kansas.[28] Wilder Metcalf was to become an officer serving with Fred in the Twentieth Kansas Volunteer Infantry formed in 1898 at the start of the Spanish-American War. The corporate officers were Charles S. Gleed, president; Frank L. Webster, secretary; Fred Funston, manager; and Paul R. Brooks, treasurer.[29]

In the October 25 issue of *The Iola Register* under the headline "Fred Funston's Coffee Plantation," Charlie Scott reported the incorporation of the company, quoting at length *The Topeka Daily Capital* article, but omitting the portion of the story identifying the officers and directors, including himself. Charlie did note that manager Fred would go about November 1 to begin the "work of improving the plantation." He had already hired 200 Mexican Indians to start clearing

400 acres which would be planted with coffee trees the following year. "The land is unimproved and is covered with a dense tropical forest. Its surface is rolling and hilly, an absolute requirement for the successful cultivation of coffee. The soil composed of the decayed vegetable matter of many centuries is from fifteen to twenty feet deep and perfectly friable and mellow."[30]

The Kansas City Star gave Fred a ringing endorsement in connection with his anticipated departure to manage "a coffee plantation, owned by himself and other Kansas men..." Although not completely factually correct, this editorial compliment to the energetic Allen County young man is of interest. Fred "is full of the spirit of adventure and enterprise, and more than that, his undertakings all have been successful. Under thirty years of age he has slept in the open air in every state and territory west of the Missouri river except one; in Alaska, and in the countries of Central America and Mexico; in other words, in the three zones north of the equator. In the Dead [sic] Valley in the United States he has endured the greatest heat man ever has encountered, and in the North Frigid zone within two degrees of the greatest cold a white man ever has encountered. Through it all he has retained the vigorous health inherited from his parents, and the information and experience he has gained in his exploration have given him a standing in the scientific world that few men attain. He is a Kansas youth and Kansas people are proud of him."[31]

The October 23 *Lawrence Daily Journal* assessed the new venture: "The Lawrence folks who have bought some fine coffee lands down in the south country, have secured a charter, and are now about ready for work. The burden will fall upon the shoulders of Fred Funston who is a hard worker and an untiring rustler. The capital is largely supplied by Lawrence men, and the new company certainly has the best wishes of all."[32]

As Frank Webster remembered years later, because of poor economic conditions, not only in Kansas but throughout the country, only about $20,000 was raised in stock subscriptions in Kansas.[33] Charlie Gleed recollected, differently, that Fred's efforts to raise funds were "so complete and satisfactory that half of the required capital was forthcoming at once in Kansas, in spite of the prevailing hard economic conditions."[34] In any event, in late 1895, Fred traveled to New York City to raise the remaining capital needed. He likely was assisted in his efforts by Charlie Gleed, who was a director of the Atchison, Topeka, and Santa Fe Railway company, and a man with important connections in New York City, where he apparently resided part of the time.

According to Frank Webster, Fred persuaded "one capitalist" to agree to invest $50,000 in the corporation.[35] I suspect this had already occurred, since a "W. J. Patterson of New York City" was one of the initial seven corporate directors, a logical position to be held by such a substantial investor. Fred returned home for Christmas and planned to stay for a week or two before returning to New York City "to complete the financial part of his Coffee Plantation project. He hopes to have everything arranged by the first of February." In reporting this to his readers, Charlie Scott maintained his silence about his own involvement in the project.[36]

Charlie Gleed claimed later that Fred "met the usual fate of modest men who came to New York for money, in that he was promptly turned down."[37] That may be a part of the story, but it is not all of it. Frank Webster recalled the fate of the capitalist who had agreed to invest the $50,000: "The 'Angel' went back to Ohio to spend the holidays and died there suddenly."[38] The net result was that it was impossible to raise the necessary capital, and The Rio Coachapa Plantation failed before ever getting off the ground. This financial obstacle was one that even the resourceful, industrious Fred Funston could not overcome.

In order to support himself while living in New York City, Fred engaged two jobs. One he was well-suited for and clearly enjoyed. He wrote articles for *Harper's Weekly*, *Scribner's Magazine*, and the *Bond Record* based on his Alaskan experiences. For *Harper's Weekly*, he wrote "Along Alaska's Eastern Boundary" which was published in the February 1, 1896, issue, and for which Fred was paid $75.

He received $50 from *Harper's* for a second article, which, he noted in June 1895, was to be published "soon."[39] Which article this was, is unknown, since no such article was published that summer. Perhaps *Harper's* saved this article for later publication, and if so, the editors benefited from Fred's national military fame a few years later. In 1899, *Harper's* published "Baseball Among the Arctic Whalers" in their children's magazine, *Harper's Round Table*, describing the author as Brig. Gen. Frederick Funston, U.S.V. (United States Volunteers). In December 1900, *Harper's Weekly* published Fred's article, "Across the Great Divide in Midwinter," the author of which was described as Brigadier General Frederick Funston. Either of these may have been the $50 article, since it is unimaginable that Fred would be writing magazine articles while fighting in the Philippines in 1899 and 1900. Also, he would not have needed the additional income as an author, since he was receiving military pay.

Fred received $50 for writing for the *Bond Record* of May 1896 his article about the resources of Alaska, "The Territory of Alaska. From a Commercial Standpoint." His most lucrative article he wrote for

Scribner's Magazine, which paid him $150.[40] The lengthy "Over The Chilkoot Pass To The Yukon" appeared in the November 1896 issue. All total, Fred's remuneration for his writings about Alaska came to $325 (about $11,000 in 2022 dollars).

Fred's other job to support himself was not to his liking. As Charlie Gleed later recollected, once Fred's personal funds ran out while he was in New York City, Gleed secured for him the position of "deputy comptroller" of the Atchison, Topeka and Santa Fe Railway, which was undergoing a reorganization in bankruptcy. Fred's sole duty for the next two or three months was to sign his name to bonds and stock certificates issued by the railway company.[41] "'My duty was to don a high hat and a Prince Albert coat every morning and go down to the Santa Fe executive offices,' said Funston, in relating the story to friends. 'All I had to do in the morning was to sign my name to hundreds of bonds and stock certificates. At noon I maintained the dignity of my position by dining at the finest hotel in New York—on my expense account—and in the afternoon I returned to my sumptuous office and signed my name a lot more. I got writer's cramp and the position was not an enjoyable one.'"[42] Fred was practical in signing his name to these securities, writing only "F. Funston."[43] For his services, he was paid $10 a day.[44] In 2022 dollars, Fred's daily pay was about $340.

In mid-April 1896, Charlie Scott characterized Fred's current situation: "For a conservative quiet man who always tries to treat everybody right Fred Funston has met with a singular series of vicissitudes. He is now signing his name as assistant secretary or something of the kind to $210,000,000 of Santa Fe bonds."[45] In his eulogy following Fred's death, Charlie Gleed observed: "I have often thought that perhaps the task of signing his name steadily for three months drove him to desperation."[46] Clearly, Fred Funston, man of independence, adventure, and action, needed a new challenge appropriate for him. It was not long before opportunity knocked:

> I happened to be in New York City in 1896, and one evening in the spring or early summer [it was May 27] was strolling past Madison Square Garden, and impelled by curiosity dropped in to see the Cuban Fair then in progress.
>
> This fair, promoted by resident Cubans and American sympathizers with the cause of Cuban independence, was held ostensibly for the purpose of raising funds for the purchase of hospital supplies for the insurgent forces in the field, but a subsequent acquaintance with what was being done on the distracted Island justifies a suspicion that more of the money was expended for dynamite and cartridges than for quinine

and bandages.

The principal attraction at the fair on the occasion of my visit was a fiery and eloquent speech by Gen. Daniel E. Sickles, well known to be one of the most valued friends of the Cubans in their struggle.

Since the outbreak of the insurrection I had taken considerable interest in its progress, and had indulged myself in a vague sort of idea that I would like to take part in it, I fear as much from a love of adventure and a desire to see some fighting as from any more worthy motive. Of course, I shared the prevailing sympathy of my countrymen with the Cubans, and believed their cause a worthy one. Whatever doubts I may previously have had on the expediency of mixing up in the rows of other people vanished after hearing General Sickles's speech, and I returned to my room that evening with my mind made up and spent a sleepless night, as befits one who has just determined on going to his first war.[47]

"Funston and His Party On a Mexican River Searching for Coffee Lands"

The Grand Cuban-American Fair (Sympathy Meeting) in New York City that Funston attended was similar to the above Chicago meeting. The large sign near the stage reads: "THERE IS HOWEVER A LIMIT AT WHICH FORBEARANCE CEASES TO BE A VIRTUE" BURKE

Santa Fe bond signed by Fred Funston and dated December 12, 1895

Napkin from the Grand Cuban-American Fair attended by Fred Funston

Chapter One Notes—*A "Highly Moral Lecture," a Coffee Plantation, and the Cuban Fair*

Epigraph: Frank Lundy Webster, "Mexican Coffee Bean Was Lucky Stone That Carried Funston On Road To Fame," *The Denver Post*, February 25, 1917 (Frederick Funston Papers, hereafter FFP) (Archives Division, Kansas State Historical Society).

1. "The Week's News," *The Iola Register*, December 28, 1894.
2. "The Week's News," *The Iola Register*, January 11, 1895. Fred hired his cousin, Burt Mitchell, as his "traveling advance agent" for the lecture tour ("The Week's News," *The Iola Register,* January 25, 1895).
3. "Carlyle," *The Iola Register*, January 4, 1895, and "Carlyle," *The Iola Register*, January 11, 1895.
4. "Geneva," *The Iola Register*, January 4, 1895.
5. "Fred Funston's Restless Life of Adventure," *The Chicago Sunday Tribune*, May 7, 1899 (FFP).
6. "Fred Funston," *The Students Journal*, January 11, 1895.
7. *The Lawrence Daily Journal,* January 11, 1895.
8. "Above The Arctic Circle," *The Lawrence Daily Journal*, January 12, 1895.
9. "Personal Mention," *The Lawrence Daily Journal*, January 11, 1895.
10. "Stories Of The Frozen Zone," *The Kansas City Star,* February 16, 1895. "Personal Matters," *The Humboldt Union*, January 19, 1895.
11. *The Chanute Daily Tribune*, January 17, 1895 (advertisement for Opera-House).
12. Frank Lundy Webster, "Mexican Coffee Bean Was Lucky Stone."
13. "Sociable," *Lawrence Daily Gazette*, April 24, 1895. The party was held on April 23, 1895.
14. "The Week's News," *The Iola Register,* May 3, 1895.
15. "The Week's News, "*The Iola Register*, May 10, 1895, quoting *Emporia Gazette*.
16. "City News," *Lawrence Daily Gazette*, May 18, 1895.
17. Quoted in "Editorial Notes," *The Iola Register*, May 24, 1895.
18. "Editorial Notes," *The Iola Register*, May 24, 1895.
19. Frank Lundy Webster, "Mexican Coffee Bean Was Lucky Stone."
20. "Funston, Fearless Fighter and Tactful Chief, Seen at Close Range," *The New York Times Magazine Section*, Section Five, February 25, 1917.
21. "The Week's News," *The Iola Register*, July 5, 1895.
22. Charles S. Gleed, "Romance and Reality In A Single Life. Gen. Frederick Funston," *The Cosmopolitan Illustrated Monthly Magazine*, July 1899.
23. "The Week's News," *The Iola Register*, September 6, 1895.
24. Fred Funston to Ann E. Funston, August 20, 1895 (Eckdall collection of letters, Allen County Historical Society, Inc., Iola, Kansas).

25. "The Week's News," *The Iola Register,* September 20, 1895.

26. "New Coffee Plantation," *The Topeka Daily Capital,* October 20, 1895. "A New Kansas Corporation," *The Kansas City Daily Journal,* October 20, 1895.

27. Charter of The Rio Coachapa Plantation Company. Office of the Secretary of State Corporations Records 1890 C-1997 C (Kansas State Historical Society).

28. Charter of The Rio Coachapa Plantation Company.

29. "New Coffee Plantation," *The Topeka Daily Capital,* October 20, 1895.

30. "Fred Funston's Coffee Plantation," *The Iola Register*, October 25, 1895.

31. "Editorial Notes," *The Iola Register*, October 25, 1895 (reprint from the "K.C. Star").

32. *Fort Scott* (Kansas) *Daily Monitor*, October 23, 1895 (reprint from "Lawrence Journal").

33. Frank Lundy Webster, "Mexican Coffee Bean Was Lucky Stone."

34. Charles S. Gleed, "Romance and Reality In A Single Life. Gen. Frederick Funston."

35. Frank Lundy Webster, "Mexican Coffee Bean Was Lucky Stone."

36. "The Week's News," *The Iola Register,* December 27, 1895.

37. Charles S. Gleed, "Romance and Reality In A Single Life. Gen. Frederick Funston."

38. Frank Lundy Webster, "Mexican Coffee Bean Was Lucky Stone."

39. Fred Funston to Edward Funston, June 22, 1896 (FFP).

40. Fred Funston to Edward Funston, June 22, 1896 (FFP).

41. C. S. Gleed, eulogy, "Report of Select Committee," *Journal of the House*, Hall of the House of Representatives, Topeka, Kansas, February 26, 1917 (FFP). The Santa Fe's corporate offices were located at 59 Cedar Street, New York City (A.E. Waterhouse, Deputy Comptroller of Atchison, Topeka and Santa Fe Railway Company, to David Potter, October 3, 1931) (Frederick Funston Papers on microfilm) (Archives Division, Kansas State Historical Society).

42. "Gained Title In Fight With Lion," *The Kansas City Journal,* February 25, 1917 (Kansas State Historical Society, *Frederick Funston Clippings*, Vol. 1).

43. These were 100-year bonds bearing 4% interest. The bond consulted is dated December 12, 1895. Fred Funston's title is shown as Assistant Secretary. See the bond illustration courtesy of Allen County Historical Society, Inc., Iola, Kansas.

44. *Kansas University Weekly*, April 10, 1896, 200.

45. "Editorial Notes," *The Iola Register*, April 17, 1896.

46. C. S. Gleed, eulogy.

47. Frederick Funston, *Memories of Two Wars: Cuba and Philippine Experiences* (New York: Charles Scribner's Sons, 1914), 3-4. This is my personal copy and bears the bookplate "Ship's Library. U.S.S. Manchuria." The 1914 edition is a reprint of the 1911 first edition. Fortunately for those interested in obtaining a copy of *Memories*, it was reprinted in a 2009 paperback edition. The date of May 27, 1896, is from David Potter, *Frederick Funston: A First Class Fighting Man: A Biography,* 107 (manuscript) (David Potter Manuscripts; 1950s, Manuscripts Division, Department of Rare Books and Special Collections, Princeton University Library).

For information about General Daniel E. Sickles, see Thomas Keneally, *American Scoundrel: The Life of the Notorious Civil War General Dan Sickles* (Nan A. Talese, Doubleday, 2002).

A current example of volunteers, in this case from all over the world, fighting in another country's war is those who have joined the Ukrainian military to help repel the Russian invaders. Near the end of March 2022, this number was estimated at 20,000 (Andy Blatchford, "Band of others: Ukraine's legions of foreign soldiers are on the frontline," *Politico*, March 24, 2022, updated March 25, 2022).

In a television interview with Ukrainian president Volodymyr Zelenskyy, he said that he was not a hero. I was immediately reminded of Fred Funston when he said to the adoring crowd in Kansas City in 1899, "I am not a hero." (See page 3 of trilogy volume one.) Both men are immensely modest.

CHAPTER TWO

Letters I, II, III, IV, and V

June 22, July 5, July 16, late July or early August, and
August 10, 1896

New York City

**Colonel Funston, after getting a taste of the climate
of Death Valley, California, believed to be unequaled
in this world, spent a winter inside the Arctic circle
for the purpose of cooling off, and then passed some
time in semi-tropical Mexico, as affording a medi-
um temperature between two extremes. Feeling refreshed sufficiently to enter upon a more active career, he sought and found it as an artillery officer in
the Army of Free Cuba.**

—*The Kansas City Star*, February 7, 1898

Ed Funston likely was surprised, and then dismayed, when he read
the June 22 letter from his son, Fred, written at 361 West 57 Street,
New York City:

Dear Pa

I am going to take a step shortly which I am afraid may
cause you and the rest of the folks some uneasiness about me,
but I am satisfied that I shall come out of it all right. I am
going to Cuba as war correspondent of Harpers [sic] Weekly
with the insurgent forces. I have for the present dropped my
Mexican plantation scheme, and during my stay in New York
have been doing some writing, and have made some money
and something of a reputation. I had an article published in
Harpers [sic] Weekly last February for which I got $75 and
wrote another which will be published soon for which I was
paid $50. I got $50 for a thing that I wrote for the <u>Bond</u> <u>Record</u>
about the resources of Alaska. It has been published and I
shall send you a copy. I also wrote article for Scribners Magazine which is to be published shortly, getting $150 for it.

So that I have been breaking in to a pretty high class of

publication and now I have the chance to make a pretty big reputation as a war correspondent and I want to take advantage of it. The business is not so dangerous as it would seem at first sight–the yellow fever being confined almost entirely to the cities occupied by the Spanish troops there being almost none of it back in the mountains where the insurgents have their headquarters.

The only way to get within the rebel lines in Cuba is to leave here on one of the filibustering vessels carrying arms to the insurgents, and arrangements have been made for me to leave on the next one. I am to be an officer on the staff of one of the Cuban generals. Of course I dont [sic] know anything about war, but they dont [sic] either, so that honors are about even. I expect to take care of myself and have no fears about coming out all right. I shall be gone probably about four months. You will hear from me occasionally, but at irregular intervals, as I shall have to take advantage of whatever opportunity offers to get word out, and if..."[1] [The balance of this letter is missing.]

Ed's letter in response is no longer extant, but its essence is clear from Fred's letter nearly two weeks later on July 5:

Dear Pa

I am still in New York, as the expedition on which I am to go to Cuba, has not yet been got ready. The Cubans have been delayed by the seizure by a U. S. revenue cutter of one of their steamers but the vessel has now been released and I think that we shall get away within a week.

Of course I appreciate your objections to my taking the trip, and in fact did not expect you to look at the project very favorably but I am pretty sure for a number of reasons that it is a good thing for me [to] do. I think you are pretty badly mistaken when you say that I will get no credit for doing it. It is going to be a big feather in the caps of the Americans who have gone down there to mix up in the row, especially if the Cubans win their independence which I think they will do in less than a year from now. The Spaniards are on the defensive, and hardly dare venture any distance from the fortified towns. The insurgents lick them every time they get at them.

There is a big sprinkling of young Americans down there now. They are nearly all officers and are very popular with the Cubans. Several of them are also correspondents for New York papers.

I shall let you know as soon as I get any definite news as to when I am to leave.

I enclose the insurance receipt which I neglected to put in my other letter.

Your son
Fred Funston[2]

Serving as a war correspondent was not limited to Americans. The Cuban revolt against Spain caught the attention of a young Englishman, 20-year-old Winston Churchill, the future British Prime Minister during World War II. Churchill, a Second Lieutenant in 4th Queen's Own Hussars, which was stationed in England, enjoyed serving in the Army but he regarded it as only a step to becoming a great statesman. In the summer of 1895, Churchill wanted to take part in a war and "systematically scoured the world map for a place where he could have as high profile an adventure as possible." He decided to go to Cuba during an upcoming ten weeks' leave and secured accreditation from Spain to accompany its forces in Cuba. To help finance his expedition, he secured a position as a war correspondent for a London newspaper with his pay based per article.

Churchill and a fellow British officer arrived in Cuba on November 18, 1895. They came under fire with the Spanish forces on December 1 when a bullet came within a foot of Churchill's head followed by heavy fire for more than ten minutes and then a day and a half of sporadic fire. His "military tourism" lasted eighteen days before the war correspondent returned to England. Although he had been with the Spanish forces, who were his hosts, Churchill's sympathies lay with the Cuban rebels, a sympathy he had to conceal from his hosts.[3] Like Fred and other Americans, Churchill was in search of adventure.

Fred's parents likely shared with his close friend, editor Charlie Scott, Fred's Cuban plans, and Charlie reported them a few days later in *The Iola Register* under the headline "Fred. Funston Gone To Cuba":

Fred. Funston, who has been in New York for several months past doing magazine and newspaper work, has agreed to go to Cuba as war correspondent for *Harper's Weekly*. And in order that he may be sure of seeing things to write about, he has engaged to join a filibustering expedition which has been enlisted to aid the insurgents, and will be sworn into the rebel army as an artillery officer, in command of a battery of Hotchkiss guns. That means that he will be in the thick of the fight, and will have to see the thing through to the bitter end.

It is a frightful risk to run. The ordinary dangers of war

would be enough to deter a less courageous soul. But in addition to the chances of being killed in battle, he faces the certainty of being put to death if made prisoner, and the possibility of contracting the fatal fevers of that country. We wish he were not going.

But since he is, God go with him and bring him safe home again! The REGISTER has faith in Fred. Funston a good deal as it has in seeing the moon over the right shoulder. He always got home before, and we believe he will this time.

And what a story he will have to tell![4]

Fred wrote Charlie less than a week later in response to this news story. Under the headline "Fred Funston's Reasons," Charlie published Fred's reasons for going to Cuba to fight, while carefully omitting those reasons which were "too personal to be printed without his consent." This letter in its entirety, with the omitted portions in brackets, reads as follows:

[My dear Scott:

[It was mighty kind of you to give me the nice send off that you did in last week's Register. I have enough of the saving grace of human vanity to like to have good things said about me, especially by one who can say them as aptly as you can.

[I have had some earnest protests from home and from friends against this trip, but those things were to be expected. But I am the only person in the world who can thoroughly understand myself and the motives that influence me and it seems to me that the motives in this case are sufficient. I want to make some sort of reputation as war correspondent. I want to see a real live war for my own satisfaction. I want to go when I can for a time, get away from some of my disappointments and bitterness against things in general] and I want to help in the task of boosting the unspeakable Spaniard body and breeches out of the unfortunate island that he has robbed and misgoverned for 400 long years. There is not a more pitiful tale in history than the story of Cuba—of the brutality, corruption and general cussedness of Spanish rule,—of her ten years struggle for independence that ended in a treaty, every solitary provision which the Spaniards have broke. This fight will be to the death and the rebels will win. I am confident that in six months it will all be over.

I have no patience with those Americans who say, as some do, that it is not our war, and that it is our duty to keep out of it. Talk of that kind comes with mighty poor grace from a people who have the example of Lafayette, Von Steuben, Dekalb and Kosciusko to look back to. It is the war of every man who wants to take part in it. [Of course I take some nasty chances, but hope that things (bullets and sich [sic]) wont [sic] come my way too fast.]

It is hard to tell just when I shall get off. The expedition has been in preparation for some time and has been delayed by the non-delivery of several of the Hotchkiss guns [little brown pets Kipling called them] with which I am to shoot holes through Prof. Weyler's justly celebrated trocha.

However, I think that we shall be off within two weeks. [My love to yourself, Mrs. Scott and the hopeful. Tell the latter young man that when his uncle Fred comes back he will trot him on his knee and tell him how he "fit" with Gomez back in '96.]

> [Faithfully,
> Fred.][5]

In his letter, Fred clearly articulated his reasons for going to Cuba as a war correspondent:

1. "[T]o make some sort of reputation as war correspondent." This is not surprising for the young man who enjoyed writing and who had been a journalist starting in his college days. As a war correspondent, he would have an employment, likely being paid for each story.
2. "[T]o see a real live war for my own satisfaction." This is also not surprising since Fred had been fascinated by all things military since he was a boy at his father's knee listening to his stories as an artilleryman in the recent Civil War. As a reader of books of military history, he had only read about war and never experienced it.
3. He wanted to get away for a time, "get away from some of my disappointments and bitterness against things in general." Likely this refers to Fred's unsuccessful coffee bean plantation plan, which had shown so much promise, but which had been ended by financial challenges that even the hard-working, resourceful Fred could not overcome. He had been forced to sign his name over and over on railroad bonds to earn a steady income. He was living in a big city—New York—not the venue for the adventurous, outdoors young man from the prairies of Kansas and from Death Valley, Alaska, and the British Northwest Territory.

Fred's disappointment in the area of romance, particularly with Maude Richards, likely was another reason for him to get away. A different world—Cuba—and a different focus—the war for independence—would change Fred's focus.

4. "I want to help in the task of boosting the unspeakable Spaniard body and breeches out of the unfortunate island that he has robbed and misgoverned for 400 long years." Fred expressed his thoughts in detail on this reason and thus this was apparently the most important reason of the four. *Cuba Libre* was a cause he believed in, realizing, however, that he would be a solider and thus taking "some nasty chances." He was undeterred nevertheless.

In a December 1896 interview with *The Kansas City Star*, Ed Funston told the reporter how Fred came to go to Cuba and showed him several of Fred's letters. The reporter asked how he felt about what Fred had done. The old Civil War veteran responded, "Oh, I don't allow myself to be worried. He'll come out all right. He is courageous but cautious. I fear yellow fever more than I do bullets. The safest place in Cuba is in the army. The Cubans fight with a sort of Fabian policy, a little fighting, a good deal of running away; but that's the way to fight. Fred's a man, 31 years old, and he'll take care of himself. I'm just looking for him to drop in any time." In this article, the reporter quoted extracts from Fred's candid letter to Charlie Scott, which Charlie had shared with the reporter. The *Star* reporter included in his article much of the letter that Charlie had omitted, though the reporter did omit Fred's desire to get away from "disappointments and bitterness."[6]

Shortly before he left New York, Fred wrote to his Lawrence friend and fellow coffee plantation investor, Frank Webster. The following extract from this letter has survived: "I have done a lot of fool things in my life, but I am now about to do what is probably the biggest fool of all. I am going to help 'Cuba Libre' by fighting the greasers."[7]

In late August, Charlie Scott advised his readers that he had received a letter from Fred "announcing that his expedition was to leave for Cuba on the 10th of August." Charlie editorialized: "So if all has gone well he is now on the island training his Gattling [sic] guns against Spanish soldiers and fighting in the cause of freedom. The dispatches from Cuba will have a mighty keen personal interest for us from this time on."[8]

What had Fred been doing while awaiting departure for Cuba? I know of no letters that exist from him telling about this period and about the details of his adventurous trip to Cuba, but we are fortunate to have his *Memories of Two Wars: Cuban and Philippine Experiences,* published in 1911, to fill in the blanks, and this is the source for most of the balance of this chapter. Only the other sources used will be cited in the notes. Interestingly, Fred described *Memories* as "nothing more than a contribution, such as it may be, to the literature of adventure."

The morning after attending the Cuban Fair, Fred approached the Cuban *Junta*, the organization of Cuban exiles, at its office located at 56 New Street to offer his services to the revolution: "[W]ithout credentials of any kind, I...inquired if I could see Mr. Palma, but did not succeed in doing so. Mr. Zayas, one of the attachés of the *Junta*, took me in hand and was most courteous, but assured me that they were sending no Americans to Cuba, and were confining their efforts in this country to raising funds and doing what they could to direct public sentiment in favor of their compatriots. I have since often wondered how I could have been so guileless as to expect them to receive me, a total stranger, with open arms. I could have been a fugitive from justice seeking a hiding-place, a worthless adventurer, or, worst of all, a spy in Spanish pay."

Fred decided to use different tactics. "Through a mutual friend [likely Charlie Gleed] I obtained a letter of introduction to General Sickles, and the next day called on the old veteran at his residence, and not only had a most pleasant chat with him, but left with a personal note to Mr. Palma in which the General stated that, though he did not know me personally, he felt justified in vouching for me on the strength of the letter I had brought him. Back to the *Junta* without loss of time, and now it was different. I was admitted without delay to the office of the kindly faced, honest old patriot [Estrada Palma] who afterward became the first president of free Cuba."

In response to the question of whether he had had any military service, Fred said that he had not, "but had read considerably along military lines and felt that I had it in me to make good." Fred acknowledged that he had "a fair reading but not a speaking acquaintance" with Spanish. The United States' position was one of neutrality on the rebellion by the Cubans against Spain, and, thus, though the *Junta* could not enlist fighters in the United States, once Fred reached Cuba, he could offer his services to the insurgents.

The *Junta* was the general legation abroad appointed by the Cuban revolutionary government in September of 1895. Its general headquarters was in New York City, and naturalized Cubans living along the Atlantic seaboard were its principal membership. The *Junta* worked with the Cuban League, which was composed of pro-Cuba Americans who helped the *Junta* to organize clubs throughout the United States. These two organizations had a common purpose: to assist the Cubans through material and moral support, both essential for insurgent success. The United States was "fertile soil for the production of both material and moral aid."

To accomplish their objectives, the *Junta* fitted filibustering expeditions to transport by boat needed materials and volunteers to Cuba. The *Junta* also raised the funds to purchase these materials. The latter was accomplished through "Sympathy Meetings," carnivals, and theatrical performances. One fund-raiser was the "Grand Cuban-American Fair" attended by Fred and which was held from May 25-30. Handbills announcing the fair noted this motto: "Cuba Appreciates Sympathy—She Must Have Assistance." These "Sympathy Meetings" were held in the most important cities in the United States.[9]

Since the Cubans were not having much success with their artillery in military actions, "largely because their people did not seem to know how to handle the guns...," it was "suggested that if I were to acquire some knowledge on that subject before sailing it might add to my welcome. This struck me favorably, as my father had been an artillery officer in the Civil War, and I had been brought up on stories of fierce struggles in which the old brass Napoleons [field guns] of that day had done their part. My own artillery experience consisted in once having seen a salute fired to President Hayes at a country fair in Kansas."

Fred was sent "to the firm of Hartley & Graham, the arms dealers from whom the Cubans purchased their implements of war, and had explained to me by one of their experts the mysteries of the Hotchkiss twelve-pounder breech-loading rifle [field gun], and was allowed to fondle that ugly looking instrument of death to my heart's content and take it apart and put it together again. A book of instructions as to its use and a lot of formidable tables of velocities at various ranges, etc., I all but committed to memory." Fred's good memory was a great asset.

His "keen interest" in the subject resulted in his instructing several of the Cubans in New York City, who were awaiting the sailing of the next expedition to Cuba. Instruction sessions were held in a small hall over a saloon where all but a few lights were turned off and all the window shades were drawn. The Cubans were primarily students. "These aspiring patriots chattered like magpies and smoked the most astounding number of cigarettes." Weekly, for a month, Fred set up the Hotchkiss twelve-pounder gun and then taught the Cubans how to take it apart, "and the breech mechanism, sights, and ammunition [were] explained. As this gun is transported in sections on mule back, as well as dragged by a shaft, the various heavy pieces were lifted up to the height of an imaginary or 'theoretical' mule and then let down again..." At the first training session, "[s]everal times the pieces were allowed to fall to the floor with a noise that should have aroused the block, and I spent a good bit of time figuring out how I would explain to the police, if they came to investigate, what I was doing with such warlike paraphernalia in peaceful New York. But we were not molested..." The lessons continued.

One day Fred and several members of the *Junta* went to the coast of Long Island to see a demonstration of the working of the recently invented Sims-Dudley dynamite gun. Looking more like a telescope on wheels than a gun, it "was fired several times out to sea, to the evident consternation of an excursion boat which made the most phenomenal speed in getting out of the way. The explosion of its nitro-gelatine-loaded shells threw water and spray a hundred feet in air." Fred was to witness in Cuba the devastating effects of this "implement of war."

"So the summer wore along, but one afternoon in August came the fateful telegram, and after all these years I can quote its every word: 'Be at Cortlandt Street Ferry at 7 P. M., ready to leave the city.'" Fred quickly prepared to depart. He dashed off a letter dated August 10 to his mother:

Dear Mother

We leave today for Cuba, and I have only a few moments in which to write you.

Now you must not worry about me, as I know perfectly well how to look out for myself. I am to do mainly newspaper work and shall not have a great deal to do with the fighting. Shall come back some time next winter and then shall not go on any more fool trips.

Do not expect all your letters to get to me promptly, as the mail facilities in Cuba just now are bad. My address will be care of O.A. Zayas, Cuban Junta 56 New Street, New York, and they will forward mail to me whenever opportunity offers. I shall write home at every opportunity.

Shall carry my newspaper credentials, so that if I am captured shall not be executed by the Spaniards.

I have been taking the Topeka Mail (weekly) and have written them to change my address to Carlyle. Wish you would file all of them and save them for me.

I leave my valises here with my landlady Mrs. B. F. Perkins. My trunk is at Prof. Snow's in Lawrence. Now dont [sic] worry about me.   Your loving son
                                          Fred.[10]

Fred may have been unduly sanguine when he assured his mother that by carrying his newspaper credentials, he would not be executed if the Spaniards captured him. Unknown to Fred, the month before, Charles Govin, an American correspondent for a Jacksonville, Florida newspaper, had been executed after his capture by the Spaniards. His "red sealed correspondent's certificate and passport" had been "scornfully" thrown on the ground by the Spanish commander, Colonel Ochoa, before he had Govin bound to a tree and macheted to death.[11]

The fact that Fred would do mainly newspaper work and not have much to do with the fighting was no protection against injury, of course. C. E. Crosby, an Englishman who had served in the French army, later built as a civil engineer a railroad in Mexico. In January of 1897, he went to Cuba "strictly" as correspondent for the *Chicago Record* and not as a combatant. On March 9 he reached the insurgent camp of the Cuban commander in chief, General Maximo Gomez, and while watching through field glasses a fight in progress with the Spanish force, Crosby was hit in the forehead by "a stray bullet" fired by a Spaniard. The "strictly" war correspondent died instantly."[12]

Before departing for Cuba, Fred went to see his close friend from Kansas, Charlie Gleed. Fred "slipped into my office as quickly as a shadow. Before the door was closed he was taking off his watch and saying: 'Give me some money and give this to my mother. I have twenty minutes to catch my train.' I handed him a roll of money and took his watch and chain for his mother. The transaction was over in perhaps a minute, perhaps two minutes, and he was gone."[13]

Fred continued the story. "[W]ith a few belongings in a small valise, and, I must acknowledge, with some sinking of the heart, I made my way to the ferry accompanied by an old friend of college days." The friend apparently was Charlie Gleed's brother, Willis Gleed, who later reported that Fred had explained his motivation for his undertaking: "Willis, I have no ambition to get rich. I wouldn't go into politics for anything. I am afraid I have no settled aim or clearly seen ambition. But nevertheless I want to cut some ice in the world, and I intend to keep hustling until my time comes."[14]

In addition to the Cubans, there were four other men who set out with Fred on the journey to join the fight: "There were Charles Huntington, a fine-looking Canadian of soldierly bearing, who had served in the Northwest Mounted Police; Walinski, an Englishman of Polish descent; Welsford, a young man from New Jersey, and Arthur Potter, a former English marine soldier who had lived in the United States for several years. Huntington was one of the bravest men I ever knew, being, in fact, absolutely reckless... Potter and Welsford were chums, careless, go-lucky young fellows..."

Traveling by train, the group reached Charleston, South Carolina, where they stayed at a hotel. There were about thirty Cubans there. "Among other guests of the hotel were some fifteen or twenty well-groomed, quiet-appearing men whom we were at once warned against having anything to do with, as they were operatives of a well-known detective agency in the employ of the Spanish minister at Washington, with the exception of a few who were said to be United States Secret Service men or United States deputy marshals. It was the duty of these men to learn what they could as to our intentions in order that they might give to the proper authorities the information necessary to enable them to seize the vessel on which we were to sail."

These men regarded the five non-Cubans as likely to disclose information, and quickly worked to become acquainted. "Two of them took me in hand and suggested that there was nothing like a mint julep to make one forget Charleston's August climate. But I told them I was from Kansas [where prohibition reigned], whereupon they suggested an ice-cream soda..." Their next suggestion was strolling a few blocks to a place that sold "cooling drinks." "It was difficult to shake them off without retiring to my room and sweltering in the terrific heat." Seeing Fred's plight, the former Canadian Mountie Huntington came over and "very genially offered to thrash both of them if they did not leave me alone. This had the desired effect."

The goal was to outwit the authorities when the Cubans and the other five men, referred to as the Americans, left the United States for Cuba. "On the afternoon of the day following our arrival the Cubans, carrying their hand baggage, began to leave the hotel in little groups, each followed by one or more 'sleuths.'" The group of five Americans was taken to the station of the Plant Line system of railways where one of the regular trains was ready to leave. "We were conducted to the rear car of the train, a day coach, where we found the Cubans who had preceded us from the hotel. Several of the detectives who attempted to secure seats in this car were told that it was a special chartered by a party of excursionists, and that we would be obliged to deny ourselves the pleasure of their company. So they found seats in the car ahead..."

The train left for a destination unknown to Fred. "I know that we pounded along over the rails at a fair rate of speed until some time late at night, when we stopped at an obscure station in the woods..." There the Cubans played their trick. "[A] locomotive backed up to our car from a siding, the car was quickly and quietly uncoupled from the train, which then proceeded on its way, while our car with its engine flew back on the track a few miles, was switched onto another line, and sped along for hours without making more than the few absolutely necessary stops. From a special car we had grown to be a special train, a small one, it is true, but none the less special. The whole plan for escaping the men following us and throwing them entirely off the scent...worked to perfection. We had many a chuckle over the chagrin that must have been felt by our attentive mentors when they found how neatly they had been 'sacked.'"

Shortly after sunrise, the train stopped at Woodbine, a little station located in some pine woods on the extreme southeastern coast of Georgia. In the "good sized sluggish river," the Satilla, was "a big [ocean-going] tug [i.e. steamer], the *Dauntless*, soon to become famous as the most successful filibuster in the Cuban service, now making her first essay in the exciting work of dodging American revenue-cutters and outrunning Spanish gun boats." From three large freight cars on a siding, the men unloaded arms and ammunition and carried them to the *Dauntless*. "There were many among the thirty-five of us who had never done a stroke of manual labor in their lives, but we five were not in that class. Nevertheless, we were heartily glad when the task was over, and all felt that we had qualified for membership in the freight-handlers' union."

The amount of arms and ammunition was large. "In five hours there had been transferred to the hold of the *Dauntless* the Hotchkiss twelve-pounder, with its pack-saddles and other gear, and 800 shells, 1,300 Mauser and Remington rifles, 100 revolvers, 1,000 cavalry machetes, 800 pounds of dynamite, several hundred saddles, half a ton of medical stores, and 460,000 rounds of small-arms ammunition. In truth, the Madison Square Garden fair for the raising of funds for the purchase of 'hospital supplies' had evidently been a howling success. I can testify that the cargo of the *Dauntless* put many a man in the hospital for every one it took out."

The *Dauntless,* with its Cuban expedition under General Cabrera, cast off about noon under the command of Captain John O'Brien, a noted filibuster (a military adventurer from the United States), who was popularly known as "Dynamite" Johnny O'Brien. He had safely transported by boat sixty tons of dynamite to a Colombian port during a severe electrical storm; hence his nickname.[15] "Captain Johnny, a most ingratiating character, had the traditional charm of the Irish and their characteristic love of adventure."[16] In Fred's words, "[h]e was an ideal man for the perilous business, cool and resourceful, and a splendid seaman. And all of these qualifications were needed for filibustering in this particular war, for if there was one thing well understood it was that every member of one of these expeditions, if captured by the Spaniards, would get the shortest shrift possible to give him. The Spaniards do not fight revolutions with rose-water, and maybe they are right. Consequently, filibustering in those days was grim and terrible business, fit occupation for lion-hearted men." The *Dauntless*, in the years 1895-1898, was to have more successful filibustering landings in Cuba than any other vessel.[17]

Once the steamer was on the Atlantic Ocean, there followed four days of rolling and pitching on the ocean's broad swells.

> [The *Dauntless*] could have made the passage in two days but for the necessity of economizing her supply of coal for the return trip to some United States port, and to have enough fuel to enable her to speed up and make a run for life if the occasion arose. Always a victim to sea-sickness, even under the most favorable circumstances, I can never forget those four days of suffering as the little steamer labored through the sea, rolling and pitching, our only home, the deck, swept from time to time by clouds of spray, with an occasional wave for good measure. We lay about day after day in our water-soaked blankets, getting such snatches of sleep as we could, and now and then staggering to the rail to make the required contribution to Neptune. We certainly were as unhappy and as unheroic-looking a lot of adventurers as ever trusted themselves to the sea.

August 16 was the big day as the *Dauntless* approached the northeast coast of Cuba. "The wind and sea now moderated somewhat, and the worn and harassed filibusters began to come to life. All realized that this was the most critical period in our voyage, as the coast was patrolled by gun-boats and armed launches, and capture meant death, swift and inevitable. We five had among ourselves talked over such a possibility, and it was pretty well understood that if worst came to worst we were to take Kipling's advice, 'Just roll to your rifle and blow out your brains, And go to your God like a soldier.'" Of course, they planned to fight first and not just surrender, and the Hotchkiss twelve-pounder was unpacked and mounted on the deck for that purpose.

As they neared the coast of Cuba, "[w]e stood on deck with beating hearts and tense faces..." Although there was no other vessel in sight, an occasional bit of smoke along the shoreline far to the east was troubling. In the end, there was no Spanish ship. The tension was great as they drew near their goal. "If I must tell all, our teeth were chattering, and not from cold, but from the terrific strain and from trying to force ourselves to be calm and cool." By now it was nighttime.

One of the volunteer Cuban pilots proved to be a traitor, attempting to run the *Dauntless* aground on a reef. Thanks to the alertness of "Dynamite" Johnny O'Brien, only the bow was briefly stuck on the reef. The traitorous pilot was executed by his fellow Cubans on their landing on the shore.[18] The *Dauntless* stopped about a half mile off shore at an inlet known as Las Nuevas Grandes, a short distance east of the entrance to Nuevitas harbor, on the coast of the province of Puerto Principe, known also as Camaguey. Using eight broad, flatbottomed skiffs, each with two pairs of oars and a steering oar, the men began transporting the cargo to the beach. Each of the five "Americans" was put in charge of a boat. The remaining three boats were under the command of three of the Cuban voyagers.

> I was able to get away first, and with a crew of four at the oars pushed toward the surf, which, owing to the darkness, could not be seen, but was distinctly audible. About half-way to the shore we could dimly make out the line of breakers. Years before, I had had some pretty stiff surf work in Indian canoes on the Alaskan coast and thought I knew something on that subject, but the prospect before us was not alluring. The greatest drawback was the darkness, which made it impossible to see whatever rocks there might be, as well as to estimate the height or violence of the surf. But it was too late to turn back, and in we went. There was a lot of pitching and bucking, and a wave or two broke over us, but as soon as we struck, oars were dropped and overboard we went, up to our waists, caught the boat by its sides, and ran up onto the beach with it on the next wave. Fortunately, it was a perfectly clean, shelving, sandy beach, and we got through with nothing worse than a superb ducking and a boat half full of water.

The work went on far into the night, with a skiff being upset occasionally, but there was no loss of life. The appearance of a Spanish torpedo gun-boat of some size forced the *Dauntless* to flee the scene before all of the war materiel was unloaded. "The engine bell rang viciously, a black column of smoke poured from the funnel of the *Dauntless*, and the race for life began." Two of the boats, including Fred's, had been unloading the *Dauntless* when it had to flee. "With heavy hearts we rowed ashore, and the members of the expedition gathered about the piles of cartridge boxes and bundles of rifles on the beach, shivered in their wet clothing, and in subdued tones discussed the situation. All were present but only about three-fourths of our own cargo had been landed. Our position was not an enviable one, as we felt morally certain that the Spaniard would return after day light and deal with us. We could, of course, escape into the bush, but all our war material [sic] would be captured."

At first light the next morning, the adventurers located a suitable gun-pit for the twelve-pounder Hotchkiss gun and set it up for battle. A fire was built, and coffee and bacon prepared, "and this with some hard bread refreshed all greatly. It was thought best to carry our tons of military stores, piled helter-skelter along the beach to some place concealed from view, and this slavish task consumed the greater part of the forenoon. Advantage was taken of low tide to recover those articles lost from the boats overturned in the surf on the previous night." Only one box of ten Remington rifles was not found. The boxes containing the small-arms ammunition were tin-lined, so their contents were not damaged, but "several cases of cartridges for the twelve-pounder were practically ruined, as we were to learn to our cost at Cascorra [sic: Cascorro] a few weeks later."

About eleven o'clock the *Dauntless* returned, having "led the gunboat a straight chase to the north for several hours, and, outdistancing her pursuer, had finally made a wide circuit and come back to get rid of the remainder of her cargo, being aided in her escape by the thick and squally weather." The remaining weapons and ammunition, about a fourth of the total, were transported to shore in about two hours. "As the last boat load pulled away, the *Dauntless*, brave as her name, gave three defiant blasts from her whistle as a parting salute and steamed away, leaving us to our own devices on a strange and inhospitable coast. As we silently watched her fade from sight we realized that we had burned our bridges behind us and were in for the war."[19]

Funston training young Cubans in New York City (*Memories of Two Wars* illustration)

This 1956 photograph of another photograph was sent to Ella (Funston) Eckdall by Albert G. Abreu, a Cuban soldier who accompanied Fred Funston to Cuba on the *Dauntless*. Abreu has identified himself and Funston standing with other men on the ship's superstructure. Ella's note on the back of this photograph indicates that the ship on which they are standing is the *Dauntless*.

I do not believe this is correct. The nameplate of the ship on which they stand does not show the name *Dauntless*. Although the name is partially obscured, the last letters are, I believe, the last letters of the word "friends," as in the name of the ocean-going tug, *The Three Friends*. The nameplate of the other ship starts with a "D," and thus this is likely the name *Dauntless*. Also, the superstructure of the ship on which the men stand appears to me to be that of *The Three Friends* (see photograph on opposite page).

The visible part of the brief history in the upper-left corner of the photograph translates as follows: "Forty-five. Ship: steam 'Dauntless.' Place and date of departure: Florida, August 12 [the "1" of "12" is not visible in the photograph], 1896. Landing place: Nueva Grandes, north coast of Camaguey. Six in the afternoon on August 16 of the same year. They finished the disembarkation and unloading at dawn on the 17th." I believe that the two ships, *Dauntless* and *The Three Friends*, rendezvoused on the coast of Florida before the *Dauntless* left for Cuba and that this photograph was taken at that time. In doing so, the filibusters gathered on *The Three Friends* to be immortalized in a photograph.

"The ocean-going tugs 'Dauntless' (above) and 'Three Friends,' used in landing Cuban expeditions."

"Overboard we went...caught the boat by its sides, and
ran up on to the beach with it on the next wave."

(*Memories of Two Wars* illustration)

"An almost ideal natural gun-pit was found near the beach" the morning after the *expedicionarios* landed in Cuba. (*Memories of Two Wars* illustration)

Chapter Two Notes—*Letters I, II, III, IV, and V*

Epigraph: *The Kansas City Star,* February 7, 1898. Editorial.

1. Fred Funston to Edward H. Funston, June 22, 1896 (Frederick Funston Papers, hereafter FFP) (Archives Division, Kansas State Historical Society).

2. Fred Funston to Edward H. Funston, July 5, 1896 (FFP).

3. Andrew Roberts, *Churchill: Walking with Destiny* (Viking, 2018), 33-38. This excellent work is the definitive biography of Churchill. For more information, see Hal Klepak, *Churchill Comes of Age: Cuba 1895* (Gloucestershire: The History Press, 2015).

4. "Fred. Funston Gone to Cuba," *The Iola Register,* July 10, 1896.

5. Weyler was the commander of the Spanish forces. In an interview of Fred in *The Kansas City Star* of April 23, 1898 ("Victory Not Easy"), Fred explained about "the great Spanish trocha extending across the western part of the province of Puerto Principe. This trocha is a ditch twenty feet wide and fifty-seven miles long. At intervals of 400 yards along its entire length are forts that are garrisoned and provided with artillery." Fred described these forts as "built of brick and earth and protected by railroad iron, the rails being set on end. The trocha is almost impenetrable. It was built to prevent the two divisions of Cuban army from communicating."
   "Fred Funston's Reasons" appeared in *The Iola Register,* July 24, 1896. The complete text of this letter of July 16, 1896, is a typed copy found in FFP and in Frederick Funston Papers on microfilm, hereafter FFP Micro (Archives Division, Kansas State Historical Society). How accurate this typed copy is, I do not know. Scott, in his published version, used the word "trachea" referring to Weyler; the typed copy indicates uncertainty as to what the word is; and the excerpt printed in *The Kansas City Star* article about Fred (see note 6 below) has the word as trocha, which makes sense.

6. "A Kansas Cuban Soldier," *The Kansas City Star,* December 13, 1896 (reprint in *The Iola Register,* December 25, 1896).

7. Frank Lundy Webster, "Mexican Coffee Bean Was Lucky Stone That Carried Funston on Road to Fame," *The Denver Post,* February 25, 1917 (FFP).

8. "The Week's News," *The Iola Register,* August 28, 1896

9. George W. Auxier, "The Propaganda Activities Of The Cuban *Junta* in Precipitating The Spanish-American War, 1895-1898," *The Hispanic American Historical Review,* August 1939, downloaded from http://read.dukepress.edu/hahr/article-pdf/19/3/286/755793/0190286.pdf on March 26, 2022.

10. Fred Funston to Ann E. Funston, August 10, 1896 (FFP).

11. Grover Flint, *Marching with Gomez: A War Correspondent's Field Note-Book Kept During Four Months With The Cuban Army* (Honolulu: University Press of the Pacific, 2004, reprinted from 1898 edition), 280-283. Ochoa allegedly wore and displayed the deceased Govin's watch and sleeve buttons.

12. "Newspaper Correspondent Killed," *The Chicago Daily Tribune,* March 30, 1897.

13. C. S. Gleed, eulogy, "Report of Select Committee," *Journal of the House*, Hall of the House of Representatives, Topeka, Kansas, February 26, 1917 (FFP).

14. "Kansas Topics—Determined to Cut Ice," *The Kansas City Journal*, May 5, 1899.

15. John O'Brien and Horace Smith, *A Captain Unafraid: The Strange Adventures of Dynamite Johnny O'Brien* (New York and London: Harper & Brothers Publishers, MCMXII; Biblio Life Reproduction Service), 47-56.

16. Horatio S. Rubens, *Liberty: The Story of Cuba* (New York: Brewer, Warren & Putnam Inc., 1932), 151.

17. Richard V. Rickenbach, "Filibustering with the 'Dauntless,'" *The Florida Historical Quarterly*, Vol. XXVIII, Number 4, April 1950.

18. John O'Brien and Horace Smith, *A Captain Unafraid: The Strange Adventures of Dynamite Johnny O'Brien*, 124-125.

19. Except as otherwise noted in the notes above, the source for this chapter is Frederick Funston, *Memories of Two Wars: Cuban and Philippine Experiences* (New York: Charles Scribner's Sons, 1914), chapter I, and page vii of Preface.

CHAPTER THREE

Letters VI and VII

August 23, 1896
Los Angeles Plantation, Province of Puerto Principe, Cuba

September 30 and October 16 (postscript), 1896
"In Camp, Province of Puerto Principe, Cuba."

**War is the game of the gods. It is thrilling. It is
fun. No kind of game thrills a man like it.**

—Fred Funston after his return from Cuba

Immediately after the *Dauntless* left the expedition of thirty-five filibusters on the beach, four of the Cubans were sent into the interior
to locate the rebel forces. After "[f]our anxious days," a scout from a
portion of General Maximo Gomez's command appeared. He was soon
followed by 600 hundred men with a large number of pack animals.

The next day, a thirty-mile march by the rebel force into the interior resulted in the newly-arrived soldiers being "about done for."
They went into camp with the approximately thousand men serving under General Maximo Gomez. According to Fred, there he met
four of his fellow countrymen: Walter M. Jones, a native of New York
State, who had lived in Cuba for ten years; Arthur Royal Joyce of
South Egremont, Massachusetts; William Smith, who was second in
command of Gomez's personal escort; and James Pennie of Washington, D.C.[1] Arthur Royal Joyce remembered this first encounter somewhat differently, since he recalled meeting the newly arrived Americans before they met up with Gomez's army. Joyce had been with the
insurgent forces four months when Fred and the others arrived on
the *Dauntless*. Joyce was with Cuban president Cisneros when news
of the arrival of General Cabrera's expedition came to the president,
who asked Joyce to go with him immediately to greet the arrivals.
Reaching their camp, president Cisneros welcomed the expedition
members, who were drawn up in line to receive him. After the president's speech, Joyce began searching for his fellow countrymen.

I discovered three, and after greeting them and extending

my tearful sympathy for their future sufferings, inquired if there were any more of them.

These were Huntington of Colorado, Potter of England and Welsford of New Jersey. Huntingon said: "Yes, there's a little fellow over here named Funston doing guard duty over the stores, lets [sic] meander over and cheer him up a bit. He will swear he is the only man on the expedition who has done his share of guard duty since we left New York."

Accordingly we meandered, and in a moment the disconsolate Funston burst upon my gaze...

This expedition was by far the most important that had then reached the island, and everything was landed, an unusual thing.

Among the arms was a twelve-pound Hotchkiss gun, which Funston had been sent down to handle. General Cabrera in making his report to the government, especially mentioned Funston and Huntington for their hard work in the disembarking.

We waited at this place one day, during which time I posted the new-comers on the peculiarities of the Cubans, their slight regard for the laws of 'Meum et tuum,' and especially cautioned them against entrusting anything of their outfit to anyone kindly offering to carry it to the next camp.

In spite of this, at the start next morning both Funston and Huntington, to save themselves a little trouble, did as all of us had done before, and allowed several of their neighbors in the cavalry column to carry part of their baggage.

Funston had an agreement with Harper's Weekly to furnish several illustrated articles, and had among his considerable personal stuff a large camera, which handicapped him considerably on the march. He also had a large rubber blanket, which caused him some trouble, and I told him to tie it on the back of my saddle, which he did.

Before I had gone very far I discovered this had fallen off, and rode back to recover it if possible; but could not find it, and, of course, none of the Cubans had seen it.

I arrived in camp somewhat late on this account and found Funston and Huntington still hopeful that their baggage would turn up.

Funston did not take the loss of his blanket as philosophically as I had hoped, but would not allow me to make up the loss to him in any way. The other baggage never came, and all attempts to find it were fruitless, and for several months thereafter when Funston would especially need one of the missing articles his language was of the vigorous, explosive kind.[2]

Billy White described Fred's swearing succinctly: He had "a wide eclectic Spanish-Texan-Kansan-and-Old English collection of oaths which he loved to juggle with in emotional moments. For he was an emotional creature."[3] Fred apparently never renounced swearing, a positive trait in the eyes of a fellow U.S. Army officer: "The dignity of the eagles [Fred's rank as general] did not take from him the prerogative of his fine, old-fashioned anger-purging profanity. He believes, I think, in the virtue of that vice, as many another man has. This human quality was, in the first days, seen the most often in his frank boyishness."[4]

In *Memories of Two Wars,* Fred carries the story forward after the *Dauntless* expedition went into camp with General Gomez's men. "The day after reporting at the always shifting headquarters of Maximo Gomez was spent by the *expedicionarios,* as all recent arrivals from the United States were called, in resting after the trying march from the coast, and in accustoming themselves to strange surroundings and to a manner of life entirely new even to those who had seen no little of rough life in the open."[5]

Fred was soon sent for by the great, 60-year-old General Gomez. Speaking through an interpreter, the two men became acquainted. "The general began by expressing his appreciation of the spirit which had impelled us foreigners to leave our homes and cast our lot with a people struggling for independence, and then bluntly asked me what I knew about artillery. I told him frankly that my accomplishments were limited, to which he replied by saying, 'Well, you cannot know any less than another American who came down here and said he knew it all.' He then stated that he would place me in charge of the gun brought down on the *Dauntless,* and also of another and smaller Hotchkiss, one of 1.65 inch caliber, that he had with him, and said further that I would have the status of an officer with the privileges pertaining thereto, but that I would not actually be commissioned until after 'making good.'"

The conversation was not limited to military matters. "Then passing from weightier subjects, he asked me if I had ever eaten sugar-cane, and I had to confess that my acquaintance with the edible properties of that plant were about on a par with my knowledge of artillery. 'Well,' he said, with a grim smile, 'you cannot be a real rebel until you know how to eat sugar-cane;' whereat he took one of several joints from the ground under his hammock, and with the fine Moorish scimitar which he carried in lieu of the omnipresent machete, showed me how to strip off the tough bark and get at the juicy pulp. He then had me try it with my own machete, and was no little amused at my awkwardness."[6]

Fred recalled Gomez's personal interest in him. "From that time he always took a great interest in me, and if we came in contact when there was an interpreter at hand he would inquire how I was getting on and how I liked being a 'mambi,' the uncomplimentary term by which the Spaniards usually referred to the insurgents. He always called me 'Capi,' an abbreviation of the Spanish word *capitan*, captain." Fred's characterization of General Gomez captured Gomez's contradictory personality: "He was a stern, hard-hearted man, with a violent temper, but had in his nature some streaks of human kindness that shone luminously by contrast. He resembled exactly the many pictures of him that were published while he was in the public eye. He was a thin, wiry man with snow-white mustache and goatee, and was of pure Spanish descent, having the swarthy complexion of most Latins."[7]

The Americans were surprised to see that nearly all of Gomez's troops were white men. This was because the province of Puerto Principe, where they were, had a smaller percentage of Blacks than any other province in Cuba.[8] The officers of Gomez's forces were generally planters, cattle raisers, farmers, or professional or business men from the towns, and were "as a class the best men of the native Cuban population." Since many of them had lived in or been educated in the United States, scores of them spoke English. At this point in the war, these officers were well mounted. They dressed neatly in white duck, which constituted the insurgents' uniform to the extent that there was one. On their hats they each wore the tri-colored Cuban badge.

In contrast to the officers, the rank and file of Gomez's army consisted largely of employees of the plantations and cattle ranches, and, among them, many small farmers and cattlemen. There also were clerks, mechanics, and laborers from the towns. They were ragged, and some actually were barefooted. They were armed with Mauser and Remington rifles, and both the mounted officers and men carried the long, cavalry machete, whose blade was about 2½ feet in length. Dismounted men carried both a rifle and the short machete. Since the insurgent forces had acquired by this time a good supply of rifles and since the Spanish troops while on the march were taking greater precaution to prevent being surprised by the Cubans, the machete was used less as a weapon of war and more to dig sweet potatoes, chop firewood, and cut up beef. All officers and men carried the indispensable hammock. Made of either canvas or gunny sacks, these hammocks were hung between two trees when the army went into camp, being used as a chair in the daytime and a bed at night.[9]

"Unless chasing Spaniards or being chased by them,..." a typical day consisted of reveille sounded at three a.m., hours before the break of day. A later bugle call in the darkness signaled the movement of the troops in a column of twos. They marched until eleven when the bugles blew "halt" and the men scattered along the margin of a wood. Horses were unsaddled and picketed for grazing. The hammocks were swung, and cooking fires started. In the early period of Fred's time in Cuba, the men ate *"aijacco"* [sic: ajiaco], an "everlasting stew of meat and vegetables." These ingredients were cut up and placed in small iron kettles to boil. On the march, men carried the kettles, or they were strapped onto saddles. After the meal was over, a two-hour nap followed. "Then the camp livened up, there were visits back and forth, card games, and some singing by those who had accomplishments in that line." The second and final meal of the day was like the first one and was eaten just after dark. "Then groups gathered about campfires and talked until late at night." After tattoo and taps, sleep followed until reveille at three a.m. and the beginning of another day's march.[10]

When Fred and the other new arrivals reached Gomez's camp, they each were provided with a horse. Fred's was to be the first of nineteen that he "was to lose in one way or another." [11] According to Fred, a few days later he and the others also received their outfits—"white duck suits, heavy shoes, leggings, and Panama hats—and we were ready for war."[12] In reality, according to Fred's fellow artilleryman, Arthur Royal Joyce, Fred refused these clothes, and "was attired in a ragged hunting coat, and badly soiled corduroy trousers." This was Fred's outfit from the Death Valley expedition and from the coffee bean plantation adventure. "He wore this costume for the next six months in spite of our daily prayers that he adopt the prevailing make."[13]

Back home in Kansas, no one had heard from Fred since his presumed arrival in Cuba in mid-August. Then, in October his mother received a letter from him dated August 23, written at Los Angeles Plantation located in the Province of Camaguey (Puerto Principe). Kept in his parents' big family Bible, this letter, as printed in the *The Kansas City Star* following the December 1896 interview with Fred's father, read as follows:

> Dear Mother—I have not time to write you much of a letter, as in a short time a courier will leave the camp to take letters to the nearest postoffice. I shall only say that I am alive and well. We left New York August 10 by rail and went to a little town on the coast of Georgia, where we boarded a small steamer that in four days landed us on the coast of Cuba. We brought an immense quantity of arms and ammunition with

us. We have been six days on the island and have had some pretty tough hardships, but things are getting better now. We are in the rebel camp, where there are several thousand troops. The president of Cuba and his cabinet are here also. It is a very interesting experience and I do not consider it very dangerous. There are no Spanish troops near here now, and even where there is fighting it is not very severe. The health of the camp is excellent and the heat is not so great as at the same season in Kansas. Don't worry about me as I shall come out all right and be home next fall or winter.[14]

In late September, *The Kansas City Journal* devoted a number of paragraphs to Fred's situation as an American in Cuba. Under the headline "A Kansas Man In Peril," the newspaper opened with these words: "The killing by Spanish soldiers of Charles Govin, an American newspaper correspondent caught with the insurgents, reminds Kansas people of the fact that one of their favorite young men is now subjected to the same danger." After discussing Fred's past adventures, the *Journal* concluded that "[i]t is probable, however, that he has at last tackled a job which will leave nothing to be desired, so far as he is concerned, in the line of trouble. It will indeed be a grief to many thousands of Mr. Funston's friends should he get into the clutches of the cruel Spaniard who seems to know as little about civilized warfare as an Apache Indian. So brilliant and courageous a young man as Mr. Funston cannot well be spared by the rising generation."[15]

After noting that Fred's mother had received a few days ago Fred's letter dated August 23, Charlie Scott on October 30 drew this conclusion for his newspaper's readers: "Evidently he has not been able to get any mail out since that time as *Harper's Weekly*, for which he is correspondent, has had nothing from him. Wish we knew what is happening to him these days!"[16] A week later *The Kansas Semi-Weekly Capital* in Topeka expressed the sentiment that "Kansas people are getting anxious to know how Fred Funston is getting on in Cuba."[17]

The fears about Fred's fate were put to rest less than two weeks later. Friends in Lawrence received a letter from him dated September 30, written "In Camp, Province of Puerto Principe, Cuba," which was then published in *The Kansas City Journal* on November 18, and reprinted by Charlie Scott two days later in *The Iola Register*. The misspelling in the newspaper of the name of the town Cascorro as Coscomo likely was from a misreading of Fred's not-always-clear handwriting. If there were any personal portions, they were omitted in the letter as published:

I have had a very hot time in the ten days just past, which I will tell you about first. I got my command as captain of artillery in the army of Maximo Gomez, and we did a lot of aimless marching about the country, finally bringing up, the 21st inst., before the town of Coscomo [sic: Cascorro], defended by three Spanish forts. The infantry and cavalry of the force surrounded the town and cut off all communication with the outside, and during the night we built a sort of fortification of mahogany rails about 600 yards from the White fort and installed therein a 12-pound Hotchkiss breech-loading rifle. I had with me only a part of my battery and a detachment of ten men, half of whom were Americans. The Spaniards did not know of our presence until, just at daybreak, Old Ephraim gave a roar and sent a shell crashing into the fort. Pretty soon there was h— to pay. Every Spaniard opened on our position and the air was alive with bullets that buzzed like bumble bees gone mad.

They rattled on the barricade and many came through. Most of them shot high, however, and the trees over our heads were shot up badly. But we gave them as good as they sent, and shell after shell tore through the walls of the fort, bringing down tons of rock and cement. It was awful. I did the aiming of the cannon and every time I stepped before the gap it seemed that every man in the fort shot at me. One bullet split open the sole of my left shoe [and knocked off the heal, inflicting a considerable bruise], and half an hour later one of my men who had been opening a box of shells handed me the screw driver and as he did so fell dead, shot through the heart. From this position we fired fifty-eight shells and on the next three days shelled the main fort from a position on the opposite side of the town, distant 1,500 yards. I did some dandy target practice at that distance. The Spaniards kept popping away at us, and we were seldom without the hum of the festive bullet in our ears. On the morning of the fifth day, the infantry having advanced their position close to the forts, we carried Old Ephraim within 300 yards of the White fort, and in half an hours [sic] time hot work tore down what remained of it. The Spaniards, plucky devils, hung onto the badly shattered main fort, and as the artillery ammunition was exhausted, we were compelled to retire, and were sent to a plantation to remain until more could be brought up from the depot in another part of the island.

We have been here four days, and will probably be for

three or four days more before we return to the siege. In the meantime, the infantry and cavalry keep the town invested. I think that when the shells get here we will make short work of the badly damaged remaining forts.

There is something about this business that I like; it is so redhot and interesting. I am so busy during the time the fighting is in progress that I dont [sic] have time to get scared; I don't feel any fear until it is all over, and then I get scared at what has been gone through. I hope that I will live through this nasty business and get through all right."[18]

Fred referred to the "sort of fortification of mahogany rails" that the Cuban forces had built. These "parapets" were known as *trincheras*. The one built for this battle was typical of those used by the artillery on subsequent occasions: "Two rows of stakes about six feet high and three feet apart were driven into the ground and the space between them filled in with tightly tamped earth, which was held in place by a revetment of poles and fence rails, laid one on top of the other inside the two rows of stakes as the earth was filled in. A gap about the size of an ordinary door was left for the gun to be fired through. There was thus protection for a few of the infantry support and for the ammunition and the men handling it, but those actually loading and aiming the piece would be completely exposed."[19]

The night before the opening of the siege of Cascorro, Fred had been unable to sleep a wink. The artillerymen, including Fred, arose at 4 a. m. and went to where the gun was situated behind the parapet. In his letter, Fred wrote that "just at daybreak, Old Ephraim gave a roar and sent a shell crashing into the fort." In *Memories of Two Wars,* Fred described the details of his first shot:

It had been left for me to decide when to open fire, and now I gave the word. The veterans, Jones, Joyce, and Pennie, rolled and lighted fresh cigarettes, Welsford sought solace in an unusually large bite from the remnant of his last plug of "store tobacco," Joyce handed an ugly looking shell to Huntington, who slipped it into the breech as Potter opened the block, Pennie took the lanyard, and I squatted behind the gun with one hand on the elevating screw and aimed at that part of the building visible, while Jones, behind me, moved the trail to the left or right as I indicated. In a few seconds I was satisfied, gave the screw a turn to lower the muzzle, and stepping from the piece, climbed on top of the parapet to the windward of the gun in order to observe the shot, yelled "Fire!" to Pennie, and the ball had begun. I had forgotten to place my hands over my ears and was almost deafened by the crash within a few feet of my head. A fraction of a second later I saw a burst of flame and smoke from the upper part of the building and saw the bricks come tumbling down. Jumping down at once from my exposed position, I landed on the back of a Cuban patriot who was lying behind the parapet and put him out of that battle, the first casualty on the siege of Cascorra [sic: Cascorro].

Fred provided insight into unexpected dangers from these guns: "These twelve-pounders, very light guns for their heavy powder charge, were nearly as dangerous toward the rear as toward the front. Despite the brake ropes, which were adjusted before every shot, I have seen them kick down a slope or along slippery ground for twenty feet, so that we soon learned to have the deepest respect for the ground in rear of one of these guns. The only time we attempted to limit these antics was by means of a bank of earth, and this experiment resulted in a broken carriage."[20]

As to feeling nervous before a battle, Fred reminisced after his return from Cuba about his nervousness at the time of his first battle following his arrival on the island:

After getting into the Cuban army I wasn't long getting into a fight. We had some hot little skirmishes and then we had one hard battle after another in quick succession. Just before the first lively battle I was in I felt nervous. The Spaniards were drawn up in battle line on a knoll about 500 yards from us. We could just catch a glimpse of them occasionally. They were in close order to prevent the cavalry charging them. Just as soon as they saw us they blazed away. They filled the air with bullets, but didn't hit anybody. We were in skirmish line, standing about as far apart as fence posts. We returned the fire and there was a general fusillade. The Spaniards had Mauser rifles and smokeless powder. There would be an occasional puff of smoke, but that was about all we could see of them. We crouched in the grass and would rise up and shoot and then duck. Every time we would catch a glimpse of a Spaniard we would crack away. Those Mauser bullets whistled through the air and made an awful shriek, but after the shooting began I forgot all about my nervousness.[21]

Fred described his mental and physical conditions candidly: "I always had the nervous jim-jams before I went into a fight, and I always had nervous prostration after it was over." Following a battle later in the Philippines, "Col. Funston fell, completely prostrated from the exertion and the exciting experiences he had undergone," wrote Charlie Scott, who compared Fred to "the blooded horse that runs until it drops!"[22]

On the evening of the second day of the siege, Fred and Walter Jones on behalf of the Americans proposed to Gomez that "if he would have a good position constructed that night from which we might effectively shell the church [occupied by Spanish soldiers in Cascorro], and give us an hour in the morning in which to destroy that building, we would gladly lead an assault on that and the tavern positions, fixing two hundred men as the number of men required for the enterprise. It was our theory that if we made the dash the Cubans would follow us, and that once in the shelter of the trenches [in front of the two buildings] we could not be driven out by fire from the redoubt..." Several Cuban officers volunteered to help lead the attack. After first nearly agreeing to the proposal, Gomez "finally came out with an abrupt 'No!' telling us that we were madmen." Instead, he ordered the construction of another parapet only 200 yards from the Spanish-occupied trenches and from which we were "literally to blow the dons [Spanish soldiers] out of the ground. Jones and I maintained a discrete silence until out of earshot, and then made a few unprintable remarks about the turn affairs had taken."

The new parapet was constructed during the night at the cost of several men's lives, the Spanish soldiers firing volleys at the slightest noise. From the new location, Fred and his men fired the Hotchkiss after dawn, sending "a shell that landed squarely on the low line of earth-filled bags that capped the low parapet of the Spanish trench... The Spaniards were replying furiously, and the worst of it was that their bullets were all coming closer down to the ground, and were aimed at the gaping port-hole which they could so plainly see. It has fallen to me to participate in a good many fights in Cuba and the Philippines, but never anywhere have I seen the equal of what was poured into us during the hour that we held this position. The air was fairly alive with the sound of bullets, and their patter against the side of the parapet was so incessant that it would have been impossible to count them. The bark on trees was cut to ribbons, and small bushes near-by on our front were destroyed."

To make matters worse, the parapet had been incorrectly designed since the barrel of the gun was so short that the muzzle would not clear the head cover connecting the tops of the two wings of the parapet. After only a few shots of the gun, which moved when fired, the head cover was blown to pieces. "Under such circumstances, aiming the gun, the only part of its service which was required to be done while it was exposed, was enough to try the nerves of any but a wooden man."

Matters got even worse. "I was aiming the fifteenth shell when a bullet struck one of the trunnions almost at my nose. My nerves had been getting pretty shaky from several narrow escapes in sighting preceding shots, and I must confess that I threw myself flat on the ground and rolled to cover. Joyce jumped over me, quickly sighted the piece, and sprang from the gun. The imperturbable Pennie, lying on the ground and smoking a cigarette, jerked the lanyard and fired the last shot from this terrible death trap." After this the Americans were ordered to abandon the gun temporarily and take cover in a nearby ravine.[23]

Fred's fellow artilleryman, Arthur Royal Joyce, provided detail both about what occurred while the artillerymen were at forced leisure on a plantation awaiting the arrival of more ammunition, and about Fred's actions after they returned to the siege of Cascorro:

> We waited five days for the gun and ammunition, and during this time Funston told us innumerable anecdotes of his trip to Alaska and on the Death valley [sic] expedition. He also regaled us with his experiences as temporary editor in Fort Smith, Ark., which has since been published in the daily papers. As we got better acquainted we discovered he was a great admirer of Kipling and needed little encouragement to recite the fragments he knew of his verses.
>
> He also liked to sing with us, but the only tunes he was absolutely sure of were "Beulah Land" and "Marching Through Georgia," the former being his favorite.
>
> Finally the summons came to rejoin General Gomez at once, and we reached the camp before Cascorro that evening.
>
> Before reporting our arrival we skirmished around the camp for something to eat, as we had had nothing that day, and while thus engaged the general sent for us and jumped on us individually and collectively, as he well knew how to do, for not coming directly to him, saying that "soldiers should be able to go a week without eating or even thinking of it, but that Americans were always wanting to eat."
>
> After this ceremony he ordered us to the trench, where we found a two-pounder Hotchkiss, with only canister for ammunition. At five minute intervals during the night we amused ourselves by firing this into the town, for no earthly reason except that we had it and were ordered to use it.
>
> At daybreak Funston took two of us to the other trench,

which, to our amazement, we found was not more than 100 yards from the big fort. Five Cubans had been killed here during the night.

Before we could begin our operations with the twelve pounder it was necessary, in order to aim it, to cut down some bushes directly in front of the trench, and a Cuban sergeant was ordered to take two men and do it. He refused, however, saying he would be surely killed, and Pennie and another American performed the task, under a shower of bullets from the fort.

We were ordered to fire every five minutes, and after about an hour of this, under very heavy fire, Funston became a bit nervous, the first and only time I ever saw a trace of it in him. He was seated on the trail of the piece, aiming at the port holes from which a volley would come every minute, striking the cannon and all around him. I will state, for the benefit of those who have never tried it, that firing with a cannon at the whites of your enemies' eyes, at 100 yards range, while scores of him are returning the courtesy, is a bit disconcerting to even the strongest nerves.

A few minutes later I got in the way of a brass covered Remington bullet and rather lost interest in the proceedings. In the afternoon twenty stalwart soldiers were detailed to carry me in my hammock to a hospital 100 miles away, and the trip, lasting two days and nights, was exceedingly joyous.[24]

The following is Fred's postscript to his letter of September 30:

Later, October 16—Did not get an opportunity to send my letter and so add this postscript. Am still alive, but in rather rocky health. We got some more shells and returned to Coscomo [sic: Cascorro] and punched up the forts some more, but in the mean time a big Spanish column had come out from [the town of] Puerto Principe to raise the siege, which they did with neatness and dispatch [on October 5]. On the 8th inst., we had a big fight with the column, known as the battle of San Miguel. As there was no ammunition for the artillery, we fought as cavalry, and much to my horror I got mixed up in some "Light brigade" business.

Just at daybreak, three hundred of us charged a body of Spanish infantry. For five minutes the scene was perfectly indescribable—a perfect hellbroth of smoke, horses and men, with a deafening noise. My horse was shot dead under me forty yards from the Spanish line and I cut my saddle off and got out. One of my American artillerymen [Potter] who rode next to me was shot through both legs and had his horse killed. It was a horrible affair and both sides were glad to quit.

This is a hard life—riding all the time and eating only once or twice a day. I get horribly tired of the fare—beef, beef, beef, with a few plantains. Have not tasted bread for two months.

Somehow I don't believe I am going to get killed in this business.

We are now in camp near Guayma, province of Puerto Principe, with 3,000 men.[25]

After the suspension of the siege of Cascorro on October 5, Fred was the leader of his fellow artillerymen, who were all armed with rifles, in battle at Machuca on October 6, where "he fought with valor." On one occasion, probably October 7, Spanish artillery landed a cannon ball in the center of where the insurgent Cuban High Command was located. Fred promptly dug the cannon ball up, and, after unscrewing the fuse, presented it to General Gomez. There had been a continuous military operation of seventeen days from September 22 through October 8.[26] For Fred personally, a benefit of the Cascorro campaign was the receipt of his commission as a captain immediately after the campaign's conclusion.[27]

GENERAL MAXIMO GOMEZ.
"This is the portrait of the renowned Commander-in-Chief of the Cuban Army. He comes from a distinguished family, to which frequent reference is made in Spanish history. His great ability as a general is equalled only by his ardent devotion to the cause of Cuban freedom. General Gomez is over seventy years of age, and is proud to devote his last days to the cause he has served so long." [1896]

"DEADLY ENCOUNTER WITH THE SWORD AND THE MACHETE.
The Machete, to which constant references are made, is the implement used in cutting sugar cane. The weapon, however, is longer and narrower than the ordinary machete, and is very deadly in the hands of the insurgents." [1896]

"SPIRITED CHARGE OF CUBAN CAVALRY.
A large number of the Insurgents are cavalrymen. They are bold riders, accustomed in the peculiar characteristics of the country, and make their attacks with great dash and courage." [1896]

"AN INSURGENT ATTACK ON A FORT MANNED BY SPANISH TROOPS.
Many Forts are scattered throughout the Island. The engraving represents a spirited attack on one of these by a detachment of the army of General Gomez." [1896]

"A CAMP OF CUBAN INSURGENTS—COOKING A PIG.
The Cuban army, being compelled to subsist on the products of the country, is not
always able to obtain such a luxury as the one here represented. The view affords
an excellent idea of the personal appearance of the patriot army and its uniform, if
such it can be called." [1896 photo]

"CUBAN INSURGENTS EAGER TO RE-ENFORCE OUR TROOPS AFTER THE [AMERICAN] LANDING NEAR BAIQUIRI—RUINS OF ROUND-HOUSE, BURNED BY FLEEING SPANIARDS, IN BACKGROUND."

A good view of what Cuban insurgents looked like during the Spanish-American War of 1898.

THE SIEGE OF CASCORRO.

"Never anywhere have I seen the equal of what was poured into us during the hour that we held this position."

—Fred Funston (*Memories of Two Wars* illustration)

Chapter Three Notes—*Letters VI and VII*

Epigraph: "Victory Not Easy," *The Kansas City Star*, April 23, 1898. Interview with Fred Funston at Iola, Kansas, on April 22, 1898.

1. Frederick Funston, *Memories of Two Wars: Cuban and Philippine Experiences* (New York: Charles Scribner's Sons, 1914), 26-27.

2. Arthur Royal Joyce, "New Stories Of Funston's Exploits In Cuba," *The Kansas City Times,* October 29, 1899 (Frederick Funston Papers, hereafter FFP) (Archives Division, Kansas State Historical Society).

3. William Allen White, *The Autobiography of William Allen White* (New York: The Macmillan Company, 1946), 143.

4. Louis Stanley Young and Henry Davenport Northrop, *Life and Heroic Deeds of Admiral Dewey* (Philadelphia: Globe Bible Publishing Co., 1899), 348. Quoted is William A. DeFord, the first commissioned officer appointed in Kansas at the outbreak of the Spanish-American War. As adjutant, he recruited the entire Twentieth Kansas Regiment.

5. Frederick Funston, *Memories of Two Wars*, 29.

6. Frederick Funston, *Memories of Two Wars*, 30.

7. Frederick Funston, *Memories of Two Wars*, 31.

8. Frederick Funston, *Memories of Two Wars*, 28.

9. Frederick Funston, *Memories of Two Wars*, 31-33.

10. Frederick Funston, *Memories of Two Wars*, 34-36.

11. Frederick Funston, *Memories of Two Wars*, 33.

12. Frederick Funston, *Memories of Two Wars*, 37.

13. Arthur Royal Joyce, "New Stories Of Funston's Exploits In Cuba."

14. "A Kansas Cuban Soldier," *The Iola Register*, December 25, 1896 (reprint from *The Kansas City Star*).

15. "A Kansas Man In Peril," *The Kansas City Journal*, September 21, 1896.

16. "The Week's News," *The Iola Register*, October 30, 1896.

17. "A Bird's-Eye View," *The Kansas Semi-Weekly Capital*, November 6, 1896.

18. "Fred Funston In Cuba," *The Iola Register,* November 20, 1896. This letter was reprinted from the *The Kansas City Journal* of November 18, 1896, which stated that it had been written to unidentified friends in Lawrence, Kansas. A shorter version, with minor changes, appeared in *Kansas University Weekly,* November 28, 1896, a student newspaper at the State University of Kansas.
   In a March 1898 lecture Fred provided more detail about the death of the man who had "handed me" the screw driver, but the detail is slightly different: "A young sophomore from the University of Pennsylvania, who was in our troop, was the first man I saw killed in battle, and it affected me a good deal, but I soon got used to it, as all old soldiers do. He was tending one of the guns and it was not working well. I got the screw driver and he had reached out his hand for it when he said something in a jerky way and fell down dead" ("Cuba As Funston Saw It," *The Kansas City Star*, March 11, 1898).

19. Frederick Funston, *Memories of Two Wars*, 41-42.

20. Frederick Funston, *Memories of Two Wars*, 43-44 and 70.

21. "Victory Not Easy," *The Kansas City Star*, April 23, 1898. Interview with Fred Funston at Iola, Kansas, on April 22, 1898.

22. "Frederick Funston," *The Iola Daily Register*, February 22, 1917 (editorial tribute by Charles F. Scott) (Kansas State Historical Society, *Frederick Funston Clippings*, Vol. 1) for Fred's quotation. "Brigadier General Funston," *The Iola Daily Register,* May 2, 1899 (editorial by Charles F. Scott).

23. Frederick Funston, *Memories of Two Wars*, 48-53.

24. Arthur Royal Joyce, "New Stories Of Funston's Exploits In Cuba."

25. "Fred Funston In Cuba," *The Iola Register,* November 20, 1896. A shorter version, with minor changes, appeared in *Kansas University Weekly,* November 28, 1896, a student newspaper at the State University of Kansas.

26. Armando Prats-Lerma, "La Actuación del Teniente Coronel Frederick Funston, (Norteamericano) en la Guerra de Independencia de 1895-1898," *Boletin del Ejercito* (Habana, Cuba, Noviembre y Diciembre de 1931), 363-364.

27. Frederick Funston, *Memories of Two Wars*, 67.

CHAPTER FOUR

"Desmayo – The Cuban Balaklava"

October 8, 1896

Desmayo was among the most notable of the battles in which Fred and the other artillerymen participated. This was the "light brigade" charge by the insurgent cavalry against the Spanish infantry on October 8, 1896, which Fred described in his letter postscript eight days later. There he called it the battle of San Miguel, likely for the nearby town of San Miguel de Nuevitas. By the following January and thereafter, he called the battle Desmayo from the name of the estate where it was fought.

Shortly after Fred's return from Cuba in January of 1898, he wrote a colorful and graphic account of this charge. In the *Harper's Weekly* article, Fred was identified as the "Late Lieutenant Colonel and Chief of Artillery of the Cuban Insurgent Army."[1] In writing this account, Fred omitted the shooting of his horse from under him that he had mentioned in the postscript of his letter, but, in the *Harper's Weekly* account reprinted below, I have inserted in brackets additional detail taken from two interviews of Fred after his return from Cuba.

* * *

DESMAYO—THE CUBAN BALAKLAVA

For twelve days, in the autumn of 1896, the Cuban insurgents had been laying siege to the little town of Cascorra [sic Cascorro], fifty miles east of the city of Puerto Principe; but although the three forts had been rendered untenable by artillery fire, the heroic little garrison, scarcely 150 men, of a Tarragona regiment, still made a stubborn defence from the trenches, and sent defiant replies to all of Gomez's communications demanding their surrender. The aged and peppery-tempered rebel chieftain fretted and fumed, and paced up and down before his tent for many an hour, but could not bring himself to throw his newly recruited infantry against that maze of barb-wire fences, exposing them to the fire of 150 Mauser rifles in the hands of men who, it was evident, meant to fight to the death.

Gomez had about 600 cavalry, 300 infantry, and a small squad of artillerymen with two Hotchkiss guns, although Spanish accounts of the engagement credit him with more than 5000 men—a most ridiculous assertion.

On the 5th of October the expected happened, and insurgent scouts guarding the roads to the westward of the beleaguered town announced the approach of a Spanish force of 2500 men coming to the relief. Gomez hastily withdrew his forces from about Cascorra [sic], and taking a position at the *potrèro* La Machuca, three miles to the westward, calmly awaited the arrival of General Castellano's column of 2500. The engagement, which began at four o'clock in the afternoon, lasted scarcely an hour, the Cubans making no attempt to force the fighting, and before nightfall the heroic garrison of Cascorra [sic] was cheering the advance guard of the relieving column. Gomez camped on the battle-field, and the next day kept his tireless scouts watching the Spaniards in Cascorra [sic].

Our two guns that had been used in besieging the town and in the engagement at La Machuca were sent away to a *perfectura* to remain until the arrival of more ammunition for them, while we artillerymen asked and received permission from General Gomez to incorporate ourselves for the time being with his cavalry escort.

At three o'clock on the morning of the 7th a scout dashed furiously into camp. Gomez was awakened and gave a few sharp orders, and in ten seconds the blare of the bugle had tumbled the men out of their hammocks, and in a surprisingly short time another blast sent them groping through the darkness to find their picketed horses.

The whole camp was a scene of confusion. A drizzling rain was falling, and the darkness was intense. The only light was a candle that Gomez's orderly was holding while the old man dressed himself.

The cause of all this uproar was that General Castellano was trying to steal a march on us by evacuating the town in the darkness, while the Cuban chief was determined to bring him to another and better fight than La Machuca. Despite the confusion, our force was on the march in half an hour after the first alarm, and picked its way through the drenched grass to the *camino real*, or main road, half a mile to the north where we remained until the break of day. The patter of shots could now be heard, as the insurgent scouts were annoying the enemy's advance. After half an hour of this desultory skirmishing scouts brought the information that the enemy had left the main road and turned to the northward, evidently intending to strike the railroad at Las Minas, instead of at Puerto Principe. They had a two hours' start; but Gomez instead of falling in behind and giving direct chase, spent the entire day trying to head off the column and force it to fight. The fact came out afterward that the Spanish commander's unwillingness to come to bay was because he believed the opposing force to number 5000 men, instead of less than one-fifth that number. Had not Gomez been encumbered by his infantry he would have succeeded in his plan, but as it was the two forces marched in a curved parallel the entire day, the scouts on the Cuban right flank and those on the Spanish left coming into contact and skirmishing at intervals. And so all day we splashed through muddy lanes, or filed across grassy *potrèros*, where herds of cattle, alarmed at the skirmish firing, stampeded and tore madly away, heads and tails in air. At nightfall the two forces halted within two miles of each other, both afraid to advance further in the darkness.

The Spanish column was in the main road leading into the town of San Miguel de Nuevitas, and about a league from that place. We merely dismounted, and picketed our horses to graze without removing the saddles. No attempt was made to prepare food, as there had been no time during the day to kill cattle, and as the insurgents are not in the habit of burdening themselves with a provision train, there was nothing in camp to be cooked. The majority of us had swung our hammocks, in the hope of obtaining a few hours' rest, and had barely got settled down, when low whistles sounded through the camp; for the blast of the bugles might disclose our whereabouts to the enemy, and word was passed along the line to remount at once. In a short time we were again in the saddle, and filed out slowly along a little path that led through the dripping woods. Orders to maintain absolute silence were passed along the line. The darkness was Egyptian [expression meaning the darkness was pitch black], but our guide knew his business well, and in an hour we were planted in the main road ahead of the Spanish column. Here we again dismounted, and seated ourselves with backs against the tree trunks, and passed what seemed an endless night.

Gomez and staff remained awake all night, and from time to time scouts came in to report that the enemy was still in camp two miles distant.

At four o'clock in the morning came the order *à caballo* (to horse), passed down the line in whispers. In less than half a minute 600 men were in the saddle, prepared for what all knew was going to be a hot fight; for Gomez's blood was up, and the old man, usually so silent and noncommittal, had announced openly that he was going to give the enemy something to talk about for the next year.

The people of the sanitary were left behind, under Doctors Molinet and Silva, and made preparations to receive and care for the wounded. With them remained such impedimenta as officers' servants and a few sick. A hundred men, under Major Guerra, were detached to protect the field hospital in case of defeat, and the remainder of us marched down the road through the woods for a mile. Gomez was at the head with his staff, followed by his escort of sixty cavalry, and behind these the first and a part of the second squadrons of Camaguey. At the first glimmer of dawn we emerged from the woods into a beautiful level savanna on the Desmayo estate. The grass was about knee high to a horse, and palmettos were scattered here and there. A line of battle, two ranks deep, was formed across the road at right angles and we sat on our restless horses awaiting the coming of day. Gomez and his staff took a position on the left wing, and did not participate in the charge that followed. Lieutenant-Colonel Bernabe Bosa, chief of the escort, who was to lead the attack in person, rode up and down in front of the line, cautioning that the most absolute silence be maintained, and ordering all to unsling their carbines and prepare for action.

Bosa was a nervous, excitable fellow, but recklessly brave in action. He rode up to where we Americans were, on the extreme right of the line, hoped that none of us would get hit, and confided to us that Gomez intended to charge the head of the Spanish column as it came marching up the road, and throw it into confusion. It is evident that he little expected to find the enemy in line of battle ready to receive him.

It was now fairly daylight, but an impenetrable fog had settled down over the landscape, and one could not see thirty feet in any direction. As we sat on our horses awaiting developments, we fell to conversing in whispers, and I noticed that the voices of all, Americans and Cubans alike, had a decided tremor. If a man's personal feelings at such a moment are of interest, I am free to confess that I would have given a handsome sum to be elsewhere. It was the long wait, the doing nothing, that unstrung the nerves of all. On account of the fog, our scouts had been withdrawn from in front of the line, lest, in case the fight opened suddenly, they be caught between two fires.

We now began to hear noises in our front, sometimes the neigh of a horse or the bray of a mule, but more than anything else the sort of undefinable sound made by more than 2000 men splashing along the muddy road, with the accompanying jingle and rattle of their arms and equipment. The rumbling grew louder and nearer, and all of us were straining our eyes to pierce the fog, when suddenly it ceased, and all was as silent as ever. At this juncture a breeze sprang up from the eastward behind us, and began to roll back the fog.

Our own line was soon uncovered, and we got a good look at ourselves for the first time, and saw a slightly curved double line about 300 yards long. Near our end of the line was the silk flag of Gomez's escort, carried by a big negro sergeant. Slowly backward rolled the fog, gradually uncovering the ground on our front, while the sun, half an hour high, showed himself for the first time and lighted up the whole scene gloriously. The nerves of all were strung to the highest pitch, for we knew that the crisis was at hand.

Finally we made out on our front, not more than 400 yards distant, something that at first looked like a hedge or a picket fence; but in a few seconds more, as the fog cleared up, it was seen to be a force of infantry in line of battle, forming two sides of a hollow square, with two field pieces at the angle ready for action. The enemy had suspected that we were on their front, and were prepared to receive us. Mingled exclamations of surprise and consternation ran up and down the line. Would the general order a charge or a retreat? Opinions on this point were about evenly divided. There was an embarrassing wait of half a minute. Gomez was taking in the situation before deciding what to do. The Spaniards, uncertain whether we were Cubans or Spanish guerillas who had come out to meet them, hesitated to open fire. But the suspense was soon over. From where Gomez and his staff were waiting came the quick, jerky ra-ta-ta-ta-ta of the headquarters bugle sounding the charge. The effect was magical and instantaneous. The moments that followed were, it seems to me, worth some years of humdrum existence, and it would be a mighty poor sort of man whose heart would not thrill as his mind went back to that wild charge across the Cuban savanna. The whole line moved forward, first at a trot, and then at a gallop. The Cubans were firing over the heads of their horses as they advanced, with Winchester and Remington carbines, while above the terrific din rose the yells of *Viva! Viva Cuba! Adelante, adelante! Arriba, arriba!*

We had covered scarcely forty yards, when a blaze of light broke along the whole front of the Spanish line, followed in a few seconds by another, and then another, while at each discharge the air about us seemed full of the spiteful crackling of Mauser bullets. The scene that followed is beyond description. Men and horses were falling on every side, while above the crash of rifle volleys and the booming of cannon rose the frantic cheers of the Cubans and the thunder of nearly two thousand hoofs. The Spaniards gave us six perfect volleys, emptying the magazines of their rifles, but their fire after that was at will and rather wild—usually too high.

But it does not take long for horses to gallop 400 yards, and in a short time we were upon them. The Cubans showed no disposition to force their horses on to the bayonets and come to close quarters with the machete, but rode furiously up and down the line at a distance of from twenty to forty yards, emptying carbines and revolvers in the faces of the Spanish infantry, and did good execution. The Spaniards, who at the beginning of the charge had done such perfect volley firing, were now shooting wildly. All had their rifles at the hip instead of at the shoulder, and were madly pumping bullets into the air; and, incredible as it may seem, even at that close range the greater part of their fire was passing over our heads. We were so close to the Spanish line that we could distinguish the features of the men whenever there was a temporary rift in the smoke. It was plain that they were excited, but there was no sign of panic or of giving way. The two Spanish cannon, that had peppered us badly with canister while crossing the open space, were now withdrawn behind the line, for fear of capture. We had held our hopeless position on the Spanish front for something more than a minute, and it seemed that, notwithstanding the bad firing of the enemy, we were to be cut to pieces, when suddenly a lively scattering fire opened on our right, and the woods 500 yards distant were being flecked with the white smoke of the Remingtons. We were certain that the new arrivals were friends, for the Mauser rifle used by the Spanish regulars makes little or no smoke, and our surmise was correct. Avelino Rosa, the Colombian, had arrived with 300 infantry, and was making a well-directed and most determined attack on that part of the Spanish half square facing the north, which hitherto had not been in action. This fire, of course, caught on the flank the side with which the cavalry was engaged, and rendered the Spanish position untenable.

The Spaniards facing the attacking infantry replied to their assailants with rapid volleys, but with little effect, owing to the fact that the Cubans were deployed in open order and were advancing stooping and crawling. The closely packed Spaniards standing upright lost more heavily, and their commander, doubtless thinking that the attacking force was a large one and that he was in danger of being surrounded, ordered a retreat, which was conducted without confusion, they carrying from the field all their wounded and the greater part of their dead, the rear-guard in the mean time keeping up a fire on Rosa.

Under ordinary circumstances this would have been the opportunity of the Cuban cavalry to use the machete, but they had been so severely punished that they were glad enough to quit.

There were scarcely a hundred mounted men left, half of those not killed or wounded having lost their horses. Within five minutes after the bugle had sounded that fatal charge the battle of Desmayo was at an end. [My horse was shot a few feet from the Spanish lines, and I busied myself with removing my saddle and bridle. Good saddles and bridles are too scarce in Cuba to lose. When I got my saddle and bridle I walked away, because I was no use there on foot, and was only in the way.[2]] [He "walked away" by tying the saddle to one of his legs and the bridle to his other leg, and then crawled on his stomach about a quarter of a mile to get away from the battle.[3]]

The Spanish loss, as we afterwards learned on good authority, was 204 between killed and wounded.

At Balaklava the Light Brigade charged against men armed with muzzle loading flintlocks and batteries of old-style cannon. In the ride of half a league they lost thirty-seven per cent of their [total] number [of about 670] in killed and wounded, and the world will never forget the story of their valor.

At Desmayo that little force of 479 Cubans rode against magazine rifles, firing twenty shots a minute, and breech-loading artillery, and held their position in the face of that pitiless fire until fifty-two per cent had tumbled from their horses, killed or wounded [251 of 479[4]].

But nobody has written a poem about us, or ever will.

* * *

The famous Charge of the Light Brigade occurred in 1854 when British Cavalry during the Crimean War charged a heavily defended Russian position. The British cavalry was slaughtered as they rode through the so-called "valley of death," and their famous charge was immortalized by poet Alfred, Lord Tennyson, in his "The Charge of the Light Brigade." That Fred, as a well-read lover of history and poetry, would see the similarities of the "light brigade" charge at Desmayo with that at Balaklava is not surprising.

What is surprising are the discrepancies between the foregoing article and *Memories of Two Wars*. Fred's account in his book of the battle at La Machuca differs significantly from that in his article, where he stated: "The engagement, which began at four o'clock in the afternoon, lasted scarcely an hour, the Cubans making no attempt to force the fighting, and before nightfall the heroic garrison of Cascorra [sic] was cheering the advance guard of the relieving column. Gomez camped on the battle-field, and the next day kept his tireless scouts watching the Spaniards in Cascorra [sic]."

In contrast, Fred described the battle in *Memories of Two Wars* as follows:

Then came the clash, the battle of La Machuca. There was no hope of preventing the relief of the town, but the general was determined to make the Spaniards know that they had had a fight, and he certainly accomplished that purpose. The day was a perfect one and the entertainment of the best. For three hours the Spanish volleys and the rattling irregular fire of the Cubans made a pandemonium, added to by the booming of the Spanish batteries. A thin film of smoke drifted above the tree tops, and all was excitement and noise. But the Spaniards broke through and entered the town. Certainly visitors were never more welcome. They camped there that night, and the Cubans fired on them incessantly. It is a safe guess that not one of them had a wink of sleep.[5]

The account in *Memories of Two Wars* about what occurred two days later, October 6, is also significantly different from the account in the article "Desmayo–The Cuban Balaklava." The book's account:

The [Spanish] garrison was increased, the ammunition supply replenished, and the defences improved, and on the evening of the next day [October 6] the Spaniards issued from the town on their return, and the Cubans were promptly upon them. They made a few miles before nightfall and bivouacked, peppered all night by their tormentors. The next morning [October 7] about three o'clock they resumed the march. The whole fifteen hundred of us were drawn up on both sides of the Camino Real to give them another fight, but the column turned to the north-westward, passed our left flank before our dispositions could be changed, and headed for the railroad between Las Minas and Nuevitas. Our infantry followed and attacked their rear-guard repeatedly, while five hundred of us mounted men, under the general himself, hung onto their left flank. It was a lively and exciting day. A few shots would grow into a heavy roll of fire, to die out in a few moments, and begin again in another quarter. And so we swept along all of a beautiful day. Just after dark, as they were going into bivouac, the last clash with the rear-guard occurred.[6]

In the article, Fred described Gomez and his army spending the entire day trying to head off the Spanish column and force it to fight. The two forces, Fred noted, "marched in a curved parallel the entire day, the scouts on the Cuban right flank and those on the Spanish left coming into contact and skirmishing at intervals." A quite different story from the book's account of the Cuban infantry attacking the Spanish rearguard "repeatedly."

The next day was October 8, the battle of Desmayo, about which Fred wrote so colorfully and in detail in his article. In contrast, in *Memories* he wrote only this: "The next morning the mounted men made a savage attack on the advance-guard, and a lively scrimmage ensued in which we had three killed and sixteen wounded. Poor Potter, one of Pagluchi's wards, had both legs shattered and had his horse killed under him, and spent the next year on his back in one of the lonely hospitals."[7]

The foregoing refers only to an attack on the Spanish "advance–guard," *not* the battle with the entire Spanish column of 2,500 men described in the article. *Memories* is thus totally silent about the Battle of Desmayo and contradicts the article's account by reporting only an attack that morning on the advance guard.

Of significance to this discrepancy is Fred's account of the battle in his October 16, 1896, letter postscript:

> On the 8th inst., we had a big fight with the column, known as the battle of San Miguel. As there was no ammunition for the artillery, we fought as cavalry, and much to my horror I got mixed up in some "Light brigade" business.
>
> Just at daybreak, three hundred of us charged a body of Spanish infantry. For five minutes the scene was perfectly indescribable—a perfect hellbroth of smoke, horses and men, with a deafening noise. My horse was shot dead under me forty yards from the Spanish line and I cut my saddle off and got out. One of my American artillerymen who rode next to me was shot through both legs and had his horse killed. It was a horrible affair and both sides were glad to quit.[8]

This contemporary account is much more consistent with Fred's 1898 article about the battle with the Spanish column than with the *Memories of Two Wars* account, which described only an attack on the Spanish advance guard that day. Interestingly, in his book account of the "scrimmage" with the Spanish "advance-guard," he noted that Potter had "both legs shattered and had his horse killed under him...," yet from his letter account of the battle with the column, we know that one of the American artillerymen who rode next to Fred "was shot through both legs and had his horse killed." Clearly, Potter was severely wounded in the battle with the column, not in a "scrimmage" with the advance guard. I believe that the 1898 article is the correct account, not the *Memories* account. Interestingly, in 1912, the year after the publication of his book, Fred prepared a "Memorandum" of his military service, which noted his participation in the battle of Desmayo as one of the 479 men in the charge, and that 251 of them had been killed or wounded.[9]

Why all of these discrepancies between the 1898 article and the 1911 book? There is no easy answer. The article is nearly contemporaneous, having been written a little over a year after the battle of Desmayo. In contrast, the book account was written nearly fifteen years later. Various thoughts come to mind. The article was written shortly after Fred's return from Cuba, a time when the battle of Desmayo was not only prominent in his memory but was a battle that had made a great impression upon him. By the time he wrote *Memories* years later, he perhaps regarded the battle as not as important as he had thought at the time. He had become a seasoned professional soldier, not a volunteer soldier with no military training. His years in the Twentieth Kansas and in the U.S. Army had shaped a professional with many combat experiences, and, thus, perhaps a different perspective on the significance of the battle of Desmayo.

At the time that Fred wrote his article, the sheer drama of the battle and its similarity to the famous charge of the light brigade undoubtedly appealed to him. It was an epic battle, and he had been a participant though, not surprisingly, he did not single himself out, including the fact that he had his horse shot under him. A gifted writer, Fred likely enjoyed drafting his account of a light brigade charge, which he viewed as equivalent to that memorialized by Alfred, Lord Tennyson.

Perhaps Fred simply got mixed up in his memory when writing *Memories*. He wrote the book under personally difficult circumstance and in "a big hurry," and these circumstances may have affected in places both the amount of detail that he included and the accuracy of his memory of certain events fifteen years later. *Memories of Two Wars* was completed in early 1910, and the Cuban portion was serialized in *Scribner's Magazine* in the fall of that year. In the summer of 1908, Fred had been assigned the demanding position of Commandant of The Army Service Schools at Fort Leavenworth, Kansas. He described The Army Service Schools as "an institution where as regards real military work West Point is completely outclassed, being a mere kindergarten in comparison."[10]

In September of 1909, Fred slipped and fell on a sidewalk, breaking his right arm. Not long before, he had broken several ribs in a fall.[11] The next month, his seven-year-old son, Arthur MacArthur Funston, died unexpectedly from whooping cough at the home of his maternal grandparents in Oakland, California, where he was staying. Because their younger son, Frederick Jr, was seriously ill with pneumonia, Fred and his wife, Eda, were unable to leave Fort Leavenworth to attend their older son's funeral and burial in San Francisco.[12] Fred "affectionately dedicated" *Memories of Two Wars* "To The Memory Of Arthur MacArthur Funston the little boy who in happy days gone by often sat on my knees and, open-eyed and wondering, listened to the story of the cruise of the *Dauntless* and to accounts of midnight rides in the Philippines; but who now sleeps forever in the national cemetery of the Presidio of San Francisco, under the shadow of the flag his childish heart so loved..."[13]

The next year, on June 24, 1910, the Associated Press reported that Fred was "dangerously ill with an attack of heart disease at his home."[14] The following day, Fred's attending physician described the report as "entirely erroneous," and stated that he was suffering from a reoccurrence of a malarial attack he had experienced several years before.[15] Seven years later, when Fred died from a heart attack, his personal physician said that Fred had had several angina attacks. "The first of them, as far as I know, occurred in 1910. It was very slight and little attention was paid to it."[16]

In early 1910, Fred corresponded with Osmun Latrobe, his former comrade in arms in Cuba, to verify certain details for *Memories*. At the end of February, Fred noted: "I have been so busy recently that I have hardly been able to keep my head above water."[17] Two years later, in 1912, Fred described the circumstances involved in writing *Memories of Two Wars*: "If I had not done the work under such adverse circumstances, a part of it while crushed by terrible bereavement, and all of it during such time as I could occasionally give to it, I am sure it would have been better, for I must say that a careful study of it in cold type shows some eruditics."[18] To longtime friend Billy White, Fred candidly wrote: "Nobody realizes [the book's] deficiencies from a literary standpoint any more than I do, but most of the work was done in a big hurry and in the face of great difficulties."[19] Whatever the reason for the omission of the Desmayo battle from *Memories of Two Wars*, the drama of the story of the charge of the light brigade, as beautifully captured by Fred, remains unchanged.

Illustration for Fred Funston's article, "Desmayo — The Cuban Balaklava".

Chapter Four Notes—*"Desmayo — The Cuban Balaklava"*

1. Frederick Funston, "Desmayo —The Cuban Balaklava," *Harper's Weekly,* March 5, 1898.

2. "Funston Is Sick and Sore," *The Kansas City Star*, January 11, 1898 (Frederick Funston Papers) (Archives Division, Kansas State Historical Society).

3. James B. Morrow, "F. Hopkinson Smith, Engineer, Artist, Author, Lecturer—'Discoverer,'" *The Washington Post*, December 8, 1907. This contains the account of an 1898 interview of Fred by Smith. After Fred became nationally famous in 1899, Smith, who built the base for the Statue of Liberty in New York Harbor, wrote to Fred in the Philippines, on May 22, 1899, telling him that he is the fourth hero with Dewey, Sampson, and Hobson. Smith expressed his intention to come, if he could, to Kansas City when Fred returned home from the war. Smith noted that "the Country will go wild when you come + you must expect to have your clothes torn off" (Frederick Funston Papers on microfilm, hereafter FFP Micro) (Archives Division, Kansas State Historical Society).

4. "Memorandum In Regard To Military Service Of Brigadier General Funston," attached to Frederick Funston to Joseph L. Bristow, October 24, 1912 (Joseph L. Bristow Papers) (Archives Division, Kansas State Historical Society).

5. Frederick Funston, *Memories of Two Wars: Cuban and Philippine Experiences* (New York: Charles Scribner's Sons, 1914), 59-60. David Potter in his biography of Fred basically follows the description in Fred's book in these words: "For an hour or more, Gomez held the Spaniards. Then the latter advanced down the Camino Real, splitting the Cuban forces apart. But the Cubans clung so obstinately to the flanks of the Spaniards that it took the latter nearly two hours to win the three miles to Cascorro" (David Potter, *Frederick Funston: A First Class Fighting Man: A Biography,* 119 (manuscript) (David Potter Manuscripts; 1950s, Manuscripts Division, Department of Rare Books and Special Collections, Princeton University Library).

   I find Potter's biography frustrating. He rarely uses notes to support his text and thus one never knows what sources he has relied on. He was a captain in the U.S. Navy and had been a friend of Fred.

6. Frederick Funston, *Memories of Two Wars*, 60-61.

7. Frederick Funston, *Memories of Two Wars,* 61.

8. See Chapter Three for the complete letter, including the postscript from which the quoted portion appears.

9. "Memorandum In Regard To Military Service Of Brigadier General Funston."

10. Frederick Funston to Woodrow Wilson, October 14, 1912 (Joseph L. Bristow Papers) (Archives Division, Kansas State Historical Society).

11. "Gen. Funston Breaks Arm In Fall to Walk," *The Leavenworth Times*, September 19, 1909.

12. "Gen. Funston's Son Dies In California," *The Leavenworth Times*, October 31, 1909.

13. Frederick Funston, *Memories of Two Wars*, dedication page.

14. "Gen. Funston Sick," *The Leavenworth Post*, June 24, 1910.

15. "Funston Not Seriously Ill," *The Leavenworth Post*, June 25, 1910.

16. "Attack Follows Dinner Party and End Comes Almost Instantaneously," unidentified San Antonio, Texas, newspaper with assumed date of February 20, 1917 (FFP Micro).

17. Frederick Funston to Osmun Latrobe, February 27, 1910 (Papers of Osmun Latrobe, 1900-1932, Manuscript Division, Library of Congress).

18. Frederick Funston to E. E. [Edwin Emery] Slosson, May 8, 1912 (Kansas Collection, RH MS P814, Spencer Research Library, University of Kansas).

19. Frederick Funston to William Allen White, February 14, 1912 (William Allen White Collection, Special Collections and Archives, Emporia State University, Emporia, Kansas).

CHAPTER FIVE

Letter VIII

November 9, 1896
"In Camp, Province of Puerto Principe, Cuba"

**I am rather glad that I am in this war. It is a
game fight and is steadily gaining.**

—Fred Funston, November 9, 1896, letter

After the brief but exciting Cascorro campaign, the thousand men
under General Gomez joined on October 13 the two thousand men
of General Calixto Garcia. They planned to lay siege to the town of
Guaimaro, which was located sixteen miles east of Cascorro. Funston
and the other Americans serving under General Gomez soon learned
that General Garcia also had two guns, and these were officered by
Americans. Fred and the others "found several likable and interesting men who were to be our comrades through many months to come.
These were Major Winchester [Win] Dana Osgood, who had won fame
as a foot-ball player at Cornell and the University of Pennsylvania;
Captain William Cox, of Philadelphia; Lieutenants Stuart S. Janney
and Osmun Latrobe, Jr., of Baltimore, and [sic] James Devine, of Texas, and Dr. Harry Danforth, of Milwaukee. All except the latter, who
served as a medical officer, belonged to the artillery, with Osgood in
command."[1]

Fred and the others serving under Gomez were soon presented to
Garcia, a veteran of the Ten Years' War (1868-1878), the unsuccessful Cuban attempt to evict the Spanish from the island. Fred vividly
described the General: "He was a man of most striking appearance,
being over six feet tall and rather heavy, and his hair and large mustache were snow-white. What at once attracted attention was the
hole in his forehead, a souvenir of the Ten Years' War. On September 3, 1874, being about to fall into the hands of the Spaniards, and
believing his execution to be a certainty, he had fired a large-calibre
revolver upward from beneath his lower jaw, the bullet making its

exit almost in the centre of his forehead. It is safe to say that not one man in ten thousand would have survived so terrible an injury. He was taken prisoner and owed his life to the skill of a Spanish surgeon, though he remained in prison until the end of the war, four years later. To the day of his death, nearly twenty-four years later, the wound never entirely healed, and he always carried a small wad of cotton in the hole in his skull."[2]

General Garcia most kindly received Fred and the others. "General Garcia was a man of the most undoubted personal courage and was a courteous and kindly gentleman. His bearing was dignified, but he was one of the most approachable of men. He seldom smiled, and I never heard him laugh but once..." There was a great contrast in personalities between Generals Gomez and Garcia: "Those of us Americans who had served under Gomez always regarded him with something akin to awe or fear, but all who came in close contact with Garcia had for him a feeling of affection. He was always so just and so considerate, and though some of us must have exasperated him at times, so far as I know he never gave one of us a harsh word. When the provocation was sufficient, however, he could be terribly severe with his own people."[3]

The Americans were fortunate since General Garcia's staff of about a dozen young Cubans spoke English. All were from the best Cuban families. In contrast with General Gomez's forces, General Garcia's troops had "a much larger proportion of negroes" since the troops came from the province of Santiago. There were several well-known Black chieftains, including Rabi and Cebreco. Fred found that some of the Black officers were "quite capable in guerilla warfare, while others were mere blusterers and blunderers." "Although the color line is drawn in Cuba in social matters, white men of the best families did not hesitate to serve under negro officers, and sometimes on their staffs."

Fred found the Cuban Blacks in the insurgent army "a most interesting study. They seemed much more forceful and aggressive than our own colored population as a rule, probably the result of most of the older ones having served in the Ten Years' War. And then, too, they had lived a more out-door life than the majority of the negroes of our Northern States, being plantation hands and small farmers, and had not been weakened and demoralized by city life." Many of the older Blacks had been born in Africa even though the slave-trade had been abolished by law "many years ago," but "it is a matter of common knowledge that up to as late as 1870 small cargoes of slaves from the west coast of Africa were run into Cuba."[4]

The combined forces of Gomez and Garcia, under the command

of General Gomez, the insurgent commander in chief, rested—both men and horses—for a few days. Then the three thousand soldiers marched toward Guaimaro. Garcia's two guns were identical to the two guns used by Gomez's artillery at the siege of Cascorro: a Hotchkiss twelve-pounder and a Hotchkiss two-pounder. These four pieces of artillery were "all steel breech-loading guns, using fixed ammunition." The combined force of artillerymen served under the command of Major Osgood, who held the highest rank, Fred holding the lower rank of captain.[5]

Fred told the story of the siege of Guaimaro in a letter dated November 9, written while he was "In Camp, Province of Puerto Principe, Cuba." That day was Fred's thirty-first birthday though he made no mention of it. Addressed to Charlie Scott, the envelope containing the letter bore "Jamaica postage" and was postmarked Kingston, Jamaica, and Boston. It took nearly three months for the letter to arrive in Iola on the following January 30.

As usual, Charlie published the latest letter in *The Iola Register*. Under the headline "It Is Now Major Fred!" and a sub-headline, "A Breezy Letter," he provided this introduction for his readers: "It is purely a personal letter, of course, but there is such keen and sympathetic eagerness for news from Fred, not only among his home folks but all over the State, that we would hardly feel justified in not making the letter public. It is a most characteristic letter, speaking lightly of greater dangers and modestly of great honors, full of confidence and hope. There is only one Fred Funston." Using the handwritten original, this letter is printed below, and, in doing so, I have compared it with the Scott publication. In brackets, I have noted where Charlie Scott deviated in his published version from the original text and also have identified in brackets the portions which were not published in the newspaper:

My dear Scott

The mail facilities in this war-wasted island are so bad that there is almost no use in writing letters at all. I have had opportunity to send to Harpers only twice, and am not sure that those got through. But I am going to try my luck at sending to you anyhow.

To start with, I cannot attempt to tell the hundredth part of what I have seen, for my three months here would fill a book.

Have been mixed up in some mighty stiff fighting but as yet have not been hit and rather hope that I wont [sic] be.

I am rather glad that I am in this war. It is a game fight and is steadily gaining. Next spring [Scott incorrectly printed "summer"] will see Cuba a free and independent nation. The prevalent notion in the states that a large proportion of the Cuban rebels are retired bandits and ex toughs, is a great error. [Scott incorrectly printed "mistake" instead of "error."] They are the best people of the island, and men of every rank and profession are fighting just as they did in our civil war. The officers are nearly all men of education and good family. The Cubans are unanimous for the war and all statements to the contrary are Spanish lies.

The situation now is this—The Spanish troops remain in the fortified towns and never venture out except in large bodies. On Oct. 8 at San Miguel we administered a hot drubbing to one of those columns and incidentally I had the pleasure of having a horse killed under me during the exercises. The Cubans roam at will over the country watching for Spanish columns and convoys, but rarely attacking the fortified towns.

We recently made an exception to this rule, however, and as a result have gained the greatest and most substantial victory of the war. Gens. Gomez and Garcia besieged the town of Guaimar [sic: Guaimaro] defended by twelve Spanish forts, and as most of the fighting was done by the artillery, I had a pretty big [Scott incorrectly printed "something of a" instead of "a pretty big"] finger in the pie. On the second day the chief of artillery Maj. Osgood (U. of Pennsylvania's famous football player) was killed and I succeeded to the command. For days we pitched shells into the forts, and on the night of Oct 27 the infantry assaulted and captured a number of the badly damaged forts. [But Lord old man,] it would take a day to tell you all about that terrible night. [Scott then added: "but the short of it is that"] We dragged cannon by hand through the streets and compelled the surrender of the barracks [Scott incorrectly printed "place" instead of "barracks"] [and had a regular Fourth of July of a time.]

We captured many rifles and great quantities of ammunition, and carried away the garrison as prisoners of war.

On account of some of the Kansas funny business done by my battery during the siege I have been promoted to major or as they call it in Spanish "comandante," and made chief of artillery of of [sic] all the forces operating in the eastern half of the island. My chances of reaching the grade of colonel are I think, very [Scott incorrectly printed "fairly" instead of "very"] good. I have in some way managed to get a pretty big "stand in" with the leaders of the revolution.

Now that the rainy season is over the conditions of life in the field are not half bad, and I certainly enjoy the responsibility and power of my position. I am furnished by the government with two servants, one to attend to my horse, and the other to cook.

We live on fresh beef, plantains, sweet potatoes and more or less vegetable bric-a-brac peculiar to the tropics. I never had better health than here, and (unless I sometime try to stop an unusually hot bullet [ )] stand a mighty [Scott deleted "mighty"] big chance of coming home in good [Scott incorrectly printed "prime" instead of "good"] condition and I want to warn you in advance that I am going to be mighty proud of the fact that I helped boost the Spanish government off from this island. [Scott incorrectly, and strangely, changed "that I helped boost the Spanish government off from this island" to "that I did what I could in my modest and retiring way to boost the Spanish from this island."] All I ask is that people dont [sic] call me "Majoh."

[I tell you old man it is a great thing to have read Kipling before one mixes up in some real fighting, and sees the bullets "kicking up the dust spots on the green" as they do in the ballad Gunga Din.

[But we shall talk about all of these things when I get back and put my feet under your mahogany as I have done many times of yore.

[By the way it seems mighty hard to get mail here and I have not had a single letter since leaving New York. Try your hand at writing me. My address is the Cuban Junta 56 New St. New York. They are suppose to forward mail to us.] We are all confident that the war will end in the spring by Spain giving up the fight, and then I am coming home to get a little Kansas ozone and good home made pie into my system. I know that I should yearn for something higher and nobler than pie, but I have become imbruted by these scenes of carnage, and I cant [sic] soar anymore. Lieut. Penny [sic: Pennie], a Washington D.C. boy who is at my side insists that the apple dumpling is a nobler bird than the pie, but then he never lived in Kansas.

[Write me a long letter.]

With much love to you and yours.

[I am your old friend]

     Fred Funston

[P.S. I swiped this piece of paper from one of the captured forts at Guaimar [sic: Guaimaro].][6]

Major Win Osgood, was, in Fred's words, "probably the foremost of American amateur athletes" and "a magnificent specimen of physical manhood."[7] The day before Osgood's death, the Cubans had captured a Spanish blockhouse, located on a hill above the town of Guaimaro. During the Spanish retreat from the blockhouse, a Spanish solder had been killed and his body lay between the abandoned blockhouse and the next blockhouse. "Not having had enough excitement during the day," adventurous and fearless Fred and Captain Jose Estrampes from New Orleans, who was a member of Gomez's staff, crawled in the darkness of the night to where the dead soldier lay "and came back ahead an excellent Mauser rifle." Also during the night, Osgood had a breach made in the first-floor wall of the blockhouse in order to bring in one of the Hotchkiss guns, and then had a port-hole made in the wall on the town side to fire the gun through.

The next morning, Osgood opened fire on the town, but due to a shortage of ammunition, only one shot per hour was allowed. When firing, Osgood sighted the gun after Latrobe, to the gun's left, placed the shell in the breech block. Janney, from the right side, pulled the lanyard to shoot the gun. Absent Americans that morning were Cox, down with fever, and Devine, who, in a horse raiding expedition the afternoon before, had been badly wounded by a shot in his hip. Janney, a man of prodigious strength, had valiantly rescued Devine from capture or death by half carrying and half dragging him up the hill before the blockhouse "under a fire that it would seem impossible a man could live through, it being especially severe after he got half-way up and he was exposed to nearly all the Spanish positions."

Fred, Jones, and Pennie had joined their fellow Americans in the blockhouse that morning. Its double walls consisted of planking and logs, six inches apart, and broken stone filled the gap between them. The first floor, where the Hotchkiss was situated, was protected by an outside earthen embankment several feet high. About every five minutes, a Spanish sharpshooter shot a bullet from the town's church tower. The shots hit either near or entered the blast-enlarged port-hole. Several spokes of the gun were hit. A Cuban passing to the gun's rear was killed. Fred was more fortunate, a bullet missing him by only an inch or two.

The morning was hot and sultry. The volleys of bullets shot by Spanish troops hit the blockhouse, grazed the earth, and a few penetrated the blockhouse above its earthen embankment. All this created a lot of dust and dirt. Osgood stripped to the waist.

Latrobe, Osgood's fellow Penn student, later wrote: "When the volleys came, slivers of stone from the blockhouse walls would fly in all directions and [Osgood] was bleeding from light cuts on head and shoulder. He was calm, determined, and the same powerful physique, which brought him fame in many hard-fought athletic contests, he still possessed—but begrimed by dust, sweat and blood. There were no thousands, this time, to yell him applause—his last fight."

Osgood sighted the Hotchkiss and started to step back. There was "the sharp, close crack of a Mauser bullet," and Osgood fell forward on the gun's trail, and then onto Latrobe who had been crouching beside the gun. The bullet had struck Osgood in his forehead and then exited a few inches beyond. He was unconscious and breathing heavily. As the "bullet course" swelled and his fellow Americans waited for a surgeon, they prayed that the wound would not prove fatal. When the surgeon arrived, "he gave no hope." Osgood's hammock was strung to a pole, and after he was placed in it, a Cuban soldier at each end carried the hammock. Their destination was a hospital hidden in the woods. Unconscious to the end, the famous Win Osgood died en route to the hospital.[8]

Osgood's unexpected and terrible death was a terrific blow to the small band of American comrades in arms. As Fred recalled in *Memories of Two Wars*, "The little group of aliens, fighting in a strange land for a cause not their own, were sore stricken. It was the first time one of our own number had been killed. Bound together by ties of race and language, and sharing the daily dangers and privations, we had become closer to each other than men ordinarily do in years of acquaintanceship under different circumstances, and now felt that the war was coming home to us. For a time we did nothing but sit in the blockhouse, well back from the fatal port-hole, and gaze in awe at the spatter of blood on the gun trail and note the devilish regularity with which the missiles from the sharpshooter's rifle whistled past us."

Fred's selection as Osgood's successor as chief of artillery was not automatic. Both Fred and William Cox were captains, the highest-ranking American officers. Cox had served under General Garcia, who favored his selection, while General Gomez preferred that Fred be designated. As Commander in Chief, Gomez prevailed over Garcia, and hence Fred became chief of artillery of the *Departamento del Oriente*.[9]

The capture of Guaimaro after a thirteen-day siege provided an opportunity for sleep. "The most of us had reached the limit of physical endurance, having been without sleep since the morning of the second day before, and sank down anywhere in the shade, letting the war take care of itself for a few hours."[10] The attitude of the Cubans toward their many captured prisoners varied depending on who they were:

> Considering the fact that the Spaniards waged a war of absolutely no quarter, even murdering the wounded who fell into their hands, it was a matter for congratulation that not a single one of the prisoners taken at Guaimaro was in any way injured. In fact the Cubans seemed to bear no hatred whatever against the Spanish regulars, knowing that they had no option either as to their participation in the war or the methods of carrying it on. But the Spanish volunteers, made up of the Spanish residents of Cuba, who had of their own volition gone into the struggle, often fared badly at their hands, while for the hated guerillas, Cuban mercenaries in the Spanish service, it was certain death to fall into the power of the insurgents. It was these wretches who in that war committed many of the horrible atrocities that brought a stain on the Spanish name. Fortunately there were neither volunteers nor guerillas in Guaimaro, so that we were spared a painful sequel to the victory. The spoils of the siege were considerable, about four hundred Mauser rifles, several hundred thousand rounds of ammunition, and subsistence and medical stores.[11]

"In the scenes of loot and destruction following the surrender Funston showed himself to be a military genius of the first order," noted Arthur Royal Joyce. "With Pennie, he devoted himself to the commissariat, and in a quiet, unostentatious manner they accumulated about all of the provisions in the town, and the artillery lived high for the next two months."[12]

The seizure of about 400 Mauser rifles and several hundred thousand rounds of ammunition was a great boon for the insurgents. Obtaining critically-needed weapons and ammunition was a never-ending challenge and worry. Some rifles and cartridges were purchased from corrupt Spanish officials. Penniless Spanish soldiers paid for the services of Cuban prostitutes with rifle cartridges which were, in turn, sold to the insurgents. Thus, these cartridges "pathetically enough, might later bring about [a Spanish soldier's] own death." The *Junta* abroad, however, was relied upon to provide the arms and ammunition, purchased through its fund-raising efforts, and which could only be delivered to the revolutionists by the *Junta's* filibustering expeditions.[13]

The pressing need for ammunition was forcefully expressed by one of Commander in Chief Maximo Gomez's generals, who wrote to him: "It is necessary that our forces do not remain inactive, so they do not lose their enthusiasm, and for this reason, I demand that they fight. I hope you will send me the ammunition I ask for." In a further communication from the general, he wrote, "It is absolutely impossible for me to face the enemy because I have no ammunition whatever to give the force until I receive some from you." Gomez supplied what arms and ammunition he could but, according to the *Junta's* lawyer, usually no one was satisfied, which created "much bitterness."[14]

This difficulty in securing sufficient arms and ammunition affected how the Cubans fought the war. Generally, they avoided pitched battles and engaged in guerrilla warfare, the Fabian fighting mentioned by Ed Funston in his December 1896 interview with *The Kansas City Star*: "The Cubans fight with a sort of Fabian policy, a little fighting, a good deal of running away; but that's the way to fight." The Cubans with their familiarity with their island had an advantage in choosing where they wanted to fight. When engaged in fighting, the Cubans fought in open order while the Spaniards fought in a line of battle or squares. They formed into a square, which offered a broad target for the Cubans. When the Cubans attacked a Spanish vanguard, it generally fell back on the main column of troops, which reacted by forming squares for action. "Thus it is that a few Cubans will harass a Spanish column for miles, retiring slowly, forcing the regulars to form time and again [into squares], inflicting numerous losses, and goading the enemy to madness at the impossibility of retaliation."[15] During Fred's seventeen months of combat, he had the broad experience of fighting in numerous skirmishes, twenty-four battles, and four sieges of fortified towns.[16]

The victorious Cubans communicated to General Castellanos, the Spanish commander at the town of Puerto Principe, that they were willing to turn the Spanish wounded over to him. The others would remain prisoner. Without waiting for Castellanos to accept this offer, on October 31 the insurgent forces, now swollen to four thousand men with the addition of other commands, set out for the proposed rendezvous point about a day's march east of Puerto Principe. It was a tough march for all involved. "It was the height of the rainy season and for months we had been accustomed to being drenched at any time day or night, so that the good night's sleep in the buildings of Guaimaro had been very much in the line of a treat. It must be remembered that there was not a tent in this whole force, and all were expected to take the weather as it came. The march was painfully slow, and the roads being in shocking condition, and much delay was caused by the slow progress of the prisoners carrying their wounded comrades in improvised litters. The rain poured in torrents, day and night, and it was almost impossible to build fires for cooking."[17]

Fred had a disconcerting experience on this march. "At our first camp a Cuban officer talking to the sorely wounded Spanish commandant just as I happened to pass, said to him, I thought with wretched taste, 'That American is the man who gave you your wound, as he personally sighted every shot at the church on the last day.' The wounded officer, a very handsome and dignified man with snow-white hair and beard, looked at me in a reproving and wondering way, and I slunk out of sight, my peace of mind pretty badly disturbed."[18]

"After four days of grueling work," the rendezvous was reached and the wounded delivered to the Spanish, who soon arrived. "The brave old commandant survived his wounds only a few days more." The insurgents then marched to the *potrero*, "Auracana," near La Yaya. There "I had the pleasure of receiving my commission as major, dating from the fall of Guaimaro, and of seeing it signed by both our chieftains."[19] In addition to promotions for several Americans, including Huntington who was promoted to the rank of captain, General Garcia "gave the large sum of $100, to be divided among the artillery, and the government supplemented this with another $100 for Funston personally."[20]

Cuban campaign marches were replete with discomforts. "In winter the horses stirred vast clouds of dust which, penetrating eyes, ears, noses, and mouths, stained everybody a forbidding red. There was intense suffering from thirst. In summer the terrific sun temperature and mud, produced by daily rains, made travel difficult. Chills were always likely after sudden showers; all the men were tempted to eat unripe fruit and drink impure water. These dangers constantly stalked the Spanish troops as well."[21]

The fall of Guaimaro to the insurgent forces had immediate consequences. Alarmed by its fall and concerned about the safety of the little garrison at Cascorro, which in September had successfully repelled the insurgent attack, the Spanish commander of the district advanced with a force of more than four thousand men. His goal was to relieve the garrison at Cascorro, and then abandon the town. "Gomez and Garcia resisted desperately with a like number, and the next week saw some of the hardest fighting that ever took place in Cuba."[22] At the battle of Lugones, on November 6, Fred fought as a part of the infantry.[23] According to Fred, the battle of Lugones was "very bloody," and "the Spanish murdered thirty-eight of our wounded on the field after the battle. We found the bodies afterward and they had actually bayoneted every wounded man they found."[24]

Fred summarized in *Memories of Two Wars* this post-Guaimaro action: "For four days it was almost one continuous battle, but limitations of space compel passing over this campaign other than to say that the Spaniards finally reached their goal, after losing several times the number of men that they had come to rescue. In this fighting, General Garcia had his magnificent saddle-horse, of which he was very fond, killed under him."[25] When the Spanish abandoned the detachments at Cascorro and San Miguel de Nuevitas, that left "the whole east side of Puerto Principe free of royalists."[26]

After the conclusion of this fighting, Garcia and Gomez divided their forces, the latter marching westward to take charge of military operations in Santa Clara province. Huntington, the former Canadian Mountie who had come to Fred's aid in Charleston when surrounded by the Spanish spies, went with Gomez, and was killed the next year in a battle with guerrillas. His body fell into the enemy's hands and was chopped to pieces. The remaining artillery officers stayed with Garcia, who also kept all of the guns. Fred assessed what had occurred: "The moral effect of the Guaimaro victory on the Cubans was very great. For the first time they had made assaults on men in trenches and protected by barb-wire entanglements. They were schooling themselves for the far bloodier work at Jiguani and Las Tunas..."[27]

GENERAL CALIXTO GARCIA.

This renowned Commander has long been a conspicuous figure in Cuban insurrections. In the latter part of 1895 he was imprisoned at Madrid. Being liberated, he returned at once to the United States, and was instrumental in organizing a formidable expedition to aid the Cuban Patriots. He is considered one of the ablest and most courageous Commanders among the Insurgents.

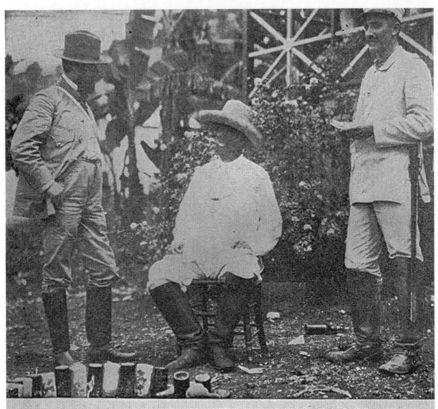

JAMES CREELMAN, WAR CORRESPONDENT, INTERVIEWING GENERAL GARCIA AND HIS SON AT SIBONEY.

Photograph taken during the Spanish-American War of 1898.
General Calixto Garcia's son was Lt. Colonel Carlos Garcia.

The Spaniards were driven from one of their blockhouses at Guaimaro. Lieutenant Luis R. Miranda climbed to the blockhouse roof and, under crossfire from all of the Spanish forts, he "slowly and painfully" drew himself up the eighteen-feet tall, four-inch thick wooden flagpole and cut loose the Spanish flag. "Every Spaniard in Guaimaro could see him, and I believe to a man tried to bring the gallant fellow down." (Fred Funston) Miranda slid down the pole with the flag, and then leapt to the ground. He was uninjured in this daring feat.

In Funston's words: "It would be difficult to imagine a feat of more reckless daring..." This is the blockhouse where Win Osgood received his fatal wound the next day.

(*Memories of Two Wars* illustration)

"Janney half-carried and half dragged the wounded man up that slope under a fire that it would seem impossible a man could live through." (*Memories of Two Wars* illustration)

"For a couple of hours, Osgood, Funston, and others shelled the Spanish-held Isabella blockhouse and others in the vicinity." (*Memories of Two Wars* illustration)

"Four thousand victorious Cuban soldiers and their Spanish prisoners
on the march after the fall of Guaimaro. 'The march was painfully slow,
the roads being in terrible condition.'"
(Fred Funston)
(*Memories of Two Wars* illustration)

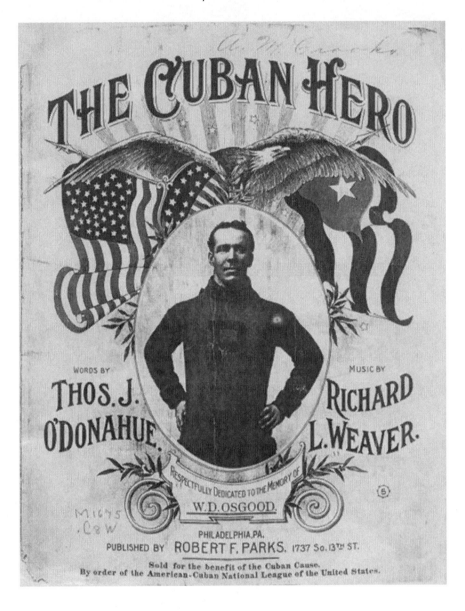

THE CUBAN HERO.

or

The Stars And Stripes Of Liberty

I Pinned Upon His Breast.

Words by THOS. J. O'DONOHUE.   Music by RICHARD L. WEAVER.

1. While stand-ing in the moonlight, My gal-lant love and I, He
2. While fight-ing with the Spaniards He was al-ways in the fore, My
3. A doz - en bal-lets pierced him, His life's blood ebb'd a - way,

95-708634

Chapter Five Notes — *Letter VIII*

Epigraph: Frederick Funston to Charles F. Scott, November 9, 1896 (see Note 6).

1. Frederick Funston, *Memories of Two Wars*, 62.
2. Frederick Funston, *Memories of Two Wars*, 63.
3. Frederick Funston, *Memories of Two Wars*, 63-64.
4. Frederick Funston, *Memories of Two Wars*, 64-65.
5. Frederick Funston, *Memories of Two Wars*, 66-67.
6. "It Is Now Major Fred!", *The Iola Register,* February 5, 1897. Photocopy of original letter of November 9, 1896, is in collection of Frederick Funston's letters from Cuba and New York City at Allen County Historical Society, Inc., Iola, Kansas.
7. "Colonel Frederick Funston Gives Some Facts About Cuba," *The St. Louis Republic*, February 7, 1898.
8. Osmun Latrobe, "The Fight at Guaimaro and the Death of Winchester Dana Osgood, '94," *The General Magazine and Historical Chronicle*, Vol. XXXIV, number 4, July 1932 (University of Pennsylvania alumni publication). For Janney's rescue of Devine, and for Funston's near miss of the sharpshooter's bullet and retrieving the dead soldier's Mauser, see Frederick Funston, *Memories of Two Wars*, 75-78.
9. Frederick Funston, *Memories of Two Wars*, 79.
10. Frederick Funston, *Memories of Two Wars*, 92.
11. Frederick Funston, *Memories of Two Wars*, 92-93.
12. Arthur Royal Joyce, "New Stories Of Funston's Exploits In Cuba," *The Kansas City Times,* October 29, 1899 (Frederick Funston Papers, hereafter FFP) (Archives Division, Kansas State Historical Society).
13. Horatio S. Rubens, "The Insurgent Government In Cuba," *The North American Review*, May 1898. For "penniless soldiers," see Horatio S. Rubens, *Liberty: The Story of Cuba* (New York: Brewer, Warren & Putnam Inc., 1932), 213.
14. Horatio S. Rubens, *Liberty: The Story of Cuba* (New York: Brewer, Warren & Putnam Inc., 1932), 268-269.
15. Horatio S. Rubens, "The Insurgent Government In Cuba," *The North American Review*, May 1898.
16. Fred Funston to Charles F. Scott, August 31, 1897. Photocopy of original letter in collection of Frederick Funston's letters from Cuba and New York City at Allen County Historical Society, Inc., Iola, Kansas. Funston noted that he had fought in twenty-two battles and four sieges. Subsequently, he fought in two more battles.
17. Frederick Funston, *Memories of Two Wars*, 94-95.
18. Frederick Funston, *Memories of Two Wars*, 95.
19. Frederick Funston, *Memories of Two Wars*, 95-96.
20. Arthur Royal Joyce, "New Stories Of Funston's Exploits In Cuba."

21. Horatio S. Rubens, *Liberty: The Story of Cuba* (New York: Brewer, Warren & Putnam Inc., 1932), 270. Rubens, an American, was the lawyer for the Cuban *Junta* and played an important role in the events of the war of independence (1895-1898).

22. Frederick Funston, *Memories of Two Wars*, 96.

23. Armando Prats-Lerma, "La Actuación del Teniente Coronel Frederick Funston, (Norteamericano) en la Guerra de Independencia de 1895-1898," *Boletin del Ejercito* (Habana, Cuba, Noviembre y Diciembre de 1931), 365 (FFP).

24. "Victory Not Easy," *The Kansas City Star*, April 23, 1898.

25. Frederick Funston, *Memories of Two Wars*, 96.

26. Armando Prats-Lerma, "La Actuación del Teniente Coronel Frederick Funston."

27. Frederick Funston, *Memories of Two Wars*, 96-97. Account of Huntington's death from Frederick Funston to Osmun Latrobe, February 27, 1910 (Papers of Osmun Latrobe, 1900-1932, Manuscript Division, Library of Congress).

CHAPTER SIX

Letters IX and X

January 1, 1897
Cuba

January 22, 1897
"Headquarters, Deptartment of the Orient, in the field near
Holguin, Cuba"

**You must not have any fears regarding my safe
return. I am satisfied that the war is nearly over
and that there will be but little more fighting.**

—Fred Funston, January 1, 1897, letter to family

After the Spaniards relieved and then abandoned Cascorro, and
after the subsequent very bloody battle of Lugones in November 1896,
Fred fought the next month in another equally bloody battle. In an
interview in February 1898 after his return to the United States from
Cuba, Fred told briefly about this Battle of Bayamo, and gave insight
into the coverage of the revolutionary battles by United States newspapers:

> Concerning the reports that are sent to the American
> newspapers by their Cuban correspondents, Colonel Funston
> declared that in a great many instances the dispatches were
> without foundation in fact. He does not charge the correspon-
> dents with deliberate "faking," but says that they are often
> misinformed, both by the Spanish and insurgents.

> Unreliable News From Cuba

> "Most of the fights that are reported by Havana and Key
> West correspondents never occur," said he. "There are no cor-
> respondents in the field, and the information that reaches the
> Havana correspondents is therefore usually unreliable. The
> biggest battle fought during the present revolution—bigger,
> even than the 10 years' war—never reached the ears of the
> correspondents and consequently did not get into the newspa-
> pers. It was the battle of Baymo [sic] and occurred in Decem-
> ber, 1896. The insurgents, 3,800 in number, under General

100

Garcia, defeated 4,500 Spanish after a five-hour hand-to-hand struggle. The Spanish made a grand bayonet charge and were repulsed. A series of ambuscades, cleverly planned and executed by the insurgents, accomplished the complete defeat of the Spanish forces. [In a later interview, Fred was quoted as stating the Spanish had 4,800 and the insurgents 3,500; he reported "[w]e lost 463 and they lost 681. We were after them hot then."[1]]

"The report of this engagement which was forwarded to the Cuban Government headquarters was probably intercepted and destroyed by the Spanish. Another report was sent but it was not as complete and accurate as the first, and very likely met the same fate. The newspapers did not have a line about this battle, although it was, in addition to being the largest, one of the most important in the entire revolution. That is a fair example of the uncertainty which attaches to the getting of Cuban news.

"Newspapers occasionally reached us in the insurgent camp, although they were always from one to three months old. The Spanish authorities do not allow American papers containing reports of the war in Cuba to pass though the lines, but the insurgent spies in the Cuban cities managed now and then to get papers to us."[2]

Come January 1 of the new year of 1897, it was time for Fred to write again to his family. His letter of this date survives, but only from its publication in *The Iola Evening News* of January 30. The letter had arrived at the Funston home on January 28, just under a month after being mailed, and thus had arrived in an unusually short period of time in comparison with other letters that Fred sent from Cuba.

Apparently, it was simply luck that resulted in the January 1 letter's publication in *The Iola Evening News*. After reprinting the letter, and likely omitting any personal aspects of it, the newspaper's editor provided this editorial comment: "It was the great pleasure of your reporter to be at the comfortable home of this cultured family when the above, to them, most welcome letter was received and read and from parts of which now and then the anxious and justly proud father, read extracts to use [sic: us] we became convinced that here was matter of much interest to your [sic: our] many readers and was permitted to extract the above."

Under the headline "Cuban Letter" and illustrated with a sketch of Fred's face and upper body, this new year's letter appeared promi-

nently on the front page of *The Iola Evening News*. This was a recently established newspaper in its first year of publication, and the fact
that it, and not its rival, Charlie Scott's *The Iola Register*, secured
from the Funston family the right to publish Fred's letter is surprising. Charlie Scott was also likely surprised, and probably displeased
about this, in view of his close friendship with Fred and the Funston
family. Charlie did not reprint Fred's letter of January 1 in *The Iola
Register,* however, likely because the day *The Iola Evening News* published Fred's letter, Scott received Fred's letter to him of November 9,
which he soon published.

The Iola Evening News reporter continued his account with great
compliments to the Funstons: "By the way your reporter here, as
elsewhere in this vicinity, was warmly and hospitably received we
were very favorably impressed. Here we found an exceedingly comfortable place to rest after our journey over the roughest roads we
ever traveled. We were royally entertained by one of our most clever
farmer families. It was our pleasure to see in this pleasant home, one
of the largest and best selected libraries to be found in our county
and it is our opinion after this stay and long conversation that these
numerous volumes are [not] kept for ornamental purposes alone. We
will ever remember our kind treatment at this home where a worthy
father and kind, loving mother guide the ship of home. It is a home in
which one loves to be and from which one is loth [sic] to depart, but
our duty to you and the News caused us to take our departure all too
soon."

Fred's location in Cuba when he wrote his letter of January 1
was not disclosed by the newspaper nor was the name of the specific
family member who was the addressee. Fred's new year's letter, as
published, is as follows:

> I think the beginning of the new year would be a good
> time to write a letter home.
>
> I have written home every two or three weeks, as often as
> I had the opportunity, but have no idea how many of my let-
> ters have gotten through the Spanish lines. So far I have not
> received a single letter from home or from any of my friends,
> though I am sure that some have been written to me. They
> are probably lying about some of the military camps or have
> been lost. All the news that we Americans have from home is
> that McKinley was elected [United States president], and we
> had a celebration in honor of the event.
>
> You must not have any fears regarding my safe return. I
> am satisfied that the war is nearly over and that there will

be but little more fighting. You know that I came down here intending to be correspondent of Harer's [sic: Harper's] Weekly, but the difficulty of getting letters out of the country, has made me practically give that up, and I have gone in for soldiering more than I intended originally.

On Oct. 28, I was promoted from Captain to Major, and am now Chief of Artillery in the Dept. of the Orient, which comprises all the eastern half of the island.

I am very glad that I came here, I have had some wonderful experiences to add to those that I have already had and have not been wasting any time either.

The greatest thing here is the numerous opportunities to make money that I have seen. The island of Cuba is rich almost beyond belief, but has never advanced much because of the wretched Spanish rule and heavy taxes. As soon as the war is over and the island free, there will be a wonderful boom and no one will stand a better chance of making money than the Americans, who helped to free the country.

I have made good friends of people in high position—the president, the members of his cabinet, and the leading generals, and have talked to them about business matters after the war, and they have given me much encouragement.

Altogether, I think my prospects are bright enough now though I surely have run some terrible risks and have been mighty near being killed several times. Did I write you that at the battle of Desmayo I had my horse killed under me?

But there is no use in attempting in a letter to tell you the incidents of the war. I shall do that when I come home in the spring.

There are a number of us American officers here and we always camp together and have many pleasant times. They are all young men of good education and are all captains or lieutenants in the Cuban army. Usually we have had plenty to eat, but just now we are in a country where provisions are scarce. We tried hard to have a good dinner on Christmas day but could get nothing but boiled beef.

But as I said before, I did a mighty good thing when I came here as you will see in the end. The hardships of the life here are not as great as I expected, especially since the rainy season is over. I have two servants, furnished me by the government, one to cook, and the other to look after my horse, but I am ragged, for it is almost impossible to get clothes. But then, one does not need much clothing here as the weather is not bad. I have never had better health than here in Cuba.

If you want to see where I am, look on a map of Cuba, about 60 miles north of the city of Manzanello, which is on the southeast coast.

Write me soon and address 56 New St. New York, care of F. E. Palma, on the lower left hand corner write, Cuartel General Departments [sic] del Oriente.[3]

Fred's January 1 letter, as printed in *The Iola Evening News*, was carried by other Kansas newspapers, including *The Topeka Weekly Capital. The Iola Evening News,* as a rival to *The Iola Register,* did not last long. By November of 1897, Charlie had eliminated the competition by purchasing it. He changed the paper from a five-column folio sheet to a daily paper.[4] Perhaps the publication of Fred's letter led a newspaper in the nearby town of Chanute to opine that "[o]ver at Iola they really believe that Fred Funston stands up and lets the Spaniards flatten their bullets on his chest."[5]

In summary, by January 1 Fred had been on the island of Cuba for just over four months. He had been forced to abandon his plan of being a journalist, with the result that he was a full-time soldier. Although still interested in helping the revolutionists obtain independence from Spain, Fred's eyes had now been opened to the economic opportunities available to the Americans, including himself, once the Cubans gained their independence. He was still alive and uninjured, and life was basically good, in part because of his belief that the war would soon be over and he would be able to return home in the spring. As he wrote, "I am very glad that I came here, I have had some wonderful experiences to add to those that I have already had and have not been wasting any time either."

It was about this time that Fred had been studying to improve his ability to speak Spanish. He did this by using a copy of Ollendorf's Spanish grammar he had picked up. Arthur Royal Joyce remembered that Fred "acquired considerable fluency in the language," but there were still language problems for him. "It used to pain him, however, to ride up to a house, and in his best Ollendorfian enquire if the 'well disposed lady would kindly give him a glass of water,' to have the said 'well disposed' turn to one of her numerous family and ask what he said, saying apologetically, to him that she did not understand English. His fluent English on these occasions was not at all flattering to the Cubans."[6]

Back home in Iola, Charlie Scott's newspaper carried on January 15 an interesting story copied from the *Lawrence Journal* about a man named G. Ewing Price. He claimed "to have returned from a long visit to Cuba, and is going to lecture in Kansas." Price further claimed never to have heard of Fred Funston, and he did not believe that Fred was in Cuba. Loyal to Fred, the *Lawrence Journal* responded bluntly to this claim: "That remark settles Mr. G. Ewing Price. A man who has been in Cuba and did not see or hear of Fred Funston is either a rank chump or else he didn't go near where Fred and the fighting were."[7]

On January 22, from "in the field near Holguin, Cuba," Fred wrote to his old Lawrence, Kansas, friend, Frank Webster, who promptly published on receipt this letter on April 10 in his newspaper, *The Lawrence Gazette*. Charlie Scott reprinted it in *The Iola Register* six days later. The original letter apparently is no longer extant, and this letter, as printed below, appears as it was published in the newspaper. Thus, like Fred's letter of January 1 published in *The Iola Evening News*, it is impossible to determine what modifications, including omissions, may have been made to this letter. It is printed here as it appeared in *The Iola Register*:

MY DEAR FRANK: —How are you and yours? By jove I am spending lots of time nowadays thinking about my old friends, and I write occasionally though the uncertainty of the mail leaving the island puts pretty much of a damper on anything like literary activity. I look longingly forward to the time when I can be home again, although I do not in the least regret coming down here.

The Cuban revolutionists are a pretty fine lot of people, much better than I expected to find them, and are putting up a mighty fine fight for their independence. The prevalent idea at home that they are a lot of bushwhackers attacking only isolated bodies of troops, is a very erroneous one. There is a permanent organization of artillery, infantry and cavalry, divided into companies, battalions, regiments and brigades with the usual number of officers. There is the strictest discipline but very little drill, only enough to enable troops to go into position without confusion. Whenever a Spanish column ventures out from the fortified towns the Cubans go at it in great style and often thrash it.

Say, old man, you ought to see a battle. There is the most infernal roar, as if all hell had broken loose and the smoke resembled that of the prairie fires that we used to have at home. On such occasions I often long for the quiet and serenity of the sumptous [sic] rooms of some old club with my friends at my side. I don't know how many of these scraps I can go through without being nipped. It does look as though my turn must come soon. I have been in two sieges, eight battles and several smaller fights, have had two horses shot under me and had the sole of my left shoe split off by a bullet. So you can see that I have been in some of the hot localities. But I shall make life a burden to you with my war stories when I return—if I do.

We occasionally hear rumors that Uncle Sam is on the point of recognizing our independence, and sincerely hope that it is true, so that the business will be wound up.

As to myself I am now chief of artillery of the department of the Oriente which comprises all the east-half of the island, and have the rank of major. I have full command of that branch of the service and have plenty to do. The hardships of the life are not very great to one who has gone through what I have. I am furnished with two servants who cook and care for my horse. We live on beef and such vegetables as we can get and often go hungry. I have not tasted bread or any thing that contains flour since leaving the states last August. But the worst hardship that I have had to undergo is that I have not received a single letter since reaching the island. Of course I do not know a thing about my home folks or any of my friends. Letters have undoubtedly been written to me, but are probably lying about some of the military camps or have been lost. My original intention of corresponding for *Harper's Weekly*, I had to abandon because of the difficulty of getting my stuff off from the island.

Yours Faithfully,

FRED. FUNSTON.[8]

There are two striking points about this letter. First, when referring to the prospect of Cuban independence, Fred describes it as "our independence." His fidelity to the cause of *Cuba Libre* was unabated. Second is the anguish that Fred endured when, after five months on the island, he had not received a single letter from home.

The publication of Fred's letter of January 22 was gladly received by Kansans. *The Kansas City Star* editorialized:

Kansas people and many others outside of Kansas are rejoicing over a letter received from young Fred Funston, in which the explorer of torrid deserts and frozen solitudes and late coffee planter in Mexico is reported as enjoying himself in Cuba with some trifling drawbacks, such as danger to life, long travel, want and woe, and the absence of wheat bread and letters from home. Frederick is now Major Funston of the

Cuban insurgent army, and possibly an inherited tendency
has led him into the artillery, as his father was a Union battery man in the civil war. He reports plenty of fighting, "lovely
fighting all along here," as Phil Kearney was accustomed to
say, with an amount of movement and noise which must seem
rather pleasant to the young man who remembers the months
of silent darkness of an Arctic winter. Every one will wish
success, independence and a safe return to the states to Major
Funston, chief of artillery of the Department of the Oriente.[9]

The general military situation between the time of the fall of
Guaimaro in October 1896 and March 1897 was described by Fred in
Memories of Two Wars (I have made two paragraphs from one long
paragraph):

> Nearly five months had passed since the victory of Guai-
> maro, and in this time the forces of Garcia had roamed at will
> through the provinces of Oriente [formerly Santiago de Cuba]
> and Camaguey [Puerto Principe]. Large convoys escorted by
> formidable bodies of Spanish troops moved slowly along the
> main roads, carrying supplies to the isolated garrisons of the
> interior, and were harassed and fought from the time of start-
> ing until their return. Occasionally a column unhampered by
> transport would sally out on operations, and move ponder-
> ously for a week or so from town to town, but it was never
> for a moment out of sight of the Cubans, who fought it or not
> as seemed most expedient. Now and then a band of gueril-
> las, well mounted and thoroughly familiar with the country,
> would dash by night out of one of the larger garrisons and
> raid through the country, cutting up such small bodies of in-
> surgents as they might encounter, and making a specialty of
> hunting out our hospitals and murdering the helpless wound-
> ed found in them.
> These detestable wretches were more mobile than the in-
> surgents themselves, their horses being better fed, and usu-
> ally managed to return to their home stations. When they
> were run down, however, it was a fight to the death, quarter
> being neither asked nor given. On one occasion Major Pablo
> Menocal, a brother of the chief of staff, while scouting with
> eighty insurgent cavalry in the Holguin district, encountered
> a band of sixty guerillas on a raid. He formed line before being
> discovered and made a furious mounted charge. The gueril-
> las fought desperately, but were driven back into a barb-wire
> fence and annihilated. Not one escaped, and there were no

wounded when it was over. In this encounter both sides had gone back to the days of the Crusades, as not a shot was fired, the long machete doing it all. But Menocal's victory cost him heavily in killed and wounded.[10]

By March of 1897, the general sufficiency of food for the Cuban people and the revolutionists had disappeared. "The days of hardship and hunger had come with a vengeance. The thousands of Cuban families living in the 'bush,' off the lines of operations of the enemy's columns, were eking out a miserable existence. All the able-bodied men being in the war, the women and children could barely raise enough vegetables to keep off starvation. Clothing could not be obtained at any price..." The days of having plenty to eat that Fred had described in his New Year's letter were no more. "The insurgent forces were barefooted and clothed in rags and tatters, and were always hungry." [11]

About fifteen years later, Fred recalled the difficult times of the revolution:

"Hardships," Great God, when I look back at some of the things that we Cuban insurgents went through in 1896 and '97... In those days we were for weeks so famished that men often became delirious from hunger. Many a day the sole "ration" consisted of a few sticks of sugar cane which we chewed swallowing the juice, and I recall how often I wakened from a troubled sleep in which my dreams had been of bacon and kindred things. There was not even a tent for the commanding general, and we simply ignored weather. I was an officer, but only five nights in a year and a half did I sleep under cover, and I had no blanket, not even for my horse; for five months I had not a stich of underwear. My outfit consisted of a hammock, poncho, revolver, machete, pair of field glasses, the clothes on my person, and not one other thing.[12]

Fred's personal situation as a revolutionist in February 1897 was vividly described after his death twenty years later by Thomas White Steep, who was a correspondent for the Scripps-McRae newspapers at the time:

Twenty years ago this month Funston, adventurer and dreamer, stood beneath a clump of cocoanut trees in interior Cuba, ragged, hungry and unknown. His long, uncombed hair stuck through the holes of an old Panama hat; his beard, unkempt, half concealed his face; he wore a loose, faded cotton shirt; his trousers were torn in shreds and hung in dangling strips below his knees; his shoes were mere sandals and he had no socks.

That was the Funston I saw, when, a year before the Spanish-American War, I came down one day into the plains of interior Cuba and found him, an unknown adventurer, attached to the staff of General Calixio Garcia's army of 2,000 half-starved Cuban revolutionists. It was before the United States contemplated intervention.

Steep noted that Fred and the other Americans talked a lot about "food and clothing, for although the Cuban days in February were hot, the nights were cold and lack of food made the blood thin. Garcia's army, like a swarm of locusts, ate up in a day everything within a radius of ten miles of camp and it was necessary to keep moving to get provisions." The lack of a particular item of clothing particularly bothered Fred, Steep remembered: "What worried Funston most was his lack of socks. He, with the other Americans, had been campaigning for months, while I had come fresh from Santiago. It was supposed, naturally, that I was well supplied. So the first thing that followed my introduction to Funston was the query from him, 'Have you got any socks?' He lifted up the shreds of his pantaloons and showed me his foot [sic: feet] pathetically naked in the worn sandals. I think he never forgave me my having no socks to spare. 'You look yellow, Funston,' I said. 'Got fever?' 'Nope,' he said, 'Bathing in the Cauto—the mud sticks to you. No towels, you see, and drying in the sun gives you that brown powdery effect.'"

Steep found supper time for the artillerists to be an interesting experience. "At night Garcia's artillerists used to hang their hammocks around a fire and eat supper. There were no tents or shelter, and you hung your hammock between two trees. Among the encircling hammocks a fire was made and supper cooked. It was all cooked in one pot—a few pieces of dried meat and yams. We had no plates, knives or forks. I can see Funston yet, stooping over in the light of that fire and eating his food from a banana leaf with a stick. 'The same food—always the same food—yams—how I hate yams!' he would say."

Steep concluded his remembrances of Fred Funston, the fighter for *Cuba Libre*, with these words: "But the portrait of Funston there in Cuba of twenty years ago was that of a man always good natured. His old Panama hat shaded a pair of kindly eyes; his scraggy beard covered a square, honest jaw, and those cotton rags were wrapped about a personality unforgettably genial. He was an adventurous dreamer, but one who knew how to paddle his canoe when high tide came."[13]

Chapter Six Notes—*Letters IX and X*

Epigraph: "Cuban Letter," *The Iola Evening News*, January 30, 1897 (Vol. I-No. 126). An original of this article was loose inside the Edward H. Funston Political Scrapbooks, photocopy of which is at Allen County Historical Society, Inc., Iola, Kansas.

1. "Victory Not Easy," *The Kansas City Star*, April 23, 1898.

2. "Colonel Frederick Funston Gives Some Facts About Cuba," *The St. Louis Republic*, February 7, 1898. Horatio S. Rubens, the American lawyer for the Cuban *Junta*, noted that there were newspaper correspondents stationed in Tampa, Key West, and Jacksonville, Florida, and in New Orleans, and that "they were not as careful about verifying rumors as they should have been, but often fixed them up with more speed than discretion and put them on the wires in interview form. Sometimes the persons to whom the interviews were credited did exist, but very often they were purely fictitious" (Horatio S. Rubens, *Liberty: The Story of Cuba* (New York: Brewer, Warren & Putnam Inc., 1932)), 203.

3. "Cuban Letter," *The Iola Evening News*, January 30, 1897 (Vol. I-No. 126). An original of this article was loose inside the Edward H. Funston Political Scrapbooks, photocopy of which is at Allen County Historical Society, Iola, Kansas. On this original, the word "not" has been handwritten, in what appears to me to be Ella (Funston) Eckdall's handwriting, in the reference to the Funston library and its numerous volumes. With the addition of the word "not," the end of the sentence reads, correctly in my opinion, "that these numerous volumes are [not] kept for ornamental purposes alone." I believe the "not" was mistakenly omitted from the newspaper story.

4. "Some of the Latest," *The Morning Sun*, Chanute, Kansas, November 11, 1897. *The Topeka Weekly Capital* article was published February 2, 1897 ("Funston Is A Major").

5. "Kansas Items Of Interest," *The Chanute Times*, Chanute, Kansas, February 26, 1897.

6. Arthur Royal Joyce, "New Stories Of Funston's Exploits In Cuba," *The Kansas City Times*, October 29, 1899 (Frederick Funston Papers, hereafter FFP) (Archives Division, Kansas State Historical Society).

7. "Loyal To Fred," *The Iola Register*, January 15, 1897 (reprint from *Lawrence Journal*).

8. "Another Letter From Fred," *The Iola Register*, April 16, 1897. In the FFP is a newspaper clipping of this letter from an unidentified newspaper. There is no publication date, but on this clipping is the handwritten date "4-10-1897." This date, not illogically, led Thomas W. Crouch in *A Yankee Guerrillero* to conclude, erroneously, that this is the letter's date, instead of January 22. This latter date was furnished by Charlie Scott when he reprinted in *The Iola Register* Fred's letter, as first published by Frank Webster in *The Lawrence Gazette* of April 10, 1897. The newspaper clipping of this letter in the FFP is titled "Another Letter From Maj. Fred Funston," and begins simply "Frank Webster, of Lawrence, received the following letter from Major Fred Funston, of the Cuban army, which will be of interest

to his many friends here." There are slight discrepancies between the two newspapers' description of the location written by Fred at the beginning of his letter. I have used *The Lawrence Gazette's* description.

9. *The Kansas City Star*, April 10, 1897. Editorial.

10. Frederick Funston, *Memories of Two Wars: Cuban and Philippine Experiences* (New York: Charles Scribner's Sons, 1914), 98-99.

11. Frederick Funston, *Memories of Two Wars*, 99-100.

12. Frederick Funston to Leonard Wood, December 1, 1913 (General Correspondence, 1913, Box 73, Leonard Wood Papers, Manuscript Division, Library of Congress). Fred's description of the hardships while fighting in Cuba was precipitated by his anger about the complaints by Army officers to newspapermen concerning the "hardships" of recently completed field exercises, which included "some fairly hard marches" that Fred ordered. "[C]ompared with real war the whole thing was a picnic."

13. Thomas White Steep, "Funston's Comrade Tells Of Fighter's Days in Rags," *New York Tribune*, February 20, 1917. The copy in the FFP does not show where and when it was published. A shorter version of this article appeared under the headline "As Funston, the Dreamer, Appeared With Garcia" (Kansas State Historical Society, *Frederick Funston Clippings,* Vol. 1).

CHAPTER SEVEN

Letters XI and XII

March 5, 1897
"Camp of the headquarters of the Departmento de Oriente Cauto river, Cuba"

March 5 and 14 (postsccript), 1897
"Headquarters, Department of the Orient, Couto [sic: Cauto] River Cuba"

This has been a great day with me for I have received my first mail since reaching the Island...

—Fred Funston to Edward H. Funston
March 5, 1897

During the almost five months after the fall of Guaimaro, the insurgent or revolutionary army under General Garcia made no attacks on Spanish towns. All changed in early March of 1897 when General Garcia ordered a part of the troops in the province of Santiago de Cuba to concentrate near the town of Jiguani in the Bayamo district. Jiguani was much larger than any town previously attacked by the insurgents and was an important commercial center. Stationed there were about 800 soldiers, consisting mostly of infantry, but there was also a detachment of artillery and a troop of guerrillas.

Since it was the dry season, it did not take long for the various military units that had been ordered to participate in the Jiguani operation to come together. By March 10, 4,200 men, "well armed but ragged and hungry," were in camp together. "On the first night after our arrival in the camp we Americans indulged ourselves in a picturesque poker game, some one having found a deck of cards. Gathered about a rubber blanket stretched on the ground, the necessary light being furnished by a few candles stuck onto bayonets, and revolver cartridges being the chips, we played far into the night, an audience of Cubans watching every move." Fred later mused, "I suppose we might have been in better business, but our recreations were certainly few enough."[1]

Arthur Royal Joyce later recalled that Fred took with him James

Pennie and Joyce himself to select the position to place the artillery.
The town's main fort was a huge, two-story castle located on top of a
hill commanding the town. "The Cubans reported the walls to be five
feet thick, of cut stone, and we doubted the power of the Hotchkiss
guns, with the poor ammunition, to do any damage to such a fortress,
and so reported to Garcia, who decided to suspend operations until
he could send for fresh ammunition and a Driggs-Schroeder steel rifle
which had come on a late expedition."[2]

While awaiting the arrival of the fresh ammunition, Garcia permitted the Americans to go into camp instead of riding around the
country. Joyce, in an article he wrote two years later, recounted how
the little group of Americans passed the time:

> While thus loafing Funston suggested that we each invoke
> the aid of the muses and evolve a song that would immortalize
> the heroic band comprising the artillery.
>
> Considerable brain matter was thus wasted in the next
> two days, and several surprising results were obtained, but
> the atrocious effort of Funston to the time [sic] of "On the
> Bowery," was the worst, and we decided to leave our claims
> to immortality to the future historians of Cuba. However, one
> undaunted genius refused to be discouraged by the jeers that
> met his first attempt, and produced the following epic, which
> was voted to be a gem:
>
>> 'Seated 'round the gleaming camp fire,
>>   In the flames red fitful glow,
>> In the beauteous Isle of Cuba,
>>   Fairest spot the earth can show,
>> Is a party, small in number,
>>   Gathered here from Freedom's shore
>> To assist our suffering brother,
>>   Rend the chains that bind him sore.
>>
>> Here for ages, all unaided,
>>   'Gainst the power that tottering stands
>> As a monument to avarice,
>>   Warning fair to other lands,
>> Cuba's sons have nobly struggled,
>>   Rising from each crushing blow
>> With the hope each day renewed
>>   That their cause would stronger grow.
>>
>> When we heard their cry for succor,
>>   Sounding through our northern land,

In the sacred name of Freedom,
    Asking for a helping hand,
From the north land from the south land,
    From the east and from the west
Came our noble band of heroes
    Each for reasons he knew best.

When the day's long march is over
    And the time has come for rest,
When around our gleaming camp fire
    Echo rings with song and jest
Then there comes a silence stealing
    Showing thoughts are far away,
Ask each then the cause that brought him
    Listen well to what they say.

First our commandante, Funston,
    Frederick is his other name,
Came to pluck from Cuba's battles,
    Added garlands to his fame.
He from Kansas' wind swept prairies
    Whence they've banished far the rum
Now he's down here, daily murmers
    "Wish to God I'd never come."

Os' Latrobe and Stuart Janney
    From Maryland, My Maryland,
What their reasons were for coming
    Easy 'tis to understand.
They were young, of course, courageous,
    Seeking in war's cruel strife
Something from the smoke of battle
    To lie about in after life.

One would scarce expect a Quaker,
    Eager for the battle's fray.
Yet William Cox of Philadelphia
    Heard the call and could not stay
When the ringing bugle calls
    To charge the aijaco*, once again
Little William's always ready,
    James Pennie, tambien**.

For ten long years upon this island
    Walter Moses Jones has dwelt.
He came down in search of lucre,

But he hasn't got it yet.
When we strive our thoughts emphatic
    To give speech in Spanish tongue
Walter Moses comes in handy,
    Let his praise be loudly sung.

When we hear some words emphatic
    Tinging blue the atmosphere,
Know we then the Texas Ranger,
    Captain James DeVine is near.
Frankly stating his opinion
    Of the Cuban's rank and file
And his language, fervent, burning,
    Seems to us a trifle mild.

There's another yet unwritten,
    Modest as the blushing rose,
He the writer of these verses
    From Connecticut's nutmeg groves,
Never murmering nor complaining
    At some real or fancied slight.
He came down because his duty
    'Twas to help the Cubans fight

*Aijaco (Ah-ee-yaco)-Beef Stew. [sic: aijaco is probably aji-aco]
**Tambien (Tom-be-yain) - Also.

These words were tried on every familiar time [sic], both sacred and profane, and then it was sadly decidedly [sic] to recite it and not sing it.

We were heartily glad when General Garcia notified us that the guns and ammunition had arrived and that the attack was to begin at once.

Joyce was modest in the above article, since he did not identify himself as the poem's author. An additional stanza at the end, which he did not include in his article, read as follows:

Valor true is always modest,
    Would ye know the writer's name,
It is writ in Cuba's history,
    Likewise on the scroll of Fame.
But for fear you will not seek it,
    I will give to you an easier choice
Of remembering, gentle reader,
    He was Arthur Royal Joyce.

In another copy of the entire poem, from which the above last stanza is copied, there is this introduction by Joyce:

THIS POEM

Is dedicated to the American Officers of the Artillery of General Garcia by the writer, one of the criminals, with the sincere hope that a daily perusal of it by each of them will tend to raise their thoughts to a higher and wider plane than that of <u>food</u>.[3]

After Joyce's death in 1910, Fred paid him this tribute: "He was a man with a lot of mighty good qualities, and you [Osmun Latrobe] recollect how his wit and his yarns used to cheer us up when things looked mighty black."[4]

By March 10, the military units had joined together for the assault on Jiguani. Five days before, Fred wrote at least two letters, one to his father and the other to his good friend, Charlie Gleed. Both letters were from headquarters on the Cauto River in the Department of the Oriente. The letter to Fred's father, which appears below, is copied from a typescript in the Frederick Funston Papers. Based upon reading originals of Fred's other letters, this typescript is questionable, in places, as far as spelling and punctuation are concerned. Fred likely wrote a separate letter, which no longer survives, at the same time to his mother. Previously, on one occasion in Alaska he had written separate, but not identical, letters to each of his parents. Each of the two letters, if written from Cuba, probably had a different focus. Not surprisingly, Fred's letter to his father was replete with military detail that Fred knew the old Civil War artillerist would appreciate reading:

Dear Pa:

This has been a great day with me for I have received my first mail since reaching the Island, Ma's letter of February the 8th and one from C. S. Gleed of Topeka. It has been a great relief to hear from home. I had almost given up hope of getting any mail. The other letters that have been written me are probably lying about some of the military camps in Cuba. All [sic: Or?] have been captured by the Spaniards. I have sent quite a number home, but from what Ma says I judge that very few of them have reached there. I long ago gave up all idea of sending matter to Harper's Weekly as it would be almost hopeless for bulky letters to get through without being opened and so I have cut it down to soldiering in real earnest and have done pretty well. I am chief of Artillery of the Department of the East Oriente which consists of the 2ⁿᵈ and 3ʳᵈ corps under Major General Calixto Garcia who was one of the leaders in the war of 1868 and 78. He has taken a great liking to me and I find my position rather enjoyable. He is almost sure to be the first President of Cuba after independence is achieved and as I have some big schemes in regard to railroad franchises in my head, I am glad to stand in with him.

The war surely cannot last much longer. The Spaniards never venture out of their fortified cities except in large columns and then only to convoy supply trains to the garrison towns of the interior. These columns usually have to fight the Cubans every foot of the way and are often driven back. The Cubans hold absolutely undisputed possession of all of the country out of gun shot of this Spanish force and their civil government is in full operation and has been for a long time.

We would take nearly all of their fortified towns if we had more ammunition for the Artillery, but we have to be very sparing on account of the scarcity of shells. Of course we have very little artillery compared with what an Army should have. I have under my command two batteries of four guns each. The guns are steel breech loading rifles of the very latest pattern and make things mighty hot for the Spaniards. The Artillery Officers under my command are Americans. There are seven of them [Joyce, Cox, Pennie, Jones, Latrobe, Janney, and Devine] and are as good fighters as I want to see. The non-commissioned officers and men are Cubans. The only reason why we have not all been killed is that the Spaniards are such rank marksmen. They use the Mauser rifle which is the very newest thing in fire arms the same as used by the German Army. It is a terribly [sic] gun. The velocity of the ball is 2,000 ft. per second twice that of the U.S. Springfield. The ball is steel instead of lead and will penetrate 40" of seasoned oak or two" of cast iron. We have had men killed at 2½ miles. The gun is a magazine rifle firing 25 times per minute. If the Spanish soldiers knew how to use their sights we could not stand their fire a minute. About one quarter of the Cubans use the same weapons while the others have the breech loading Remington, a very good gun.

The Cuban Army numbers about 35,000 men all they can get arms for. The Spanish 175,000 outnumbering us 5 to one. Our force has not done much fighting recently, but now General Garcia is camped here with 4,000 men preparing to attach [sic] the town of Jiegnani [sic] a day's march from here. The place is defended by 22 forts large and small. I shall have entire charge of the Artillery during the siege and we have no doubt of taking the place. If we do, I will probably be promoted to Lieut.-Colonel. I don't consider that I am wasting my time down here at all. The first money raised after the recognition of independence goes to pay the Army and there is now due me $1200.00 as I get 220.00 per month American gold. I have such good luck so far and the War is so near over that I have no idea of being killed. I have gone through two long sieges, 8 battles and a number of smaller fights without a scratch although I have had two horses killed under me.

    I wish you would all write to me often,

Your son,
Fred.[5]

In contrast to the letter to "Pa," which has survived only as a typescript, the original of Fred's letter of March 5 to Charlie Gleed is in the Frederick Funston Papers and appears verbatim below. This letter was published by Gleed in *The Kansas City Journal* of June 24, and Scott reprinted it the next day in *The Iola Register*. Gleed did not print this letter exactly as written, but these variances are largely insignificant except for the brief portions of the letter which were not published by Gleed and which are identified by brackets below:

My dear Gleed

    This has been the greatest day since I struck Cuba, for I have just received my first mail in nearly seven long months— your letter of Feb. 3, one from my mother, and Dale Plumb's wedding card. Lord, Lord, Old man, I've just been coltish all day. I hope now that my mail will continue to come through without delay. It has been fairly sickening when I knew that letters were being written to me to have them lost or gobbled by the Spaniards. There is not much to say about myself except that the wheels in my head continue to buzz in several directions as they have been doing for some years. I am in superb health, fat and ragged. Washington at Valley Forge was a church social business compared with the way this aggregation of Cuban patriots is togged out. I have neither a shirt nor any manner of undergarment a state of affairs that jars on my sense of the proprieties. Suppose that I should try to stop a Spanish shell and be thus rudely yanked up before the bar of judgement [sic] and have to spend half an hour proving that I was neither a populist nor a Bowery tough, but a high minded Cuban patriot.

    And then the matter of eats is another painful subject.

Whenever I get my mind onto some really ethereal subject I find it wandering into the realms of cherry pie. The other day the commanding general invited me in my capacity of chief of artillery to a council of war and while there surrounded by an aggregation of military geniuses I kept thinking of how I could knock the spots off from a Holland House dinner. What in the devil is the matter with the United States that it does not recognize our independence. The Spaniards are shut up in the fortified towns and never venture out of them except in strong force, and then have to fight every foot of the way. The government of Spain is wiped out except within the walls of the fortified towns, and no pretence [sic] made of enforcing it.

The Cuban civil government is in full operation and exercises over 19/20 of the soil of Cuba all the functions of government. There is no [illegible] of any other. [U. S. President Grover] Cleveland, in his ludicrous message, said that it was a government on paper only. He also suggested "Autonomy." Great God but that makes our blood boil. Is that for what these Cubans have turned the country into a slaughter pen, burned their own homes, and faced the Spaniards on 200 battle fields? Let me tell you that I know these people awfully well and that they will not lay down their arms until the hated red and yellow flag has been driven from the island forever. nothing [sic] is so hopeless as Spain's struggle to impose her unjust government on these people whom she has robbed and plundered for generations. If necessary they will fight her twenty years.

[If any body ever tries to tell you anything about Cuban matters throw this at them and tell them that I know.]

We are camped on the Couto [sic: Cauto] river in eastern Cuba with 4,000 men preparing to attack the town of Jiguani, a days [sic] march from here. The place is very strong and defended by 22 forts. The most of the work will fall on the artillery of which I am in command, and rest assured that I intend to give them some of the Kansas funny business that took Guimaro [sic: Guaimaro].

If the war is not over by May I shall ask leave to come home for the summer but we all have strong hopes that the dons will come to their senses before then and accept the inevitable. And O, wont [sic] I be glad to get back to Kansas and New York and see dozens of people.

Be sure to write me again. You cant [sic] imagine what a comfort it is to hear from you.

[Lovingly, Fred]

[In the above, I have omitted Fred's address in New York in care of the Cuban *Junta*.]

Later, March 14

We had our fight—attacked the Jiguani forts on the 13th and Got Licked. O Lord it was awful. My artillery battered four forts into a cocked hat (it took 121 shells to bring one of them down) then, ammunition running short Gen. Garcia ordered an assault on the remaining forts. The Cubans went at it handsomely but were mowed down, and retreated. I never want to see the like again.

During the bombardment an ill mannered Spanish shell exploded near me and a fragment knocked me down. I am going to bring it home as a relic of the war.

[Lovingly Fred.][6]

One wonders how "fat" Fred really was on March 5 in view of the general scarcity of food by then. Perhaps like his clothing, he was contrasting unfavorably his situation with the forces at Valley Forge in the American Revolution, which lacked food and clothing in the winter of 1777-1778. Also, he described "the matter of eats" as "another painful subject." Most notably, Fred shared that "the wheels in my head continue to buzz in several directions as they have been doing for some years." That Fred was still uncertain what to do with his life presumably was no surprise to his longtime good friend, Charlie Gleed.

In a letter to his sister, Ella, written two months later, on May 10, Fred provided additional information about the "ill-mannered Spanish shell": "On March 13 I was slightly wounded by the explosion near me of a Spanish shell. A fragment struck me in the chest knocking me down and making a bad bruise but in a week I was all right. I picked up the ugly looking piece of iron and shall bring it home with me as a memento of the war."[7]

Fred's injury occurred as a part of the artillery duel involving the insurgents' new twelve-pounder Driggs-Schroeder naval landing gun, which they called Cayo Hueso after the town of Key West (Cayo Hueso), Florida, whose Cuban residents had raised the purchase funds. The other duelist was the Spaniards' Krupp gun. This duel continued at different times during the first day of battle on March 13, during which Fred and his comrades learned how to do a lifesaving "dive to cover or vigorous side-stepping" maneuver:[8]

> The enemy's gun did not seem to be so accurate as ours, but its shooting was by no means wild, every shell coming

in close, and an occasional one making a hit on the parapet [where Fred and the other artillerists were]. At a burst of smoke from the Castle the one of us on lookout would call out "Down," and every one, no matter what he might be doing, would throw himself flat on the ground. In a couple of seconds the shell would strike and burst, and then we would leap to our feet and try to give them a couple before they could fire again. The discovery was made that by watching carefully we could discern the enemy's shells up in the air when about half-way to us, and several times when we saw that they had a line on the parapet we succeeded in avoiding them by quick jumping to either the right or left. Before the day was over we had become quite expert in judging the shells and getting out of the way of them. The gun that they were being fired from was a Krupp of one of the older models and of low velocity compared with ours, or this could not have been done.[9]

About ten that morning, Fred took a break from the fighting. "A few yards to the left of the parapet was a tree the shade of which was very inviting, and I went over and sat down under it, leaning against the trunk. In a short time I felt something bite the back of my neck and discovered that a lot of little black ants were scurrying up and down, and so shifted my position away from the tree a foot or two. Not two seconds later a bullet hit the trunk at a point where it would have gone through my body. I suppose I should be a friend of ants, but am not."[10]

It was in the late afternoon that day that Fred received the injury that he described in his letters to Charlie Gleed and Ella, but in *Memories of Two Wars,* he typically did not disclose the details of his injury:

But as certain as fate in a few moments the black muzzle [of the Krupp] would reappear for an instant and be followed by a puff of smoke. Our gun, already being loaded and aimed, would be fired, and we would run into the open in order to be able to the more easily jump out of the way of the shell. As our parapet had by this time been badly battered, and all the enemy's shots were aimed at it in the hope of dismounting our gun, the open was much the safer place. There was one thing that impressed itself on our minds, and that was that side-stepping shells from a breech-loading rifle at eight hundred yards range was no business for rheumatics. Joyce finally got tired of these jumps to the open and announced that he was going to stand his ground. So when the next warning yell came he sat down with his back to the parapet. The shell landed squarely on the top, and burst about two feet above his head. Joyce was fairly covered with a few shovels-full of earth, and a couple of fragments fell in his lap. He arose very deliberately and began to brush his clothes, remarking in a bored way that it was no way to treat a man who had gone to the trouble to dress neatly for this occasion. But the next time he accompanied the rest of us. In front of our parapet about ten feet, and just enough to the left of Cayo Hueso's line of fire not to be injured by its blast, stood a young palm tree about twenty feet high. Shells had barely missed it many times, and we had speculated on the probability of its surviving the battle, but now its turn came, it being struck about three feet above the ground and cut down. The shell exploded from the force of the blow and threw fragments all over Jones and myself, we having jumped to the left when we saw where it was going to strike.[11]

Fred recorded the details in *Memories of Two Wars* of the balance of the unsuccessful assault on Jiguani. Word came that Spanish reinforcements were on the way to aid Jiguani's defenders. "Before daybreak it was all over, and we brought the guns back to the general rendezvous."[12] This was on March 14, the date of Fred's postscript on his letter to Gleed.

Thomas W. Crouch, in his admirable, ground-breaking study, *A Yankee Guerrillero*, believes that Fred received a serious wound to his left arm on March 14.[13] I believe this is incorrect, since the battle was over before daylight on March 14 and the artillery did not fight during the night when the insurgent infantry stormed Jiguani. Instead of his left arm being wounded at Jiguani, I believe this serious injury occurred not long thereafter in a battle at Monte Alto. Crouch described the injury to Fred's left arm as caused by a fragment of a Spanish shell: "The jagged hot metal shredded his left arm, broke a bone, and left the appendage dangling at his side."[14] In one of his lectures in 1898 after his return from Cuba, Fred provided this detail: "My first wound was inflicted by a piece of a bursting shell. I saw a dark object coming toward me. Involuntarily I threw my hands to my eyes. There was a dull explosion, and my left arm fell mangled to my side. But the battle was on, and it was an hour till I could get a substitute and leave the field."[15] Charlie Scott later described "Fred's left arm broken by a fragment from a shell." When Fred enrolled as Colonel of the Twentieth Kansas in May of 1898 after his return from Cuba, the surgeon's medical examination revealed "scar of fracture of left ulna."[16]

Although Fred claimed in his lecture that this was his first wound, that does not appear to be correct. In some interviews, he described his first injury as being shot through the arm.[17] This is confirmed by his letter of August 31, 1897, to Charlie Scott, where Fred informed him that he "was shot through the arm last winter."[18] Presumably, Fred was shot with a Mauser bullet, and the result consequently was not a serious wound, the steel-tipped bullet making a clean, tiny entry hole and an equally small exit hole. The wound would have closed quickly and with little hemorrhage.[19]

The details about Fred's being "shot through the arm last winter" are unknown. When Fred wrote to Charlie Scott about this in late August 1897, he also stated that, in order not to alarm his parents, he had "never told" about his injury. Assuming that last winter would be before Fred wrote his father on March 5, it is perplexing why Fred stated in his letter that "I have gone through two long sieges, 8 battles and a number of smaller fights without a scratch although I have had two horses killed under me." In order to reassure his parents about his well-being, I believe Fred carefully chose his words. A bullet wound is not a "scratch," and thus Fred could truthfully write that he had fought without receiving a scratch. At the same time, since the phrase "without a scratch" means without an injury or wound, he could use the phrase to reassure his parents, knowing they likely would interpret it as meaning he was without any injury. Recalling that Fred took to Alaska a dictionary for his nearly eighteen months there, it is easy to believe Fred was a master in his use of words to produce a technically truthful report that had a calming, reassuring effect.

Combat wounds were not the only threat to the health of Fred and his comrades-in-arms. "Malaria is the dread disease, but quinine properly administered will keep it off," Fred remembered. "When I was in the Cuban army we could only get quinine occasionally. I contracted the malaria after I had been in the country about nine months [about mid–April 1897]. It is a strange thing that the Americans who were with the insurgents stood the climate better than even the Cubans themselves."[20] Attacks of malaria were frequent. "All the Americans in the expedition suffered from tropical malaria, which laid them out with fever, chills and delirium every other day as a matter of course. When a man felt an attack coming on he got someone else to relieve him at his cannon, stumbled into his tent and passed a few hours in fevered ravings, sank into sleep and when he woke returned to his place."[21]

But where was Fred when his left arm was mangled and broken? After the unsuccessful siege of Jiguani, "Commander Funston received the order to situate himself in Monte Alto."[22] The poster advertising one of his lectures in early 1898 stated that Fred was "desperately wounded" in the battles of Monte Alto and Sama."[23] I have been unable to find details about the battle at Monte Alto, including its date, but believe that this is where this injury occurred, and, for reasons discussed in Chapter Nine, I do not believe the arm injury occurred at the battle of Sama.

Fred's timetable for the month of March becomes very tight if, in fact, that is the month in which the battle of Monte Alto and his injury occurred. According to Arthur Royal Joyce, even though the insurgent army had been unsuccessful at Jiguani, General Garcia was pleased with the Americans' performance. After leaving Jiguani on March 14, "[w]e marched all night and in the morning General Garcia sent for us and said that his unsuccessful effort was in no way due to us, and that our work was greatly appreciated. He also said we would not be needed for a month, and advised us to go up on the north coast and get some clothes through one of his agents and at the same time giving us twenty dollars apiece. Funston, in deference to his superior rank, getting twenty-five. Funston discarded his old suit and appeared in new raiment from his head down."[24]

On March 21, Cuban army officer Carlos Roloff's expedition landed at the Bay of Banes, bringing arms and ammunition to the insurgents. When Fred and his fellow artillerymen received word of this, probably a few days later, they were still on the north coast on leave. "I was a great distance from where the expedition disembarked, but I just hit the high places getting there, riding for seventeen consecutive days."[25] The battle of Monte Alto must have occurred then about the middle of March and after Garcia had authorized the Americans to go to the north coast. If Fred was wounded there, he would have still been suffering when he and his fellow Americans went to the north coast, and then, presumably, continued to suffer on the 17-day ride to reach where the Roloff expedition had disembarked.

In *Memories of Two Wars,* Fred described the next events. General Garcia and nearly 4,000 men marched to the Bay of Banes, "to meet the third expedition of the filibuster *Laurada...*" There followed fighting "between the Cubans and the Spanish gun-boat *Jorge Juan,* anchored close to shore, the encounters with General Luque's powerful column sent to take the expedition referred to, the blowing up by means of a mine of a small Spanish gun-boat on the Cauto River, resulting in the death of every one of her crew of thirty-four, the all but successful attempt on a transport at the entrance of the Bay of Banes, our disastrous attack on the town of Sama, and many other stirring events [which] cannot be told here."[26]

The Battle of Jiguani
(*Memories of Two Wars* illustration)

"A mule train with ammunition en route to the front between
Siboney and El Pozo."
This photograph was taken during the Spanish-American War of 1898
and shows how ammunition was transported by the revolutionists.

"To the dynamite gun was given the honor of leading the ball" on the first day
of the attack on Victoria de las Tunas." (*Memories of Two Wars* illustration)

"How the Spaniards fought under cover—they hid in trenches, behind
barbed-wire fences, where they could not be seen and could be reached
only with great difficulty."
(This photograph was taken during Spanish-American War of 1898.)

Chapter Seven Notes—*Letters XI and XII*

Epigraph: Frederick Funston to Edward H. Funston, March 5, 1897. Typescript (Frederick Funston Papers, hereafter FFP) (Archives Division, Kansas State Historical Society).

1. Frederick Funston, *Memories of Two Wars: Cuban and Philippine Experiences* (New York: Charles Scribner's Sons, 1914), 98-101.

2. Arthur Royal Joyce, "New Stories Of Funston's Exploits In Cuba," *The Kansas City Times*, October 29, 1899 (FFP).

3. Arthur Royal Joyce's poem is found in FFP and in Joyce's article (see note 2). In the FFP, it is a typed copy on stationery of one James W. Mays, Attorney at Law, in Los Angeles, California. This copy and the one included in Joyce's article are not exactly the same, but the differences are largely insignificant. The Mays copy has the introduction "This Poem." The version in Joyce's article is the one reprinted in this chapter.

   The same matter of insignificant differences is true of the version of the poem published in *The Lawrence Daily Journal* of January 6, 1900, submitted by "Chas. Elwell," who had obtained a copy from "De Vinne," who would be the James Devine (DeVine) referred to by both Fred and Joyce. In this version of the poem, Devine's surname appears as DeVinne. This version lacks the introduction, but includes the last stanza included in the copy in FFP. It does have a title, however: "Soldiers of Forture." Elwell submitted this to the newspaper by letter dated December 22, 1899, from Santiago de Cuba where he had met DeVinne.

   The word "aijaco" is spelled ajiaco in the Mays copy, and "tamblien" is spelled "Tombien" in the Mays copy. In the Elwell copy, "aijaco" is "Yacka."

4. Frederick Funston to Osmun Latrobe, February 27, 1910 (Papers of Osmun Latrobe, 1900-1932 file, Manuscript Division, Library of Congress). Fred noted: "Only about half of our little band of adventurers are left, and we certainly were about as husky a lot of land pirates as ever lived."

5. Fred Funston to Edward H. Funston, March 5, 1897. All mail from the United States went through the Cuban *Junta* in New York City. George Reno, an American, carried in November 1897 the mail to the Cuban revolutionary government located at La Esperanza. The bag of mail weighed about eighty pounds, and upon Reno's arrival at La Esperanza, as "the bearer of long-delayed missives from over the sea, I was given a most hearty welcome. A vacant little palm-thatched house of one room was instantly converted into a post-office, and hundreds of men who had mothers, wives, sisters and sweethearts in the United States held their breath, each in hungry hope that his name would next be called" (George Reno, "Operating An 'Underground' Route To Cuba," *The Cosmopolitan Illustrated Monthly Magazine*, August 1899).

6. Fred Funston to Charles S. Gleed, March 5 and March 14 (postscript), 1897 (FFP). Published in "Kansas Topics," *The Kansas City Journal*, June 24, 1897 (Fred Funston to C. S. Gleed, March 5, 1897), and in "Fred Funston Again," *The Iola Register*, June 25, 1897.

7. Fred Funston to Ella Funston, May 10, 1897 (FFP).

8. Frederick Funston, *Memories of Two Wars*, 107.

9. Frederick Funston, *Memories of Two Wars*, 105-106.

10. Frederick Funston, *Memories of Two Wars*, 109.

11. Frederick Funston, *Memories of Two Wars*, 110-111.

12. Frederick Funston, *Memories of Two Wars*, 115.

13. Thomas W. Crouch, *A Yankee Guerrillero: Frederick Funston and The Cuban Insurrection, 1896-1897* (Memphis State University Press, 1975), 99-100.

14. Thomas W. Crouch, *A Yankee Guerrillero*, 100.

15. "Fred Funston Tells of Cuba," *The Topeka Daily Capital*, March 4, 1898.

16. Charles F. Scott, "Frederick Funston," *The Independent*, April 11, 1901. "Field and Staff Muster-in Roll, 20 Reg't Kansas Infantry," for Colonel Frederick Funston (RG94 (Records of Adjutant General Office), pi17, entry 522, Frederick Funston, combined military service record, 20th Kansas Volunteer Infantry, Spanish American War, arc 300400) (National Archives). This includes notes based on Fred's medical examination.

17. "Fred Funston In New York," unidentified newspaper, January 11, 1898 (FFP). "Funston Is Sick and Sore," *The Kansas City Star*, January 11, 1898 (FFP).

18. Fred Funston to Charles F. Scott, August 31, 1897. Photocopy of original letter in collection of Frederick Funston's letters from Cuba and New York City at Allen County Historical Society, Inc., Iola, Kansas.

19. Funston explained in an interview in 1898 about the effects of being shot by a Mauser bullet ("Funston Is Sick And Sore," *The Kansas City Star*, January 11, 1898) (FFP). See in Chapter Nine a discussion of this subject.

20. "Victory Not Easy," *The Kansas City Star*, April 23, 1898. Interview with Fred Funston at Iola, Kansas, on April 22, 1898.

21. "Fred Funston, Darling of the Gods," *The Kansas City Star*, March 19, 1916 (Eckdall Scrapbook III, 40).

22. Armando Prats-Lerma, "La Actuación del Teniente Coronel Frederick Funston, (Norteamericano) en la Guerra de Independencia de 1895-1898," *Boletin del Ejercito* (Habana, Cuba, Noviembre y Diciembre de 1931), 366 (FFP).

23. "On the Inside of the Cuban Revolution" poster for lecture by Frederick Funston (Charles A. Arand Papers) (Archives Division, Kansas State Historical Society).

24. Arthur Royal Joyce, "New Stories Of Funston's Exploits In Cuba."

25. Fred Funston to Charles F. Scott, May 10, 1897. Photocopy of original letter in collection of Frederick Funston's letters from Cuba and New York City at Allen County Historical Society, Inc., Iola, Kansas.

26. Frederick Funston, *Memories of Two Wars*, 117. Perhaps the following event occurred at this time: "Among the many interesting stories told by Fred Funston there is one that well illustrates human nature and the horrors of war. The insurgents under General Garcia had laid a mine under a railroad track for the purpose of blowing up a train load of Spanish soldiers.

The electrician was an American, and had everything in readiness. The small squad of men, among whom were Garcia, Funston and the electrician concealed themselves in the wood some distance from the track. The train was heard coming, and at the same time a woman stepped upon the track a short distance away, and walked toward the concealed mine. As the train approached it became evident that she would meet it at the exact spot where the mine was. The woman stepped aside to let the train pass. The electrician hesitated, his hand on the key. 'General,' he said, 'If I press this key that woman will be killed.' There was no thought of the hundreds of soldiers who would be blown into eternity, no pity, no hesitation on their account; but every man there save one wavered, and would have allowed the train to go unharmed. Garcia looked once, and then in a calm voice said, 'This is war, senor. Press the key,' and in the next instant the air was filled with iron, steel, splinters and mangled bodies ("Echoes From Old Iola," *The Iola Daily Register*, February 21, 1923, reprint from *Lawrence Journal*).

According to George Clarke Musgrave, the Cubans frequently tried to blow up train engines and troop cars, sparing passenger cars. Soldiers marched ahead of the engine, using long poles to prod the railroad tracks for dynamite. The Spaniards were forced to utilize "thousands of men to guard the tracks and trains," troops which otherwise would have been in the field fighting the rebel forces (George Clarke Musgrave, *Under Three Flags In Cuba: A Personal Account of the Cuban Insurrection and Spanish-American War* (Boston: Little, Brown, and Company, 1899; reprint by Forgotten Books, 2012)), 132-133. Musgrave was an Englishman who was a supporter of Cuban independence.

CHAPTER EIGHT

Letters XIII and XIV

March 10, 1897
"In Camp Headquarters Department of Oriente Mejia Cuba"

March 10, 1897
"In Camp Headquarters Dept. of Oriente, Mejia, Cuba"

The best of my life is behind me...
—Fred Funston to Edward H. Funston
March 5, 1897

On May 10, Fred wrote two letters from camp headquarters of the Department of Oriente. One was addressed to his sister, Ella, the other to Charlie Scott. In his letter to Ella, Fred omitted the news of his mangled left arm, but did tell of the slight wound from the exploding shell. I believe he did this so that his sister and other family members would feel relieved that Fred had escaped serious injury, not knowing that he did not tell all of the story.

My dear Ella

The departure of several officers for New York gives me the opportunity to again send out some mail. There is not much to say except that I am alive and reasonably well and that I would a good deal rather be home than here. I had hoped that by this time the war would be over, but it still drags its weary length along. If it is not finished by October I am going home anyhow, and let them fight it out among themselves. I have been in three sieges, fourteen battles and a number of smaller fights. On March 13 I was slightly wounded by the explosion near me of a Spanish shell. A fragment struck me in the chest knocking me down and making a bad bruise, but in a week I was all right. I picked up the ugly looking piece of iron and shall bring it home with me as a memento of the war.

Of course we hear but very little news from the outside world as the island is blockaded and it is very difficult for mail to get in. I have had four letters, one each from Ma, Charlie Scott, Charlie Gleed of Topeka and Burt Mitchell. I suppose I

131

was a pretty big fool to come down here and mix up in this war but I am here now, and am going to stay until fall when I shall surely be home and I think I shall have seen enough to not go on any more such trips.

I shall not try to tell you any war stories in this letter but save them until I get home. It is such slavish work to write letters when one has no table, and then anyhow I dont [sic] think that young women care much for war anyhow, at least they ought not to. By the time I get home I shall have been gone two years. That is a long time isn't it? It really hardly seems that I have been gone as long as my last trip to Alaska, but I have. Cuba is a most beautiful and fertile country and the climate superb just about like a Kansas June the whole year. It seems a shame that so beautiful a country is being devastated by war.

We all thought six months ago that by this time the war would be over, but the end is not yet in sight.

I wish that you would write a much longer letter than I have written you and tell me all about the folks at home and any news you may know about our Lawrence friends. I suppose you will go up to commencement and see many of them.

    Your loving brother

        Fred

Give my love to all the folks and Uncle Asa's folks.[1]

[I have omitted "Commandante" Frederick Funston, Jefe de la Artilleria's New York address in care of the Cuban *Junta*.]

Extracts from Fred's letter to Charlie Scott were published by him in *The Iola Register*. The personal portions were omitted from publication, but a photocopy of the original letter is extant. This is most fortunate, because the omitted passages provide significant insight into Fred's troubled state of mind. The halcyon days of late 1896 and early 1897 were clearly gone. The Ed and Effie referred to are Fred's close friend, Ed "Buck" Franklin, and Charlie's sister, Effie June Scott, who were soon to tie the knot. The entire letter is printed below. I have placed in brackets the significant omissions in the published letter, ignoring minor discrepancies that Scott created in the published version.

My dear Scott

One of the greatest pleasures that I have had on the island was the receipt of your good letter of Feb. 8 which reached the island on the Roloff expedition which ran the blockade and on March 21 landed an enormous supply of war materiel. Three weeks later I had your letter as I was a great distance from where the expedition disembarked, but I just hit the high places getting there, riding for seventeen consecutive days.

A party of officers is leaving the camp today bound for New York and this letter will go with them. They go on important business and are to put to sea in an open boat and reach Jamaica, thence taking the mail steamer. I could have gone with them, but the commander of the department Maj Gen. Calixto Garcia pressed me so strongly to remain with him until fall that I have consented. He has planned some big operations in which artillery will play a prominent part, and it would look pretty bad for the chief of that corps to leave when most needed.

[But it was a bitter pill for me to miss the wedding of Ed. and Effie and wouldn't I like to be with you in Willow Park. I would like to camp out where I would not have to roll out of my hammock at the blare of a bugle every morning at 5 a.m.

[But as to the prospective wedding. For Ed's sake and for Effie's, I am mighty glad for they are it seems to me eminently suited to each other, but I am selfish enough to be a little bit sorry on my own account. Of my four old chums yourself, White, Franklin and Kellogg, only the latter is left and it seems my luck to see him only every two years on an average. A man is never so thoroughly a chum after he is married as before, and it is only right that he should not be, because he has other and higher obligations.

[I cant [sic] make new chums because I have gone past that period in my life where I made new friendships and I tell you it would take a mighty fine man to occupy one small corner of Franklin's spot in my heart. I tell you Old Man I am beginning to feel pretty sore about those things, and to see that I am soon to be alone in the world. Yesterday I thought of this so hard that I shed some unmanly tears, the first since I lay down on my bunk at Rampart House three years ago and nearly cried my eyes out from sheer lonliness [sic]. The best of my life is behind me, nothing can ever occur that can make me thoroughly happy, that is I mean absolutely happy, but there can come about plenty of hard luck, disappointments, and heartaches. Would it be such an awful thing after all if I met the fate of my predecessor Osgood who in half a second went from the full vigor of manhood into eternity. I think that is a whole lot better and more dignified than dying of dyspepsia or pneumonia, and having some unctuous divine who knew nothing about you bore his congregation and stultify himself trying to prove to his hearers that you would not spend an indefinite number of years in hell. I would rather have said over me things that our lion hearted old chieftan Maximo Gomez said when they lowered Osgood's uncoffined body into the grave under a beautiful mango tree near Guaimaro.]

As to this war, it drags its weary length along. All the world thought six months ago that ere this Spain would have given up a fight that she can never win, but she seems determined to spend her last dollar and shed her last drop of blood to keep in the family her wayward daughter the Queen of the Antilles. A plucky dame is that grim old mother of nations. All predictions as to when the war will end are now mere guesswork. Of the ultimate result there can be no doubt. Cuba will win her independence, but if not before a year the island will be all but ruined. It is an awful shame. The United States is playing a damnable dirty part in this business. She would flare up like an old hen if any European nation tried to interfere here and put a stop to this hellish business, but she folds her arms while within sight almost of her own shores there is being carried on one of the most merciless and cruel wars in the history of mankind. Do you know that on the part of the Spaniards this is a war of no quarter? An Apache is a refined gentleman compared with these white devils that we are fighting.

They kill every man they capture wounded or not, usually as soon as taken, but sometimes save them for the farce of a drum head court martial.

They raid our hospitals and <u>machete</u> the poor sick and fever stricken wretches that they find and <u>kill the women nurses</u>. But God, I cant [sic] write about such things without cursing. As to the other side, the Cubans are trying to win the respect and sympathy of the world by observing the rules of civilized warfare. They always release prisoners or keep them as prisoners of war and treat them with kindness. The Spanish wounded that fall into our hands are cared for as well as our own. A while back Gen. Garcia captured a number of wounded Spaniards and had them carried to a Spanish town and delivered under a flag of truce. But some day the Cubans will get tired of turning the other cheek and do a little Apache business on their own hook.

[My last fight was about six weeks ago when we made an unsuccessful attack on the forts defending the town of

Jiguani. We destroyed four of them with artillery fire, but night came on and there arrived news of the near approach of a Spanish force outnumbering us greatly, and being short of ammunition we had to withdraw with the job half done.

[We now have plenty of ammunition the next two months will see some hot work in this department.

[By the way an article in a N.Y. Herald of March 22, when [sic: which] was brought to us from one of the seaport towns, give [sic] a great send off to the Americans in the Cuban army, and says some very nice things about me.

[Write me a long letter and tell me everything.

[My love to all of your family and my heartiest congratulations to Effie.

[Faithfully yours,

[Fred][2]

The *New York Herald* article did, indeed, say "some very nice things" about Fred: "Major Funston, of Kansas, is a young man who made a trip to Alaska to collect specimens for the Smithsonian Institution. He landed with the expedition of Braulio Tena, in company with several other Americans, who came to form a battery. On the death of Major Osgood, during the siege of Guaimaro, he received the command of a twelve pounder, and out of 110 shots he only missed his mark once. General Gomez, in recognition of his excellent record, made him chief of artillery, and at present he is with Calixto Garcia in the east."[3]

On May 15, *The Iola Evening News* carried a startling story under the headline "Funston Starving." This article reported that Thomas W. Steeps [sic], "a special correspondent of the Scripps McRae League of newspapers," had telegraphed from Jamaica a plea on behalf of the Americans fighting with the insurgent army. This is the same Thomas W. Steep who had visited Fred and his comrades in arms in February in their camp. He claimed that they asked him to appeal to the State Department "to do something for their relief." Steep asserted that the Americans "are in a most deplorable condition, living on roots and herbs." This would not be true, based on what Steep recollected twenty years later as previously noted. Steep further alleged that they were starving, and that they wanted to get back home.[4]

The reaction in Kansas to Steep's claims was negative. *The Lawrence Daily Journal* opined that "[a]s Fred Funston has never been known to make an 'appeal' the story has somewhat of doubtful sound."[5] *The Lawrence Daily World* was blunt in reporting this story, which it attributed to the *Kansas City World*: "That dispatch must have been manufactured in the World office. The people here believe that Fred Funston can get out of anything without a scratch and they never dreamed of his calling for help to let go. Fred is not that kind of fellow."[6]

The final word on the subject may have been Ed Funston's, who wrote a rebuttal letter which appeared on the first page of *The Iola Evening News* four days later. Ed noted that he had a letter from Fred dated March 5, which showed "the reported dispatch from Jamaica to be absolutely false in every particular." Ed then quoted positive language from Fred's letter, concluding that "[n]ot one word is written about hard living or scarcity of food..."[7] Fred, in my opinion, had carefully omitted any report on those subjects, likely believing that such news would distress his parents.

Chapter Eight Notes—*Letters XIII and XIV*

Epigraph: Fred Funston to Charles F. Scott, May 10, 1897. Photocopy of original letter in collection of Frederick Funston's letters from Cuba and New York City at Allen County Historical Society, Inc., Iola, Kansas. Typescript in Frederick Funston Papers on microfilm (Archives Division, Kansas State Historical Society). Published as "Fred Still Fighting," *The Iola Register*, July 16, 1897.

1. Fred Funston to Ella Funston, May 10, 1897 (Frederick Funston Papers, hereafter FFP) (Archives Division, Kansas State Historical Society).

2. Fred Funston to Charles F. Scott, May 10, 1897.

3. "Word From Major Fred.," *The Iola Register*, March 26, 1897. This contained the paragraph about Funston in the *New York Herald,* which had published "a special dispatch from its Cuban correspondent."

4. "Funston Starving," *The Iola Evening News*, May 15, 1897. There is a copy of this article in the FFP, but without any notation of the name of the newspaper. Since the font is identical in the two articles, it is obvious that *The Iola Evening News* is the source of the FFP copy.

5. "Localities," *The Lawrence Daily Journal,* May 15, 1897.

6. *The Lawrence Daily World and Evening Gazette,* May 18, 1897. Editorial.

7. "Letter From E. H. Funston," *The Iola Evening News*, May 19, 1897.

CHAPTER NINE

Letters XV and XVI

August 31, 1897
"Las Tunas, Oriente, Cuba"

September 6, 1897
Cuba

[The insurgent attack] was like the battles of the story books and it was worth years of humdrum life to see it.

~ ~ ~

We artillery men are the heroes of the day and nothing is too good for us. The Spanish officers say that they are fairly thunderstruck by the way our cannon used them.

—Fred Funston to Charles F. Scott,
August 31, 1897

By late summer of 1897, Fred's family and friends were undoubtedly worried about him. The last letters that had been received were the two dated May 10, one to Charlie Scott and one to Fred's sister, Ella. Scott received his in mid-July, and presumably Ella's arrived about the same time. Since then, there had been only silence. Whether Fred had ceased writing letters, or whether he had continued to write letters that failed to arrive, was unknowable by his Kansas kin and friends.

On August 20, Charlie Scott publicly expressed his concern through his newspaper: "Will some one please locate Fred Funston and thereby relieve the anxiety of all of his friends. Some of the papers keep insisting that he has left Cuba and gone to Klondike [for the Alaska gold rush], while others say it is a fake.[1] We have about come to the conclusion that they don't any of them know any more about it than we do,—and that isn't much."[2] On August 6, the *Kansas Semi-Weekly Capital* noted that "[s]ome enterprising newspaper man would do his friends in Kansas a great favor by locating Fred Funston definitely."[3] A week later, the same newspaper claimed that "[a] carrier pigeon is hourly expected conveying a definite report of the whereabouts of Fred Funston."[4]

The silence and anxiety continued for two more months. Then, in mid-October, Charlie Scott received the long-awaited letter from Fred. Eight pages in length, it was dated August 31 at "Las Tunas, Oriente, Cuba." In the October 15 issue of his newspaper, Charlie introduced extracts from this letter with these words: "The editor of the REGISTER has just received a letter from Fred Funston, the first word that has come from him to any one in this country since the 10th of last May." After providing the date and place of origin of this letter, Charlie noted that "while much of it is purely personal, the following extracts, describing in the most graphic way the last great battle, are of too great interest to all his friends to justify their being kept private, and we therefore give them publication."[5] The entire letter is reprinted here since a photocopy of the original letter exists. The portions in brackets are those which were not published in the newspaper, including the letter's shocking conclusion:

[My dear Scott

[I have not had opportunity to write for a couple of months for very good reasons. A few days ago I received your very good letter of July 15 and read it many times. It did me a whole lot of good. I hope that all the plans, the wedding, the Estes Park outing ect [sic] came off on schedule time, and that Ed and Effie[6] do not go to Costa Rica. These yellow legged countries are frauds when it comes to staying too long in them.]

We have just won the biggest victory of this or the former revolution by capturing the city of Las Tunas with its twenty-one forts and taking the entire garrison with a great quantity of rifles, ammunition ect [sic]. The fight lasted three days and two nights and was a fearfully bloody affair. On the night of the 27th inst. we constructed fortifications in the way of strong intrenchments on the south side of the town, the nearest fort being distant 400 yards, and placed therein four steel, breech-loading field guns and a Sims-Dudley pneumatic dynamite gun. At the dawn of day on the 28 we opened on six of the forts within range, and they replied most vigorously, peppering us with all sorts of hardware from Krupp shells to Mauser bullets. They tore our intrenchments to pieces and it was with the greatest difficulty that we held the men to their work. It was something awful, shells exploding near us

constantly and our losses were heavy. The pneumatic dynamite gun did wonders, wrecking the cavalry headquarters
and in two shots blowing the top off from Fort Concepcion.
At 10 A.M. Lieut. Col. Calixto Enamorado with a few men
carried the latter work by assault losing one third of his men
by the fire of adjoining forts. But at twelve occurred the grand
feature of the siege. The strong fort called the "cavalry headquarters," because it had once been used as such, had suffered much from our fire when chief of Staff Menocal ordered
the bugler to sound the charge. Hardly had the notes died
away before the same lieutenant colonel with 200 men left
the shelter of the hillcrest and started for the fort. Many men
fell but on they pushed until checked by the tangle of barb-
wire fences where in the open the[y] held their position firing
at the Spaniards in the trenches of the fort until Lieut. Col.
Carlos Garcia, son of the general, led up 150 men—there was
a wild rush for the fort, the men cut the barb wire fences with
machetes and Lieut. Col. Garcia with the Cuban flag in one
hand and sword in the other leaped the moat and the men
followed him like a flock of sheep. It was like the battles of the
story books and it was worth years of humdrum life to see it.
All was over in a moment and when the hated red and yellow
flag gave place to the Cuban banner we in the intrenchments
only 400 yards away cheered ourselves hoarse. All the rest of
the fearfully hot day we pitched shells at the Spanish forts
and dodged those they sent at us. The cannonading ceased at
nightfall, but a terrific racket was kept up by the infantry who
assaulted and took two more forts.

The next day we put the guns in one of the captured works
and at a distance of 150 yards shelled the great fort known as
the "Infantry Cuartel" but with little effect as the walls were
very strong. Even the dynamite gun had but little effect here.
With darkness the uproar ceased and the wearied men on
both sides got what snatches of sleep they could. The morning
of the 30th, yesterday, saw the end at hand. After an hour's
bombardment the flag of truce was sent to the Infantry Cuartel, and the plucky commander having been killed his men
surrendered. We then cut our way through several blocks of
stone houses and threw up barricades in the streets to attack
the only remaining fort the "Cuartel General" more than a
dozen forts having surrendered with the "Cuartel Infanteria."
After a few shots and some flag of truce business they gave
in and the fight was over, but at a fearful cost, one third of

the Cubans having fallen. But the Spaniards had fought as heroes losing in the defense 40 per cent of the garrison.

We captured 21 forts 1,050 rifles with 1,000,000 rounds of ammunition two Krupp cannon and a train load of prisoners, I dont [sic] know how many besides great quantities of general stores. The Cubans are wild with joy and say it settles the war, but I dont [sic] know about that. We artillery men are the heroes of the day and nothing is too good for us. The Spanish officers say that they are fairly thunderstruck by the way our cannon used them. Of us nine officers two were killed and three wounded while half of our men were killed or disabled.

I have been given the gold star of a lieutenant colonel and on my commission the general has interlined a few words that will make pretty pleasant reading for my friends, but I shall not quote them now.

———

I have been so broken down by the hardships that I have undergone that I am coming home for good thinking that I have done my share for Cuban independence. In a few weeks I shall ask for my leave and shall be home for Christmas possibly before. I don't like to quit now but a man who has fought through four sieges and twenty-two battles ought to rest a bit.

———

Tell the Boy[7] of whom I often think that when his Uncle Fred gets home he will tell him all about the baby donky [sic] that wasn't afraid at the battle of the "Hill of Iiom." [Now Scott dont [sic] let anybody see this part of the letter at present.

[The reason why I did not write for three months is because on June 20th in a battle I was shot through the body the ball piercing both lungs and missing my heart a scant three quarters of an inch. I am now quite well but my folks must not know about this for fear of alarming them. For the same reason I have never told that I was shot through the arm last winter. But dont [sic] let any body know this. I'll tell it when I get home. Dont [sic] write me again as I shall start before your letter will reach me.

[Faithfully
[Fred Funston][8]

Fred mentioned in his letter the pneumatic dynamite gun, a new addition to the artillery. This was the first time that such a weapon had been used in warfare and had been brought to Cuba by the Roloff expedition in March 1897. "The projectile of this weapon consisted of a cylindrical brass case about two inches in diameter and eighteen inches long, containing a bursting charge of five pounds of nitro-gel-atin..." In the air, the shell resembled "a swallow in flight." "Against earthworks and massive buildings the gun was not of much use other than for its terrifying effect, but it blew blockhouses and the weaker class of buildings to rubbish in a few shots." In describing his experiences in learning how to operate the Sims-Dudley dynamite gun, Fred was typically self-deprecating:

> Well, I looked her over and prodded around her for a day or two till I found from the printed directions that came with her which end was the shooting end. I didn't let the Cubans know that I was scared, but I was. We got into a little mix-up one day, and the old man sent for the dynamite. I waltzed her out, kept the directions in my head as well as I could and loaded her up. When the order came I sighted her and let her go.
>
> For a second she seemed to wheeze; it's all up, I thought; the Cubans ran; but I didn't dare to; it was only a second and then she coughed, and the air in the Spanish fort was filled with misfit logs, and debris, and I knew that it was all right. I turned around and grinned like the cat that had swallowed the canary, and no one knew that I had just finished making four or five kinds of a fool of myself. After they had set 'em up in the other alley we rolled 'em again.[9]

There is confusion about the date and place that Fred received his wound to his lungs. In lectures after his return to the United States in January 1898, he consistently stated that his lung wound occurred in May 1897 at the battle of Sama (or Sima, according to one published account).[10] In contrast, he stated June 20 as the date in his letter to Charlie Scott. The battle of Sama began on the morning of May 10 but, on the fifth shot of the insurgents' cannon, it was disabled. The artillerymen were forced to go some thirty miles to the nearest repair shop and thus missed the next four days of the infantry battle. Fred was among the artillerymen, and it is on that same date of May 10 that he wrote his letters to Ella and to Charlie Scott. He had had the unexpected opportunity to write to his kin and friend.

If Fred had received his severe lung wound at the battle of Sama, it would have had to have occurred during the first five cannon shots before the artillerymen took the disabled cannon for repair thirty miles away. Obviously, the wound did not occur then, since Fred would have been in no shape to have written his two letters home. A further fact indicating that Fred was not injured at the battle of Sama comes from the 1898 article written by a fellow American, Emory Fenn, who was a major in the Cuban Army and who was chief of the torpedo department. Fenn, in his account of the battle of Sama, singled out the arrival, before the battle, of Fred as commander of General Garcia's artillery. If Fred had, in fact, been shot through both lungs at the battle of Sama, then Fenn surely would have noted such a significant event in his article. He did not. I believe Fred's specificity two months after the event in stating the date as June 20 for his wounding is correct, rather than his memory six months later when he stated the date as May and at the battle of Sama.

David Potter, who wrote Funston's biography, stated that Fred received his wound to his lungs at Sama on May 11 when he was withdrawing his guns before the advancing Spanish forces from Gibara, thirty miles west of Sama. This was the same day that the siege of Sama had begun, according to Potter, rather than May 10 as stated by Fenn, which I find more credible. Also, according to Potter, because of this wound, Fred was to miss the Cuban attack under Garcia on Gibara on June 20. This, of course, is the date stated by Fred in his letter about his wound to his lungs. Hence, this must be the battle where the wounding occurred.[11] I know no details about this battle.

Regardless of the date, the physical consequences to Fred were the same. Fred's lung wound was caused by a bullet shot from a Mauser rifle, which was extremely fortunate for him, as he later explained: "[My wound] healed up in a few weeks, not to say a few days. It was a Mauser bullet, which at the right range will harmlessly pierce almost any organ except the heart. I have seen men shot through the stomach and even the brain and recover rapidly. The small caliber, high power bullet, except at point blank range and long range, makes such a clean, tiny wound that it closes up instantly and there is hardly any hemorrhage."[12] He also explained the futility of attempting to hide from Mauser bullets: "It isn't much use to get behind a tree or any obstruction when the Mausers are talking, for the bullets go at a velocity of 2,000 feet a second [for a distance of three miles]. They will pierce a large tree and kill a man who is behind it."[13] And that is exactly what happened when the bullet exited Fred's body after passing through his lungs and scarcely missing his heart. The bullet then passed through a tree and killed a Cuban who was hiding behind it for protection.[14]

In contrast to the "humane" wound caused by a Mauser bullet, "when the wounds are from Remingtons with the ordinary lead ball, or the lead ball with a thin brass jacket (explosive ball), they often prove fatal, and if the patient recovers, the improvement is slow."[15] Fred would later recall that it was a Remington brass-covered ball which struck Arthur Royal Joyce at the siege of Cascorro. When Joyce was hit by the bullet, Fred noted that he said "with the utmost self-possession; 'Well, this reminds me of a little story.' A man who can make such an off-hand remark as a bullet tears a big hole in his thigh probably deserves the palm for self-possession."[16] Joyce later wrote: "In the afternoon twenty stalwart soldiers were detailed to carry me in my hammock to a hospital 100 miles away and the trip, lasting two days and nights, was exceedingly joyous."[17] It was to be about two months before he "emerged from [his] retirement in the so called hospital, and joined Funston..."[18]

After being wounded through his lungs, Fred was taken to a hospital for treatment. According to Emory Fenn, there was an insufficient number of Cuban doctors to attend the wounded properly:

> One doctor, and in some cases two, are assigned to an entire division. These doctors appoint assistants from the men in the ranks, who, after a little instruction, are given a few bandages, cotton, carbolic acid, quinine, etc., and assigned to the various regiments in the division. These men are expected to give the first aid to the wounded, and administer such medicines as they may have when they are required; but even then it often happens that they are not present when the men are wounded, and it is necessary to take them many miles on horseback, or in hammocks hung on a long pole, before their wounds are dressed. Owing to this delay, small wounds often prove very serious. After their wounds are attended to, they are taken, as soon as practicable, to one of the many small hospitals in the woods, where they are given every attention possible under the circumstances.
>
> These hospitals are nothing more than deserted country houses, with beds made by driving four forked sticks into the ground, two at the head and two at the foot; a heavy stick is then laid in each pair of forks, and thin sticks, laid lengthwise of the bed, rest on these. The frame is then covered with banana-leaves, and, if it is possible to procure it, a sheet completes the bed. These hospitals are in charge of a *practicante,* but under the general supervision of the doctor, who visits them as often as possible; and in some cases, as after a heavy engagement, a doctor or several doctors are assigned to them, and remain as long as their services are required. As soon as

a new patient arrives he is placed on a new bed, as the same bed is never used twice, and is given an attendant to do his cooking and attend to his wants.

These hospitals are well supplied with bandages and medicine, and the prefect is required to keep them supplied with vegetables, sugar, milk, etc. The general in whose division they are furnishes meat, and the country people bring chickens, eggs, and any little dainties they may have.[19]

Although Fred had been lucky being shot by a Mauser bullet, and not a Remington one, his luck ran out in the hospital—"typhoid fever came to assist his convalescence from the wound..."[20] He lay in a bullhide hammock. Both Charlie Scott and William Allen White claimed Fred spent three months in the hospital, but approximately two months, the time period between June 20 and the beginning of the battle of Las Tunas on August 28, makes more sense.[21] In any event, Fred performed heroically at Las Tunas. As had happened to him at the siege of Jiguani, when he had been knocked down by the force of an exploding shell, at Las Tunas a Krupp shell "ricocheted off the Loma del Cura trench with such force that an enormous piece of rock hit Funston on the chest, putting him out of combat. Once Funston recovered an hour later, he went back to his post, with his usual valor, not before producing a booming battle cry: LONG LIVE FREE CUBA!"[22]

At Las Tunas, Fred once again dodged enemy shells. He later described the memorable first day of the three-day battle:

It will be recalled that at Jiguani we had taken pride in our ability to get out of the way of the shells from the Krupp used there, but these guns were of much higher velocity. At the ranges at which they had been fought earlier in the day the shell would follow the flash so quickly that one scarcely had time to move, but now at twelve hundred yards one could dive to cover if he lost no time. Immediately after sighting Cayo Hueso I had been climbing part-way up on the parapet to the windward of the smoke to observe the effects of my own shots. Whenever in this position I saw the flash of the enemy's gun I would yell "Down!" and would drop into one of the short ditches with the others. Finally I took a foolish notion that this getting down with such haste looked undignified, and that I would do no more of it. So when the next flash came I gave the warning cry and stood my ground. A couple of seconds later I was literally hurled backward through the air for fifteen or twenty feet, landing on my head and shoulders and being half buried under earth and poles, and at almost the same instant heard the explosion of the shell. I heard Menocal cry out, "My God, he is cut in two!" and a second or so later was half drowned under a deluge of filthy water. Colonel Garcia had picked up a bucket containing the water in which the sponge used in swabbing out one of the guns from time to time had been dipped, and had poured it over me. About a year ago I inquired of him as to the object of this well-meant attention, and was informed that it had been the only thing handy, and that water is always good for people. This having been the color and something like the consistency of printers' ink, I certainly was not a very inspiring object when helped to my feet, and was not fit to appear in polite society without a change of raiment and a bath. The shell had pierced the parapet about two feet from me, and had burst some twenty feet beyond. But my revenge was coming, and in about two shots more the offending gun was dismounted and the enemy left without artillery.[23]

In *Memories* Fred described the reaction of the Americans to being under fire: "All of this time we were being pelted by shells as fast as the two Krupp breech-loaders could be served. Shells were bursting all about us, and occasionally one will wreck a portion of the parapet. I hope it will not be taken as unseemly boasting, but as stating an absolute fact, when I say that far from feeling any uneasiness we were as cool as cucumbers, and considered we were having the time of our lives. But it had taken the participation in a good many stiff fights to bring us to such a state of mind."

The first day of battle saw the death of American lieutenant-colonel Joseph Napoleon Chapleau. "As his name would indicate, Chapleau was of French descent, and he had all of the characteristics of his race. He was volatile and dashing, and had made a reputation for dare-devil exploits." In an infantry charge, Chapleau "using a rifle and encouraging the men with him, received a wound that cut a blood vessel in his neck...the blood gushed in torrents from the wounded man's throat, drenching the surgeon who was attempting in vain to stop its flow. Chapleau, perfectly conscious, was muttering, 'It is finished,' 'It is finished,' 'It is all over,' his voice growing gradually weaker until his head sank down on his breast, and another brave man had died a solider's death."[24]

The old health problem of malaria raised its ugly head at the battle of Las Tunas. Fred's recent battle with typhoid likely left his body further weakened, and thus more susceptible to malaria. The first day of the battle was further complicated for him by this illness:

> All of us Americans, in common with many of our Cuban
> comrades, were suffering from a very severe form of malaria,
> and took it as a matter of course that about every other day
> we were to go through the racking experience of a burning
> fever with its accompanying delirium and the depressing chill
> in which it seemed that every man was trying to shake his
> teeth out. At this juncture I felt mine coming, and knew that
> in a short time I must be unconscious and delirious, and so
> turned the battery over to Janney, and led by my faithful or-
> derly, fifteen-year-old Sergeant Cecilio Betancourt, stumbled
> back to the head-quarters camp, distant half a mile. During
> my ravings, while imagining I was another person, I could
> hear a long-continued roar of infantry fire punctuated by can-
> non shots. Finally came the welcome unconsciousness, and
> when I awoke late at night there were no people near except
> Sergeant Betancourt and my striker, Juan Gonzalez. About
> ten o'clock I felt able to mount my horse, and riding back to
> the artillery position found that all the guns were gone. A
> few men who happened to be in the vicinity informed me that
> they had been taken into the town. We rode down past the
> ruins of the *Cuartel de la Caballeria*, making inquiries from
> persons encountered en route, and I finally rejoined my com-
> mand. The roar heard during my delirium was occasioned by
> the Spanish sortie, made in an attempt to retake the works
> lost and probably with the intention, if successful, of sweeping
> over the artillery position. The attack had been repulsed after
> severe fighting.[25]

By the second day of battle, August 29, the artillerymen were
having a difficult time during the firing of their big guns. "And so it
went on all of a long, tiresome, and dreary day," recalled Fred. "From
illness and hunger and as a result of the exhausting work of the preceding day, we were in a half-dazed condition, and could keep on our
feet with difficulty. Yesterday had been my day with the fever, and
to-day some of my comrades took their turn, and sank on the floor to
let it work its devilish will."[26]

As Fred had written in his letter to Charlie Scott, the end of the
battle came on the third day, August 30. In a captured barracks early
that morning, Fred discovered food. "I was so hungry that I pretty
nearly lost all regard for the proprieties, and made a quick run for the
kitchen, a Spanish soldier showing me where the officers' provisions
were kept. The first thing I found was some sausages in cans, and

cutting one of these open by one blow of my machete, began to eat the contents in the most primitive way imaginable." [27]

That morning there were two blockhouses occupied by the local detachment of the hated guerrillas:

> The defenders of these two positions saw the fall of the *Cuartel de la Infanteria*, and knew that it was only a question of time until the deadly dynamite gun from the shelter of near-by houses would blow their flimsy blockhouses to bits. They were in a terrible position, as they could not expect the quarter given the Spanish regulars. Their captain came out to ask what terms would be given them. The laconic reply was, "The same that you have given the helpless wounded in our hospitals." It was merely a choice of the form of death, so they marched out, threw down their arms, and to their credit met their fate with courage. They were cut down with the machete. It was a shocking spectacle, but it was retributive justice if there is such a thing, for these men had never known what mercy was. [28]

By 8 a.m. only the Telegraph Fort remained held by the Spanish. All the rest of the city had fallen to the insurgents. In an April 1898 interview with *The Kansas City Star,* Fred described a surreal experience that had occurred in this final battle. In doing so, he suddenly "burst into laughter..." as he described the actions of the Cuban soldier with the alliterative name of Barney Bueno (Barney may have been a nickname). Intrigued by Fred's short story of an incident of "such dramatic power," the reporter spoke again with Fred a few days later to obtain more details. This resulted in a lengthy *The Kansas City Star* story on May 1 devoted to what had occurred. Fred had been present and thus was "an eye witness of the whole scene." A summary of that account follows.

Across the street from the huge stone Telegraph Fort was one of the finest houses in the city. It was constructed of white bricks, and "the interior was finished with the finest woods and the furnishings were exquisite." This house, owned by a surgeon and lieutenant colonel of the Spanish army named Mendez, had been abandoned by him, and he was holed up in Fort Telegraph. Up the marble steps and into the inside of the house the Cubans lugged a twelve-pound Hotchkiss gun, and placed it in one of the two, high parlor windows facing the fort after first tearing out the wall below the windowsill so that the gun muzzle would fit there. The Cubans began clearing the room of its valuable furniture and bric-a-brac.

When the Hotchkiss gun was fired, the wind blowing from the

fort meant the smoke from the gun drifted back and filled the room. "The men at the Hotchkiss gun fired slowly and carefully; the rest of the battery outside took up the fire with the cannons and the dynamite gun. The Cubans in the house, huddled on the floor, could hear the five-pound dynamite shells drop and explode inside the fort and could see occasionally through the breach of their own wall the havoc they created. The return from the fort was directed mainly at the house and at the gun that spat its balls through the gaping wall."

The smoke got thicker in the room. "In the midst of this storm of powder smoke a man rose up from the floor and staggered across the room. It was Barney Bueno, a captain of infantry, a big, fine, dashing fellow. He was an educated Cuban of the better class, a graduate of the Polytechnic school of Troy, N.Y., an accomplished musician and singer. Barney had been drinking too frequently at a bottle he had found in one of the rooms, and the liquor had just begun to seep into his brain." Barney began to sing a Cuban air, but decided he wanted to play a piano.

> Just then the smoke lifted a bit and he saw his instrument. It was a Grand piano and bore the inscription, "'Otto,' Berlin." He threw back the lid and drew up the stool... [H]e played and sang a racy song he had often sung in camp....
>
> The men at the windows turned and started through the swirling smoke.
>
> "Why, it's Captain Barney," they cried in delighted surprise. "Sing it again, Captain Barney; sing it again!"
>
> "Mind your guns and hold your tongues," shouted Barney, "and I'll sing it again."
>
> He sang it again and again at every splendid shot the Hotchkiss made.
>
> The bullets were dropping steadily about him. He heard the tinkle of falling vases and the crash of glass bookcases. Chairs were knocked to pieces and pictures dropped from the walls.

The battle continued. The fort's walls crumbled. "And Barney played all the while—airs from 'El Capitan,' 'The Serenade' and 'Trovatore'— sang ballads of the camp and rhymes that will not bear printing." After twenty minutes, the fort surrendered.[29]

Surprisingly, Fred's account in *Memories of Two Wars* not only lacked the rich detail of what had occurred, but changed some facts:

> We of the artillery, gathered in the parlor of the residence of the surgeon, breached the wall from the inside and looked through at our expected target, distant only sixty feet. Men

had been sent to bring up a gun, and while we were waiting Captain "Barney" Bueno of the staff sat down to the piano and played the "Bayames," "Yankee Doodle," and the "Washington Post March." A lot of our men were sprawled about the floor looking at the pictures in some French periodicals. Outside there was still some exchange of rifle shots. The Spanish commander knew that we had him in a trap, and rather than have his men uselessly slaughtered, hauled down his flag, and at nine o'clock the fight was over, having lasted without cessation for fifty-one hours. To say we were glad of the end but mildly expresses our feelings.[30]

It is difficult to understand why Fred would change some facts. Perhaps, in looking back on what had occurred more than a decade earlier, Fred did not believe that all the details of Barney Bueno's actions, including his inebriation, should be recorded for the larger book-reading audience, and thus altered the record. Fred's assertion that the Spanish surrendered without a battle, instead of after the battle he had previously described, is puzzling. Perhaps Fred simply did not later remember correctly what he had so graphically described a few months after its occurrence. There is also the important aspect that Fred stated about writing *Memories:* "most of the work was done in a big hurry and in the face of great difficulties." (See the discussion at the end of Chapter Four about Fred's circumstances when he wrote *Memories*.)

Fred attained his highest rank in the Cuban Army as a reward for his actions with the artillery in the battle of Las Tunas. As he had written Charlie Scott, "I have been given the gold star of a lieutenant colonel and on my commission the general has interlined a few words that will make pretty pleasant reading for my friends but I shall not quote them now." Unfortunately, the copies of Fred's three commissions in the Frederick Funston Papers are from official Cuban archives, and are thus not the originals. General Garcia's interlineation is lost forever. Fred valued highly these commissions, noted a reporter in an April 1898 interview: "Turning upon his Cuban experience Colonel Funston drew from his pocket a bundle of papers. Carefully unfolding them he produced three strange looking official documents, elaborately inscribed in the Spanish language. They were his commissions as lieutenant [sic: captain?], major and lieutenant colonel in the Cuban army. Each bore the signatures of General Gomez and Calixto Garcia. 'Those will be great souvenirs some day,' he said proudly. 'See, they bear the seal of the Cuban republic. I prize them very highly and if I go back to Cuba I shall leave them in Washington to be taken care of. They cost me some hard fighting and some blood, but I had lots of fun.'"[31]

The Spanish captured Fred when he was leaving Cuba in December 1897. Since the Spanish found no identification on him, he did not have these commissions then. Likely, they were sent to his family from Cuba by his friend and comrade in arms, James Pennie, who had evaded capture by the Spanish when Fred was apprehended, and, who, when he returned to the rebel camp, decided to mail them to Fred's family.

All of the artillery officers were promoted one grade by General Garcia in appreciation of their service. "Our first sergeant was a negro as black as night," wrote Fred. "He was a brave and faithful fellow and had long ago deserved promotion in the organization in which he had served, but our chief had feared that we Americans would resent such action. But Las Tunas settled it with us, and we went to the general in a body and said we would be glad to have him as a fellow-officer. He was glad to comply, and it was my pleasant task to surprise the gallant soldier by handing him his commission as second lieutenant."[32]

On September 6, Fred wrote a brief note to one of his Lawrence friends, which Charlie Scott characterized for his newspaper's readers as "wholly personal and of interest to the public only as it conveyed the agreeable news that he was in excellent health and spirits and expects to reach home before Christmas. 'I have agreed to remain through one more operation with the army which is to take place in October,' he writes, 'and then I shall consider that I have done my share and try to reach home.'"[33] If Fred wrote that he was in "excellent health," which appear to be Charlie Scott's words, not Fred's, then he did not disclose to the letter's addressee his true situation that he had candidly described in his letter of August 31 to Charlie Scott: "I have been so broken down by the hardships that I have undergone..." Since the original letter is apparently no longer extant, we do not know precisely what Fred wrote.

Fred received one more wound before leaving Cuba, but it was a very different one than that caused by a bursting shell or Mauser bullet. "'In the first place, my severest wound,' he said [in January 1898], 'was not received in battle as reported. I was trying to ride away from a rain storm when my horse slipped on a high bank and fell on me. My hip was contused between the weight of the horse and a gnarled stick, and a chronic inflammation has set in. It gives me infinitely more trouble than the shot through the lungs. That healed up in a few weeks, not to say a few days.'"[34] The stick injury occurred in October. As a result, Fred walked with a painful limp, an unpleasant and frustrating handicap for a man of action. His final battle came only a few weeks later while he was serving in the cavalry. "I distinguished myself greatly by running my horse into a barb wire fence in the mad attempt to increase the distance between myself and a body of pursuing Spanish cavalry. I was not mentioned in the official report."[35]

In October, Spanish troop columns crossed the eastern territory of Cuba with the goal of supplying the different posts that they still controlled, since these places supported the Spanish troops. "[G]reat convoys of provisions were transported despite the continuous rains and the rising of the rivers, which were extraordinary that October."[36] On November 28, General Garcia and his insurgent army attacked Guisa, a strongly defended town. Since Fred was reported to be ill, he did not participate in the attack and subsequent siege of Guisa.[37] Fred's deteriorating physical condition was increasingly desperate, and he and James Pennie decided that the time had come to return to the United States. A 1931 Cuban account, based on official records and written by a Cuban revolutionist who had known Fred, told the sequence of events which then unfolded:

> Funston asked General Garcia for a pass to go cure himself in his home country, with the condition that he would return to Cuba as soon as his condition permitted it, since he fervently desired to keep serving Cuba until its independence was achieved. Major General Calixto Garcia, Chief of the Oriental Department, did not hesitate one moment to concede Funston's request, since Funston was gravely ill, due to the terrible hit he took in the chest during the taking of Las Tunas; and in the war fields there were no mediums for his cure. Along with Funston also left his subaltern Lieutenant James Pennie, who suffered from malaria.
>
> Since Funston was enamored by the Revolution, he wanted to leave Cuba with a document that identified him as a Cuban revolutionary, so when he got to Camagüey he addressed the Government—which was encamped in Aguará—with the following request:
>
> To the Government Council of the Republic of Cuba
>
> The exponents—citizens Lieutenant Colonel Chief of Artillery Frederick Funston and Lieutenant of the same division James Pennie—respectfully address this high worthy corporation, in order to manifest that:
>
> They have shared in union with the good sons of Cuba the sorrows of the campaign for sixteen months the first one [Funston] and twenty months the second [Pennie], always under

the orders of Major General Calixto Garcia, Chief of the Department. And although they are both satisfied and thankful for the good reception and treatment that they received, they both extremely regret to have to ask for a permit to return to their home country, the United States of America, due to the fact that both of them are in dire health conditions, and also extenuated by the rigors of the weather.

They both came to Cuba because of their sympathy for a just cause, without the ambition for any sort of reward; and only with the desire to help it [Cuba] to soon see it free from the tyrannical Spanish oppression.

Attached is their chief's permit, who said that it would be forever valid; and since they are still ill, they have not had a chance to go and renew it. They both hope that the triumphs of the Liberating forces continue, and that the Council of Government have success in guiding the nation to the greatest prosperity and to the most complete union.

La Esperanza, December 4th, 1897.

Frederick Funston,   James Pennie,

Lieutenant Colonel.   Lieutenant.

The War Secretary informed that "considering that this was not an urgent matter, the permit would be denied," and thus the petition was denied to those valiant and generous Americans that, gravely ill, without medicine, without beds, were lying on the grass.

A week later, Funston and Pennie, made use of their safe-conduct—granted to them by the Deputy General of the Army and Chief of the Oriental Department, Mayor General Calixto Garcia Yñiguez—and left to heal in the United States.[38]

Why the War Secretary, José B. Aleman, would regard the legitimate request of Fred and James Pennie as "not an urgent matter" is difficult to understand. Perhaps the War Secretary felt that since the Cubans themselves could not leave the island for health reasons, then the Americans should not be allowed to do so either. Much more probable, however, was that the military services of the Americans were regarded as so essential that they must remain to fight for the revolution.

In any event, and as noted in the foregoing account, the two Americans decided to leave anyway, armed with the safe-conduct pass issued by General Garcia. Fred's departure was to be anything but uneventful. After his return in January 1898 to the United States,

Fred told in interviews and lectures some of the details of what had occurred, the amount of the detail varying from account to account. The following four accounts, the fourth being the most detailed, provide a fairly complete story, though there are some inconsistencies among them:

(1) I have a passing regret that my connection with the Cuban war did not close more auspiciously. When six Spanish soldiers rose upon me from the bush, I felt that in this day and date [December 12[39]] it was not needful to strike an attitude of defiance and be shot dead or to appear with proud defiance before a court-martial and not in a Spanish prison, so I simply announced that I was on my way to accept amnesty and, as I chewed and swallowed the only incriminating paper I had, the Spanish officers reported there was no evidence to the contrary and I was sent to Havana and turned over to Consul General Lee.[40]

(2) [M]y departure from Cuba was fraught with even more danger than my arrival. You see, when I applied for the furlough I had reached the rank of lieutenant colonel and hence my superior referred my application to the insurgent civil government. Lieutenant Penny [sic] of the United States army, who is a lieutenant in the Cuban army, accompanied me upon my journey to the government officials. As luck would have it, we ran into a party of six Spanish soldiers. There was a skirmish, but seeing we were outnumbered three to one, we finally turned our horses and fled. Lieutenant Penny [sic] escaped, but I, weak and crippled from my wounds, as I was, fell into the hands of the pursuing Spaniards.

At first I thought "it was all up with me," to use a somewhat inelegant but very expressive slang phrase. But as a last resort I determined to bluff it out if possible. I told my captors that I was a presentado [one accepting amnesty] coming in to surrender. Fortunately I had no papers on me to disclose my rank or identity. All I had to do was to give a false name [Bernard Malloy[41]] and stick to my story. If I hadn't done it and if my identity had been discovered I would have been shot on the spot. As it was my captors did not put any too much faith in my story.

They bound me hand and foot and took me to Los Ninas and thence to Porto [sic] Principe, where I was brought before General Castellano, the Spanish commander. To him I repeated my story. He convened a special board of inquiry, consisting of six members. For the third time I represented myself as a presentado. As I was not in uniform and had no papers upon me, the story went and I was released upon my oath that I would never fight against Spain.[42]

(3) I was going to the Cuban capital, Las Guymas, and was crossing a railroad track at night when I was ambushed by a squad of the enemy. I had no idea anyone was near when I was challenged and heard the click of their rifle locks. I knew I was captured and I said in Spanish "I surrender." I told them that I was on my way to the Spanish lines to give up and I stuck to the story. They believed it. I was taken to Puerto Principe and tried by a military commission. [I had one officer appointed to defend me and one to prosecute. After two hours investigation the court decided that I was probably guilty of being an irreconcilable insurgent, but that they could not prove it. So I had to chose [sic] between signing a parole and lying in prison till the close of the war. It would have done Cuba no good to do the latter, so I signed the parole...[43]] I was very decently treated and released on parole.[44]

(4) In the month of September, 1897, I asked General Garcia for a five-month furlough, and he replied that he was very sorry to lose me and that it did not, under the law, lie in his power to grant a furlough, but that he would refer me to the civil government, about ten days' ride from where we then were, at Victoria de las Tunas. I knew that this was merely an evasion on the general's part, but of course would not say so to him. He, however, gave me a sort of conditional furlough for five months. When I say conditional I mean that it had to be ratified by President Salvador Cisneros. General Garcia then expressed the desire that, before presenting the furlough to the president, I remain with him until the close of the campaign that he was then engaged in. This I did and participated in the battles of La Gaza and of the farm Jesus Maria.

In November General Garcia, leaving the artillery, of which I was in command, at Las Pilionas, set out in pursuit of a Spanish column near Bayamo, many miles away. I waited in vain for his return before starting to the seat of the civil government and finally heard, through one of his staff officers, that General Garcia had left for Palma Soriano, near Santiago, and that I would probably not see him again for some months. It would, with the uncertain and irregular postal service that the Cubans had, take a month to communicate with General Garcia and get a reply. I considered that, having remained with him for more than six weeks after he had given me permission to go to the civil government to have my leave ratified, I was justified in leaving for La Esperanza, the seat of the provisional government, without further parley.

I accordingly wrote Brigadier General Menocol, the nearest officer of high rank in the vicinity, and asked him to notify General Garcia of my departure.

The next day I called on the officers of the Tunas brigade, commanded by Capote, bade them good-bye and told them that I was going first to La Esperanza and then home. They gave me their good wishes and a number of them mounted their horses and rode with me for a mile.

My only companion was James Pennie, an American, a second lieutenant of artillery, who expected to return to our camp and was merely going with me for the trip. We knew the country so well that no guide was required and in eight days we reached the point where it was necessary for us to cross the fortified railroad line from Puerto Principe to Nuevitas, extending half way across the island, or make a detour of many miles. The line was protected by blockhouses at intervals of 800 yards and was occasionally patrolled by small squads of soldiers.

We approached the railway line about midway between two blockhouses just at dusk. As two horses splashing along the muddy road would make more noise than one I suggested to Pennie that he remain about 150 yards from the line, concealed in the brush, while I rode forward to ascertain if the track was clear. As I approached the cleared right of way I heard the challenge of a sentry "Halt! Who goes there?"' of course in Spanish, and six Spanish soldiers who had heard me approaching rose from the brush with leveled Mausers and compelled me to throw up my hands. I could in the gathering dusk barely make out the dim outlines of the nearest blockhouse distant probably 350 yards.

I saw that the only way to save myself from execution was to pretend to my captors that I was on my way up to the blockhouse to surrender. When they took me to the lieutenant, who searched me at the blockhouse, to the Spanish commandant at Las Minas, and before the court-martial that tried me, at Puerto Principe, I stuck to this story through thick and thin; so they eventually believed it, and I was deported to the United States on my promise that I would have nothing further to do with the Cuban insurgents.[45]

In the first account above, Fred stated that he had "chewed and swallowed the only incriminating paper [he] had..." after he was captured. Perhaps the most extensive account of Fred's swallowing of this safe conduct pass from General Garcia appeared in *The St. Louis Republic*. On his train trip home from New York, Fred stopped briefly in St. Louis where he was the guest of former State University of Kansas student, Mary Norris Berry, the young woman with the beautiful singing voice about whom Fred had written his good friend, Buck Franklin, several years earlier.[46]

Fred told the story of his Cuban experiences "only after the most persistent urging, both by his hostess and the newspaper man," and the result was a very extensive article. Although this article quoted some detail given by Fred about his swallowing of the pass, the reporter was so intrigued by this episode that he wrote a subsequent article dealing solely with this episode:

"I was injured during the early part of December [sic: October] and found that it would be necessary to go to the hospital for treatment, as I was completely disabled. From General Garcia I obtained a permit to leave the ranks and go to one of the insurgent towns for treatment. It was necessary to get this permit approved by the civil officials. I started on my way, suffering considerable pain but hoping that I might elude the Spanish soldiers and reach my destination safely. It was my ill luck while crossing a railroad track to run into a picket of six Spanish soldiers."

"Of course," said the Colonel, "I might have drawn my pistols, shot right and left and perished bravely for the cause, but I didn't. I concluded discretion was the better part of valor, when it was a case of six to one, so I surrendered and handed over my weapons, telling them I was an American and on my way to the Spanish headquarters to surrender, anyhow. They seemed disposed to treat me as a joke. But I knew the funny part would cease when we reached the nearest post, whither they were taking me, walking my horse along in their midst. I had just one damaging bit of evidence on my person that would give the direct lie to my story, and that was a small strip of paper about as long as my hand, saying:

'Pass Colonel Funston through the lines,' and signed 'Garcia.' All other passports I had taken the precaution to leave behind me. But this one lay in the bottom of my right pocket in my linen coat, and I knew that I must get rid of it in some way and before we reached the post. So, still talking with the men and holding my reins in the left hand, I put my right hand down into the pocket and with my fingers folded the paper into a tight wad. This I worked into the palm, and then bringing out my hand with this same pink-bordered handkerchief on top of the paper, I passed it across my mouth, got the paper inside, chewed it slowly and swallowed it just as we came in sight of the Spanish commander's quarters. When they searched me, as they proceeded to do the first thing, I had no tell-tale documents, nothing about me to prove that I was other than I represented myself to be, and instead of being imprisoned and eventually executed—my certain fate had they found Garcia's pass—I was confined only two weeks in a very comfortable sort of prison, then released on parole and finally came North, as you see.

"But the pink-bordered handkerchief—it did the work. I captured that handkerchief, too. We took a small interior town one day and looted it, of course. In a dry goods store I found a small box of handkerchiefs which nobody else seemed to want, and which I needed very badly. The pink was among the lot."

Fred had shown the reporter the life-saving handkerchief, which the reporter described as "a crumpled, pink-bordered, very badly soiled pocket handkerchief, which, I hope he will frame some time soon, for it saved his life."[47]

At no time after his return to the United States, including in the foregoing four accounts of his departure from Cuba, did Fred disclose what the Cuban government documents confirm—he had, in fact, made it to the Cuban capital, and there the government had denied his request to leave Cuba. Simply put, he lied. I believe that Fred was concerned about his reputation, which he felt would be damaged if it was known that he had deserted the Cuban army, even though he had the greatest justifications to do so—his seriously deteriorating health and his status as only a volunteer in the Cuban Liberation Army, to which he had given invaluable assistance for more than a year.

The charge of desertion was leveled against him by some U. S.

soldiers returning from Cuba in the summer of 1898 based on stories that they had heard there. At that time, Fred publicly defended, in a lengthy letter published in *The Kansas City Star*, his departure from Cuba, and part of that detailed defense is the fourth and final account set out above. It, like all of the others, gave no hint that the Cuban government had denied Fred's and Pennie's furlough requests. In fact, in his letter Fred speculated that had he reached the civil government, he was "sure" that Garcia's pass "would have been ratified." Untrue, of course. He did provide in his published defense, however, additional insight into what had happened:

In all of the Cuban towns held by Spaniards were many Cubans secretly aiding the rebels in the field and having constant communication with them. Of course, the story soon got into the country districts among the rebels that the Spaniards had an American deserter, for that is what I was pretending to be in order to save myself.

Eventually I reached the United States and reported to Estrada Palma, the Cuban delegate in New York, to whom I explained in full the circumstances of my leaving the island. Mr. Palma expressed himself as fully satisfied that I was captured and had not deserted, and said that as I had given my word to the Spaniards they would not ask me to do further service in the insurgent army. He promised that he would at once write to General Garcia, explaining my disappearance and accounting for me. A week later Mr. Palma told me that he had done this. That the Cuban junta did not regard me as a deserter is evident from the fact that they voluntarily sent me to one of the sanitariums in New York and got an expensive surgeon to care for me.

It was not until I was in Tampa, Fla., with General Miles at the time of the concentration there of the army, that I learned that the Cubans thought I had taken "French leave." Lieutenant Colonel Hernandez of Garcia's staff had just arrived there from Cuba and I discussed the matter with him. Hernandez said that Pennie came back to camp about New Year's day and said that I had ridden up to the track to reconnoiter; that he had heard some loud conversation and had heard me reply to the challenge, "Alto, Quien Vive?" with "The Unpresentado," which means one who is coming in to give himself up. It does not seem to have occurred to these people that a man would be quick-witted enough to save himself when captured, by pretending that he was coming in to surrender.

Hernandez told me that Pennie himself appeared to be at a loss to understand whether I had been captured or had given myself up. He further said that Garcia had never received a single word from Palma on the subject, which is not to be wondered at considering the wretched mail communication between the rebels and the outside world. I was not much worried by what Hernandez told me at Tampa, as I then expected to go to Cuba with General Miles and knew that I would see Garcia and straighten out my record. I talked of the matter at Tampa with a number of friends in the army, among them Captains Dickman and Cavanaugh, and they seemed to think the matter scarcely worth noticing. Unless I am mistaken I also told Mr. Whelpley of The [Kansas City] Star the story.

To close with the desertion matter, I never was under any obligation to fight for the Cubans. I am an American, and I think that a fairly ornery American is better than a ten-acre field full of Cubans. I went into the war without the hope of any reward and without the slightest obligation. I never took any oath of allegiance. I served for nearly two years in a cause which was just, principally because a Cuban is only one or two degrees less worthless than a Spaniard. I suffered for nearly two long, dreary years what the men of our army suffered before Santiago for one month [in the Spanish-American War of 1898], and I do not wish to disparage the splendid achievements or the heroism of our regulars. I survived wounds, starvation, sickness and capture by a merciless enemy, only to have my reputation blackened in my absence from home by some irresponsible cur with nothing but rumor to base his stories on, assisted by the worse than blackguard newspapers that have aided him.[48]

Not only did the stories that American soldiers brought back from Cuba allege desertion by Fred, some stories claimed that he was never in the insurgent army while others said that he had never been wounded "and so on ad nauseum." As to those soldiers who had "been very industriously circulating" these negative stories, Fred observed in his letter to *The Kansas City Star:* "These individuals have had apparently great weakness for rushing into print and having themselves interviewed."

As for the story that Fred had never been wounded, he also dealt with this subject in his letter to the *Star*:

The best reply that I can make to the story that I was

never wounded is to append an extract from my discription [sic] in the original muster-in-roll of the Twentieth Kansas made by the army surgeon who examined me. The extract is certified to by Major Whitman of this regiment. Have any of the people who have known me all my life ever heard of my being shot or having an arm broken anywhere but in Cuba?

THE SURGEON'S TESTIMONY

I certify that the following is a true extract copy of remarks set opposite Colonel Funstons' [sic] name on the original muster roll of the Twentieth Kansas infantry, U. S. V. * * * "Scar. Gunshot wound on right side, exit on left side. Scar of fracture of left ulna." F. H. Whitman, Maj. Twentieth Kansas Inf'ty U. S. Vol's

Fred concluded his defense against the several allegations against him: "I hope that the papers that have been giving circulation to these rumors will be fair enough to publish my reply, and I thank The Star in advance for allowing such an imposition on its space in a purely personal matter."[49]

Even with the report of the surgeon based on his physical examination of Fred after his return from Cuba, one wonders if some of Fred's critics are like the Apostle Thomas, who would not believe the other apostles when they said that Christ had been resurrected until he saw and felt Christ's wounds. Obviously not possible now in Fred's case. I believe even without seeing, however. The contemporary evidence—Fred's 1897 letter to Charlie Scott about his wounds, the surgeon's report of the visible evidence of a through-and-through gunshot wound—militates for the conclusion that Fred was, in fact, wounded in battle.

In stark contrast, the rumors in Cuba are just that—rumors without evidence. Their repetition by some American soldiers does not make them any more credible. The only contrary evidence I have seen is *not* contemporaneous and involves Fred's fellow *expedicionarios*, Osmun Latrobe and Stuart Janney. In 1932, David Potter, the author that Eda Funston had hired to write Fred's biography, contacted Latrobe "seeking final data on certain points" since his manuscript was almost completed.

His questions related to identification of the battle in which "Funston was shot through the lungs" and of the Cuban bush-hospital to which he was carried. Also, Potter asked about the circumstances under which Fred was wounded. Both Latrobe and Janney, to whom Latrobe had written about these questions, replied that Fred was not wounded in any battle, Latrobe specifically stating that "Funston was not shot through the lungs." Potter, on Latrobe's response to him, wrote this rebuttal: "Funston's letter to Charles Scott 1897 expressly mentions this wound." This is, of course, true.

Why would neither man, Latrobe now a colonel in the U. S. Cavalry and Janney now a prominent Baltimore attorney, not remember this event? Perhaps the answer lies in Janney's answer to another question asked by Potter: "(d) who commanded the artillery during Funston's absence, i. e. during the summer of 1897 up to the fight at Victoria de las Tunas? Was it Joyce? Cox?" Latrobe answered by referring to Janney's response: "In reply to question (d) I would say that Funston was never absent except temporarily during the summer of 1897 up to the fight de las Tunas. At any rate there was no formal change."[50]

Although noting it, Janney does not explain Fred's temporary absence "during the summer of 1897." As we know, horrible as such a wound sounds, Fred's wound to his lungs by the Mauser bullet "healed up in a few weeks, not to say a few days." A rapid recovery from a Mauser bullet shot at the right range was not uncommon. But in Fred's case, he caught the feared typhoid fever in the hospital. This clearly lengthened his hospital stay to approximately two months. In a world before antibiotics—the only effective treatment—typhoid fever was a deadly disease, its victims including First Lady Abigail Adams and the eponym for Stanford University, Leland Stanford Jr, who died at age fifteen in 1884.

Grover Flint was an American war correspondent for four months with General Gomez's army. He confirmed Fred's description of the frequently relatively benign effects of being shot by a Mauser bullet. It "traverses the human anatomy, leaving (at ordinary ranges) a wound scarcely larger at the point of exit than at the point of entrance, and causing only a trifling hemorrhage. Unless it ricochets, or bursts its nickel cap..., it never carries particles of clothing into the flesh, and if it encounters a bone on its way, rarely splintering, shattering, or causing dangerous complications."

Flint most surprisingly observed: "So slight is the fear of Mauser wounds among the Cuban forces that it has become rather a discredit to a soldier not to have one or more wounds, and for this reason you frequently see men expose themselves needlessly to fire..."[51] In contrast, a wound from a lead bullet shot by a Remington carbine usually caused horrific damage.

Since, in reality, the wound to the lungs was insignificant in comparison to a lengthy battle with typhoid fever, which kept Fred in the hospital for a long period, I believe that Janney and Latrobe in 1932, thirty-five years after the event, had in their respective minds Fred's typhoid fever which had kept him in the hospital for so long, forgetting the easily recoverable Mauser wound that landed Fred there in the first place. The evidence—contemporary writing substantiated by the physical evidence of the entrance and exit of a bullet—is overwhelming that Fred was wounded in battle.

In *Memories of Two Wars*, Fred devoted four chapters to his Cuban experiences. The final chapter, "A Defeat and a Victory," ended with the taking of Las Tunas in August 1897. He does not discuss the subject of his subsequent departure from Cuba or his gunshot wounds.

How did General Garcia feel about Fred's departure without governmental approval? And why, in fact, did the Cuban government deny Fred's and Pennie's furlough requests? The answers come from H. J. Allen, the editor of *The Evening Herald* in Ottawa, Kansas, and future Governor of Kansas (1919-1923). He had interviewed Fred in Ottawa in April 1898 before his lecture about his Cuban war experiences, and traveled to Cuba after the start of the Spanish-American War in the spring of 1898. Hearing there that Fred had deserted the Cuban army, Allen asked General Garcia himself about this, and he "simply said that Mr. Funston had never been given any permission to come home." This, of course, is true based on the Cuban record set out above.

General Garcia referred the editor to a member of his staff, Dr. Castillo, the surgeon-general of the Cuban army, who "told us that Funston was the most valuable American who ever engaged with the insurgents; that he was a brave and effective artilleryman and that the refusal of the Cuban government to grant him a furlough arose from the value of his services; the Cuban officers have nothing but praise for his conduct as an officer of their army—and their criticism of him for deserting is not severe. They recognize the fact that Funston had a moral right to come home when he wanted to come, and they criticize the Cuban government for withholding a formal permission." Fred was vindicated by the Cuban officers themselves! As for General Garcia, when told that Fred might soon be returning to Cuba with the American forces, the General "announced to his staff officers that he would receive Funston heartily, and that no account whatever would be taken of the manner in which he left the army."[52]

In 1906, the United States intervened militarily in Cuban affairs, and Brigadier General Funston was dispatched briefly to Cuba by the United States government. The canard that he had deserted the Cuban army was still alive in some quarters. He dealt directly with the charge in a newspaper interview that fall, and, this time, acknowledged that the Cuban revolutionary government had not authorized his departure from the island:

> The soldiers in the field don't think me a deserter; that comes from the civilian crowd around [Cuban president Estrada] Palma [who resigned as president on September 28, 1906]. When I was with Garcia's army my health broke down completely; I had an abcess and other troubles, and had to leave the island. Garcia granted permission to return to the States, and I applied to these civil authorities for leave to go on a small boat they controlled. They refused it, not because it was I who applied, but because they were opposed to Garcia. So I told'em I would go through the Spanish lines, and I did, but I ran into the arms of a Spanish patrol and was captured. They'd have shot me, and I palmed myself off as a deserter to save myself. How the real Cuban fighting men feel toward me was shown by the banquet they gave me [recently], said to be one of the finest ever given there. [53]

In *Memories of Two Wars,* Fred concluded his account of the Cuban war of independence by describing this 1906 banquet:

> A pleasant sequel of my own service came a few years ago when I was the guest of honor at a banquet given in Havana by my old comrades of the revolution. The present Cuban minister to the United States, General Carlos Garcia, was toastmaster, and at the table were eighty-one former insurgent officers, one of them being the present president of the republic [Jose Miguel Gomez]. Sixty-five had been old comrades of the *Departamento del Oriente.* It was hard to realize that those well-groomed men in evening dress were the worn and wasted men who had led the Cubans at Cascorra [sic], at La Machuca, and many another good fight, and had stormed the ridge at Jiguani and led their men through the wire entanglements at Victoria de las Tunas; or were the same comrades, always kindly and considerate, who in the grim days of hunger always saw that the American *mambis* got their share when food strayed into camp. That one evening of reminiscence and good-fellowship was pay enough for it all.[54]

Fred had stated that he was "very decently treated" following his capture. After he had convinced the Spanish authorities that he was simply an American who had accepted amnesty, he was lodged, under guard, in the Hotel Telegrafo in Nuevitas. He was described later by a fellow lodger as "thin and emaciated," and the fellow lodger "feared he was going home to die."[55] The next day, on January 4,

Fred was taken to Havana. "I was in the uniform of a rebel and was a pretty seedy looking specimen. The Spaniards stared at me on the streets and a gang of kids followed me around shouting 'Mambecia!' which means rebel. No one bothered me, though. I dropped into General [Fitzhugh] Lee's office [the American consul and a Confederate officer in the Civil War] and he sized me up with the remark: 'Are you a rebel?' I said I was. 'Well,' said he, 'I was a rebel thirty-five years ago, but I never was as tough looking as you are.' I had no money and he furnished me funds to buy clothes and get to New York. I had not time to wait to have a suit of clothes made, and the only thing I could buy was an ice cream suit, straw hat and tan shoes. I landed in New York on January 10, 1898, rigged out in that outfit. It was very cold and I was a curiosity."[56]

"With cries of 'Al machete,' the Cubans rushed into the barbwire protecting the cavalry barracks at Victoria de Las Tunas. With machete they hacked at the barbwire, and in a few moments had cut through it." (Fred Funston)
(*Memories of Two Wars* illustration)

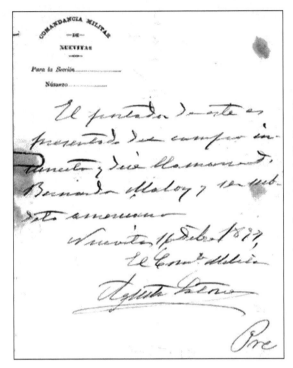

Spanish "passport" issued to Bernard Malloy, Funston's false name that he gave to his Spanish captors after his capture by them on December 12, 1897. On the backside an official has noted "Malloy's" passage through the city of Caibarien on his way to Havana where the Spaniards took him to the American consul.

Translation:

Military Command of Nuevitas

The bearer is a presentado from the insurrection camp named Bernard Malloy who is an American.

Nuevitas 16 December 1897

The Military Commandant August Latorre

Translation of the reverse side (continued from front side with "Pre"):
Presentado today going to Havana.
Caibarien January 1, 1898
Don Garcia
(Seal) Municipal Alcaldía of Caibarien

Chapter Nine Notes—*Letters XV and XVI*

Epigraph: Fred Funston to Charles F. Scott, August 31, 1897. Photocopy of original letter in collection of Frederick Funston's letters from Cuba and New York City at Allen County Historical Society, Inc., Iola, Kansas.

1. A lengthy, purported interview with Fred was published in *The San Francisco Call* of July 23, 1897. It claimed that Fred had left San Francisco by train the prior evening for Portland, Oregon, and from there to "the newly discovered gold fields of the far north" ("He Will Try It Again," *The San Francisco Call*, July 23, 1897). *The Kansas City Journal* of July 30, 1897, noted that Lute Thrasher, "a former Kansas newspaperman," was the staff member of the *Call* who did the interview. The *Journal* then editorially stated the obvious: "The friends of Funston cannot imagine that he would prefer vulgar gold to the blood of the brutal Spanish. Then they cannot understand how it is Funston could have heard about Klondike and reached San Francisco so soon. They can understand, however, how a story might be written for space rate purposes" ("Brief Bits of News," *The Kansas City Journal*, July 30, 1897). The mystifying part of this story to me is that Lute Thrasher was from Iola, and thus, presumably, would have recognized anyone impersonating Fred. I speculate that, for unknown reasons, Thrasher himself perpetrated this hoax.

2. "The Week's News," *The Iola Register*, August 20, 1897.

3. "Sunflower State Gossip," *The Kansas Semi-Weekly Capital*, August 6, 1897.

4. "Sunflower State Gossip," *The Kansas Semi-Weekly Capital*, August 13, 1897.

5. "It Is Colonel Fred Now," *The Iola Register*, October 15, 1897.

6. "Prof. E. C. Franklin of the department of chemistry at Kansas University, Lawrence, was married [in Denver, Colorado, on July 22, 1897]...to Miss Effie June Scott, of the department of French and German of the same school." They soon went to Estes Park, where they joined "the Kansas crowd" camped there ("Us and Others" with a subheadline of "Chemistry and French Professors United In Marriage at Denver," *The Iola Register*, July 30, 1897).

7. The "Boy" was Charlie Scott's small son, Ewing C. Scott.

8. Fred Funston to Charles F. Scott, August 31, 1897

9. For description of the weapon, see Frederick Funston, *Memories of Two Wars*, 119. William Allen White, "The Hero Of The Philippines," *The St. Louis Republic Magazine Section*, May 21, 1899, for the account of Fred's experiences in learning about the Sims-Dudley dynamite gun.

10. For example, see "Fred Funston In New York," January 11, 1898 (unknown newspaper) (Frederick Funston Papers, hereafter FFP) (Archives Division, Kansas State Historical Society); "Fred Funston Tells Of Cuba," *Topeka Capital*, March 4, 1898 (FFP). Also, the poster advertising Fred's lecture stated that he was "desperately wounded" at two battles, Monte Alto and Sama (Charles A. Arand Papers, Archives Division, Kansas State Historical Society).

11. Except for my paragraph concerning David Potter's book, all details are from Emory W. Fenn, "Ten Months With The Cuban Insurgents," *Century Magazine*, June 1898. David Potter, *Frederick Funston: A First Class Fighting Man: A Biography,* 131 (manuscript) (David Potter Manuscripts; 1950s, Manuscripts Division, Department of Rare Books and Special Collections, Princeton University Library).

12. "Funston Is Sick And Sore," *The Kansas City Star*, January 11, 1898 (FFP).

13. "Victory Not Easy," *The Kansas City Star,* April 23, 1898.

14. "Gained Title In Fight With Lion," *The Kansas City Journal*, February 25, 1917 (Kansas State Historical Society, *Frederick Funston Clippings,* Vol. 1).

15. Emory W. Fenn, "Ten Months With The Cuban Insurgents."

16. Frederick Funston, *Memories of Two Wars,* 59.

17. Arthur Royal Joyce, "New Stories Of Funston's Exploits In Cuba," *The Kansas City Times*, October 29, 1899 (FFP).

18. Arthur Royal Joyce, "New Stories Of Funston's Exploits In Cuba." Joyce did not lose his aplomb in the Cuban hospital where he and Cuban soldiers waited for medical attention. A reporter for *The New York World* subsequently reported:

    There were a large number of patients who in turn had to undergo the extremely painful and, in Cuba, the very necessary operation of having their wounds cauterized.

    Joyce asked them what they were yelling about. They said: "You just wait till the doctor burns yours."

    Then they got mad and said to the surgeons: "Why don't you burn the Yankee?"

    Finally Joyce's turn came. He braced up for the ordeal and endured the exquisite torture of the caustic upon his quivering lacerations without a whimper. In fact, he laughed, talked and cracked jokes. The surgeons even were surprised, and the other patients were thunderstruck.

    One of the surgeons involuntarily asked: "Doesn't it hurt you?"

    Joyce leaned over and whispered: "Why, you cheerful idiot, of course it does; but do you think I'll show it?"

    The other patients asked in awestruck admiration: "Are all the Americans like you?"

    Then young Joyce sat straight up in bed, his lacerated thigh burned as if from a thousand white-hot needles and he lied magnificently.

    "Listen, you fellows. You might take the whole American people, put 'em in a field and shoot 'em full of holes—you'd never hear a whimper" ("Heroes Of The Cuban War," *Florida Times Union,* Jacksonville, June 15, 1897. Reprint from *New York World*).

19. Emory W. Fenn, "Ten Months With The Cuban Insurgents."

20. Charles F. Scott, "Frederick Funston," *The Independent*, April 11, 1901.

21. Charles F. Scott, "Frederick Funston," *The Independent*, April 11, 1901, and William Allen White, *The Autobiography of William Allen White* (New York: The Macmillan Company, 1946), 306. See White for the bullhide hammock.

22. Armando Prats-Lerma, "La Actuación del Teniente Coronel Frederick Fun-

ston, (Norteamericano) en la Guerra de Independencia de 1895-1898," *Boletin del Ejercito* (Habana, Cuba, Noviembre y Diciembre de 1931), 369 (FFP).

23. Frederick Funston, *Memories of Two Wars,* 129-130.

24. Frederick Funston, *Memories of Two Wars,* 123-125.

25. Frederick Funston, *Memories of Two Wars,* 132-133.

26. Frederick Funston, *Memories of Two Wars,* 135.

27. Frederick Funston, *Memories of Two Wars,* 137.

28. Frederick Funston, *Memories of Two Wars,* 138. One of the stories written about Fred, after he became famous in 1899, was that Fred had begged for the lives of the guerrillas, and when his request was rejected, he was "enraged" and that is why he left the Cuban forces. I have found no evidence to support this allegation, and, in view of Fred's bad physical condition and what he wrote in his letter to Charles F. Scott, I give no credence to this allegation. See "Daring Little Col. Funston," *The New York Times*, April 30, 1899, for an example of this story.

29. "Victory Not Easy," *The Kansas City Star*, April 23, 1898, for "laughter," and then see "Music Amid Battle's Roar," *The Kansas City Star*, May 1, 1898.

30. Frederick Funston, *Memories of Two Wars,* 139.

31. "Victory Not Easy," *The Kansas City Star*, April 23, 1898.

32. Frederick Funston, *Memories of Two Wars,* 141.

33. "Latest From Col. Fred," *The Iola Register*, December 3, 1897. The letter's envelope was not postmarked in New York City until November 10, 1897.

34. "Funston Is Sick And Sore," *The Kansas City Star*, January 11, 1898 (FFP).

35. "A Letter From Major Fred Funston," *The Lawrence Daily Journal*, January 17, 1898.

36. Armando Prats-Lerma, "La Actuación del Teniente Coronel Frederick Funston," 374 (FFP).

37. Armando Prats-Lerma, "La Actuación del Teniente Coronel Frederick Funston," 374-376 (FFP). Guisa was basically an outpost for the town of Bayamo. It "was well protected at sixteen points, with the usual arrangements for cross fire, and, as was common, with the church edifice doing duty as a fort." During the battle for the town, the Cuban General Rabi accused the leader of the headquarters band of cowardice. In response, the band leader and his musicians assembled in the plaza where the church stood, and played the "Bayames," the Cuban national hymn, while under constant fire from the Spanish soldiers inside the church. General Garcia ended this reckless demonstration abruptly when informed about it.
    After the Spaniards surrendered Guisa, the town was leveled just as Victoria de las Tunas had been following its surrender. The Spaniards were thus deprived of the use of both towns as a local headquarters (Horatio S. Rubens, *Liberty: The Story of Cuba* (New York: Brewer, Warren & Putnam Inc., 1932)), 307.

38. Armando Prats-Lerma, "La Actuación del Teniente Coronel Frederick Funston," 376-377 (FFP).

39. "Frederick Funston," *Harper's Weekly*, March 5, 1898. December 12, 1898, was the date Funston was captured.

40. "Funston Is Sick And Sore," *The Kansas City Star*, January 11, 1898 (FFP).

41. On December 16, 1897, the Spanish Military Commandant, August Latorre, issued to Funston in the Spanish name of "Bernardo Maloy"(Bernard Malloy) what amounted to a passport identifying him as a "presentado" (FFP).

42. "Funston Is Sick And Sore," *The Kansas City Star*, January 11, 1898 (FFP).

43. "Fred Funston Tells Of Cuba," *The Topeka Daily Capital*, March 4, 1898.

44. "Victory Not Easy," *The Kansas City Star,* April 23, 1898.

45. "How Funston Left Cuba," *The Kansas City Star*, no date shown but it is September 4, 1898, at "Camp Merriam, Presidio, San Francisco, Aug. 29 [1898]" (*Wilder Stevens Metcalf and Frederick Funston With the Twentieth Kansas in the Philippines During the Spanish–American War)* (scrapbook of newspaper clippings, Spencer Research Library, University of Kansas). This is Funston's lengthy letter defending himself against allegations that he had never fought in the insurgent army; that he had never been wounded; and that he had been in the rebel army but had deserted. "Funston, "Brig. Gen., U.S.V.," *The Kansas City Star*, May 7, 1899, contains a portion of Funston's lengthy letter (FFP).

46. Frederick Funston to Edward C. Franklin, November 27, 1892 (FFP). Fred wrote: "By Jove, I came near to getting stuck on young Berry, the night she was at Sutliff's [sic] and sang for us. She is a smooth little girl and not so infernally cyclonic as her older sister."

47. The first paragraph quoted is from "Colonel Frederick Funston Gives Some Facts About Cuba," *The St. Louis Republic*, February 7, 1898. The next three paragraphs quoted are from "A Corner On Gossip," *The St. Louis Republic*, February 11, 1898.

48. "How Funston Left Cuba," *The Kansas City Star*, no date shown but it is September 4, 1898, at "Camp Merriam, Presidio, San Francisco, Aug. 29 [1898]."

49. "How Funston Left Cuba." The actual medical record appears in "Field and Staff Muster-in Roll, 20 Reg't Kansas Infantry," for Colonel Frederick Funston (RG94 (Records of Adjutant General Office), pi17, entry 522, Frederick Funston, combined military service record, 20ᵗʰ Kansas Volunteer Infantry, Spanish American War, arc 300400) (National Archives and Records Administration).

50. David Potter to Colonel Osmun Latrobe, November 4, 1932; Osmun Latrobe to Captain David Potter, November 28, 1932; Stuart S. Janney to Colonel Osmun Latrobe, November 26, 1932 (all Frederick Funston Papers on microfilm, Archives Division, Kansas State Historical Society).

51. Grover Flint, *Marching with Gomez: A War Correspondent's Field Note-Book Kept During Four Months With The Cuban Army* (Honolulu: University Press of the Pacific, 2004, reprinted from 1898 edition), 287. Appendix E, "The Effects of the Modern Mauser Bullet," contains accounts of Mauser victims who quickly recovered from being shot.

52. "Colonel Funston's Cuban Record," *The Evening Herald*, Ottawa, Kansas, August 23, 1898. Allen spoke not only to Garcia and Dr. Castillo, but also to "General Castillo and several members of Garcia's staff." Fred was not sent with the American forces to Cuba in 1898, and thus he never saw Garcia, who died from pneumonia in December of 1898, again.

53. "General Funston Explains," *The Los Angeles Times*, November 6, 1906. The *Times* credited its story to "Army and Navy Journal." Estrada Palma was the same man Fred dealt with in 1896 at the Cuban *Junta*. See the letters of Leonard Wood and Frank McCoy for examples of the canard that Fred had deserted (Leonard Wood to Frank McCoy, September 24,1906; Frank R. McCoy to Leonard Wood, November 16, 1906; Box 12, Frank Ross McCoy Papers, Manuscript Division, Library of Congress).

54. Frederick Funston, *Memories of Two Wars,* 145-146. In a letter to Osman Latrobe in 1910, Fred wrote: "I had the pleasure last year of entertaining Carlos Garcia and Charlie Hernandez at my house. I pulled off a smoker for them, and we had a great time talking over the old days in the bush. At the time of the revolution against Palma [1906], Carlos promptly got into jail and I visited with him there, and induced Mr. [William Howard] Taft who had just taken over the government to let him out. The evening before I left Havana the Cubans pulled off for me the finest banquet, so the papers said that had ever been given in the city, Carlos was toastmaster, and among those present were Mario Menocal, both the Cardenas boys, Miranda, Estrampes and a lot others that we knew. Of the 81 guests, 65 had been officers in the Oriente, and among those present was the present president of their two by four republic. I forgot to say that General Collazo was there in a boiled shirt, and got pretty well 'corned' before the thing was over. The cane juice was a little too strong for him" (Partial letter with presumed date of early 1910, Frederick Funston to Osmun Latrobe, Osmun Latrobe Papers, 1900-1932, Manuscript Division, Library of Congress).

55. George Clarke Musgrave, *Under Three Flags In Cuba: A Personal Account of the Cuban Insurrection and Spanish-American War* (Boston: Little, Brown, and Company, 1899; reprint by Forgotten Books, 2012), 130-131. Musgrave, an Englishman who was a supporter of Cuban independence, stayed at the same hotel as Fred, who was identified to him, likely by Cuban supporters. Musgrave did not attempt to communicate with Fred, since it might have compromised both of them. Fred's true identity was unknown to his Spanish guards. Musgrave, a war correspondent who had been refused a pass to travel by the Spanish, had registered at the hotel under an assumed name. Thus, each had much to lose should his true identity be discovered. On page 209 of his book, Musgrave included a photograph of "General Garcia and Staff." There are fourteen men shown.

On the back row on the left end a bearded young man is identified as "Col. Funston." This is not correct. The man does not look like Fred Funston, including his eyes. The astonishing part of this group photograph is a man identified as "Capt. Musgrave." Presumably, this is the author himself, who was not a member of Garcia's staff. The University of Miami has two copies of this photograph in their collection. Both include all of the same men in the same physical positions as in the Musgrave book's photograph except

171

for "Capt. Musgrave," who is not included. As I understand Musgrave's book, he was with Garcia's forces in the spring of 1898, which is after Fred left them. Apparently Musgrave wanted to be immortalized by appearing in a photograph with the great general and his staff.

56. "Victory Not Easy," *The Kansas City Star,* April 23, 1898.

CHAPTER TEN

Letters XVII, XVIII, XIX, and XX

January 13, 14, 18, and 24, 1898
New York City

If there ever was a hero in this country it is Fred Funston. He is a born wanderer, a knight of the sixteenth century, who has come on the stage too late. He has in his veins the chivalric blood that made Raleigh a knightly character in history. He is brave, gentle and generous and he deserves every kindness that has come to him.
—William Allen White
Emporia Daily Gazette, March 5, 1898

[Funston] spoke laughingly of his wounds, modestly of his achievements, but enthusiastically of the devotion and bravery of the struggling Cubans.
—*The Kansas City Star,* January 11, 1898

In a front-page story headlined "Funston Is Back," *The Kansas City Journal* announced Fred's return to New York City, which he had left nearly a year and a half before:

> A short, thick-set man, with a straggling, wiry beard, limped slowly down the gangplank of the Ward line steamer City of Washington when she came to her pier at the foot of Wall street [sic] to-day [January 10]. He was Frederick Funston, of Kansas, back from Cuba, and prison, and death.
>
> His face was pale, his cheeks sunken and hollow. Some sympathetic friends met him on the pier in a carriage. They drove him away to a hospital, where an operation will be performed that may or may not save his life, for Frederick Funston is a very sick man. He is suffering from wounds he received in fighting for Cuba. A tumor in his hip makes one leg practically helpless, and his left arm is shattered by a rifle bullet.[1]

173

The Kansas City Star reported on its front page an extensive interview by its New York correspondent with the debilitated Fred:

Colonel Fred Funston of the Cuban army and of Kansas, who returned sick and disabled from the Cuban war yesterday, was unable to start for his Western home last night. The first breath of crisp, bracing January air that greeted him on his arrival here was fine, but later in the day he fell very ill, and this morning was weary and suffering.

"I did not expect to have an attack of jungle fever in New York," Funston said. "A spell I had last night was as severe as my last experience with it in Cuba. This yellow color of my skin is not the bronze of camp and field, but the fever. I did intend to go to a Kansas City hospital at once, but I can't travel, and shall remain in New York for the present."

NOT DISABLED IN A BATTLE

Perhaps it was the illness that made him do it, but lying twisted up in his bed, the hero of four sieges, twenty-four battles and one wild cavalry charge proceeded to skin the romance from the Cuban war. "In the first place, my severest wound," he said, "was not received in battle as reported. I was trying to ride away from a rain storm when my horse slipped on a high bank and fell on me. My hip was contused between the weight of the horse and a gnarled stick, and a chronic inflammation has set in. It gives me infinitely more trouble than the shot through the lungs. That healed up in a few weeks, not to say a few days..."

Except for the strong voice and good eyes of humor, Colonel Funston would seem a pitiful wreck of a man. It is evident that he is disappointed with this Cuban war.

"Does the Cuban junta take any interest in returned American soldiers?" Funston asked.

"One of the junta remarked about Ona Melton [American war correspondent who had been imprisoned by the Spanish] that he could go where he pleased. It was nothing to them," replied the correspondent for The Star, "and last night Estrada Palma asked: "Colonel Funston—who is he? I never head [sic: heard] of him.""

"Hum," was all the wounded soldier of liberty replied. Then he leaned back and laughed. Except for catching at his chest with his hands the laugh had a good, healthy ring to it.

"Well, I didn't get anything out of the war except broken health and wounds," Funston said, "and I don't expect to get anything. We all served without pay. I can't go back, because I am a paroled prisoner of war, and I have given my word of honor not to fight again...."

Asked to describe his battles, Colonel Funston painfully got an easier position in the bed, saying: "By the way, it's not the Mauser through my lungs or the cracked elbow that bothers me, it's the rain storm hurt. Remember that. The battles were all alike—nobody in sight at all. When you see soldiers in Cuba there's no battle going on. Where there's smoke in the brush—that's Cubans with Remingtons. In the brush you'll find patriots on their stomachs like sunfish, avoiding bullets. Where the tree tops are being riddled with bullets, that's opposite where the Spaniards are. That's a battle in Cuba."

Colonel Funston expects to be in Kansas City in about three weeks. He says he can cure the jungle fever himself.

RATHER COOLY RECEIVED

Strange to say, Funston's arrival in New York did not create the stir that could have been expected from his rank and the splendid service he has done the cause. The newspapers all greeted him in their columns as the Yankee hero from Cuba, but they did not go into ecstasy over him, nor was he feted, as others have been, who, as a matter of fact, were much less deserving of such attention as he.

ESTRADA PALMA KNEW HIM NOT

Strangest of all, when a correspondent for The Star saw Signor Thomas Estrada Palma, the head and front of the Cuban junta in New York, at the Astor house yesterday, and asked him about the gallant young American who has risked his life a thousand times for the struggling Cubans, and who has risen to a higher rank in the patriot army than any other American, he shrugged his shoulders depreciatingly and replied: "I do not know the gentleman, sir; have never seen him."

Such is honor, such the gratitude of nations! The fact seems to be, however, that the public is surfeited with Cuban news at the present time. Too many contradictory stories have been published of late about the island's struggle for liberty, and too many imposters have reaped glory and gain from the alleged connection with the cause. Now the public seem blind to real merit, and fail to honor the brave man whose unselfish heroism entitles him to all the honor that can possibly be bestowed on him....

When he left Kansas he was a splendid specimen of perfect physical manhood, strong and lithe, every limb sound, every faculty developed, he had never known illness; but now, after eighteen months of service in the field, what a change. As he stood on the Ward line dock yesterday he was shivering with malaria. A bullet had passed through both his lungs, another through his arm. His limbs, too, terribly injured by a fall some months ago, ached and tortured him; but withal the gallant young fellow was light and gay of spirit. He spoke laughingly of his wounds, modestly of his achievements; but enthusiastically of the devotion and bravery of the struggling Cubans.[2]

Two days after the interview with the *Star*, Fred wrote Charlie Scott on January 13 from 18 West 32 Street, New York City. In publishing the non-personal parts of this letter, Charlie provided this introduction: "Under ordinary circumstances the publication of so personal a letter as the following, which came yesterday to the editor of the REGISTER could hardly be justified. But the sympathetic interest in Col. Funston is so general and genuine that it would seem selfish to keep to one's self any communication from him at this time."[3] A photocopy of the original letter exists, and the entire letter is printed below. The portions of his letter omitted from publication and significant errors made by Scott in the published letter are shown in brackets:

My dear Boy

You may have seen ere this in the papers that I have got in, as a lot of fellows have been around interviewing me. On the day of my arrival, the 10th, I wrote a few short letters home among them one to you, and then found yesterday evening [Scott printed "morning"] that I had forgotten to mail them.

I shall not be home for three weeks or a month as I have to go into a hospital and be cut up into small slices, and then lie in bed until I grow together again. My bullet wounds about which I wrote you sometime ago have healed perfectly and do not trouble me anymore, but the present injury to my hip is caused by a horse falling on me three months ago. In addition to that I am in a bad fix physically. People here who knew me say I have aged ten years and I certainly feel pretty old.

The story of how I happen to be here is too long a one to think of writing in the fix I am in now, but the whole thing is an "interestin' readin" as they say in Lawrence. Within a month I have been captured by the Spaniards [Scott printed "Spanish"], tried by court martial under a false name, released because nothing could be proven against me and have made my way to Havana and New York. The cold hard facts are that I lied to that court martial in a way that ought to stultify me forever. It is not a handsome thing to say that I did, but just after my acquittal I borrowed a copy of the statutes of Mesopotamia and found the following paragraph, "Lying is bad business, but it is better that a string of whoppers be told than that a Kansas man should spend many months in a Spanish jail."

[I wish you would write to me at the above address, tell me the home news all about yourself and folks and send me a few back numbers of the Register, the more recent ones. I am mighty anxious to see you, Wont [sic] we have some great old talks?]

It is a rank shame that I cant [sic] go home right away but there is no doubt that the only way for me to come out of this thing is to be treated in a good hospital.

[My love to Mrs. Scott and the Boy, as well as to yourself,
[Lovingly]
Fred Funston[4]

Fred was incensed about some of the misreporting about his physical condition and about Estrada Palma's not knowing him. In his next letter to Charlie Scott on January 18, Fred vented his feelings while providing facts:

My dear Old Boy

Your good letter of the 13th has just reached me. I am mighty wroth about that "crippled for life" business. I have never said or intimated such a thing to anybody, and in a month from now I can outrun every one of the lying reporters who put those words in my mouth. If I were crippled for life I would keep it mightily to myself. I am badly knocked out but getting better every day under good treatment. But it came about this way. On the day that I reached New York I had to talk to 18 reporters of city and outside papers. These men found me in bed and in great pain for my crippled hip was just whooping things up on that day, and some of them made it as sensational as they could although I told them that my injury was only temporary. The most of them however confined themselves to facts.

The way that Mr. Palma did not know about me was that a couple hours after the arrival of the steamship from Havana a wild eyed young ass of a reporter rushed into Mr. Palma's office and asked if he knew anybody by the name of <u>Thurston</u>. Of course he did not. The same reporter afterward found me at my room, got my name right and then telegraphed all over the country that Mr. Palma had never heard of me.

When I was able to report at the office of the Junta I was mighty cordially received and they proceeded to do the right thing by me. However, it is just as well that you shook the old man up a bit. He is a trifle slow. Harpers and Scribners are after me hard to write them some stuff and when this cursed pain lets up on me I shall try to dish them up something for the money that is in it.

Shall be home in ten days or so.

Lovingly,
Fred[5]

Rather than sharing with his readers this descriptive and blunt letter, Charlie Scott chose in the *Register* of January 24 to summarize it in one brief paragraph, totally ignoring the Palma issue at this point: "A letter from Fred Funston to the editor of the REGISTER says that the talk about him being a 'cripple for life' all came from the lively imagination of some reporter. He isn't crippled and does not intend to be, and if he were he wouldn't tell anybody. He is gaining fast and hopes to be home within ten days. All of which is mighty good news."[6] In the *Register* two days later, Charlie wrote about Palma's claim not to know Fred, which made Fred's friends "surprised and indignant." One of them, Charlie himself though he did not so identify himself in the article, wrote Palma "suggesting rather sharply that Col. Funston was a mighty good man for him to get acquainted with." Charlie then quoted for his readers Fred's explanation about the confusion concerning Fred's surname.[7]

On January 14, Fred wrote to Frank Webster, his old friend in Lawrence, and this letter, as published, is as follows:

MY DEAR FRANK: I was mighty glad to receive your letter welcoming me home. I am more than glad to be out of that hell-hole, and to say that I look forward keenly to coming out to Kansas is expressing it pretty mildly.

I wish to arise in my seat and say with an earnestness bordering on profanity that it is good to again be in the United States. Lord! old man, what a fearful price I have paid for my boyish folly of mixing up with that war. I am a battle-scarred and malaria laden wreck of my old self, and I am only out of pain when asleep. There is no doubt of my ultimate recovery, however.

My son, if anyone ever attempts to inveigle you into a war invite him to climb to the top of the Lawrence water tower, with you and then while he is panting to recover his breath just kick him off and then go down and make insulting remarks to his remains.

The last battle that I participated in was last November. I distinguished myself greatly by running my horse into a barb wire fence in the mad attempt to increase the distance between myself and a body of pursuing Spanish cavalry. I was not mentioned in the official report.[8]

The Cuban *Junta* sent Fred to a New York sanitarium and "got an expensive surgeon" to care for him. After surgery on his hip, Fred wrote Charlie Scott one more time on January 24. Charlie shared portions of Fred's letter with his readers, providing this introduction: "The latest letter from Fred Funston contains so unusual a description of a surgical operation, and gives so good a report of his rapid recovery, that it will be read by all his friends with the greatest satisfaction."[9] The portions deleted in the published letter are in brackets, and also in brackets are additions by me:

My dear Scott

[Your good letter of the 18th, the second I have received from you would have been answered sooner but for the fact that I have been stretched out on my back a bad position for letter writing.]

A large rude surgeon, who when a small boy no doubt amused himself pulling the legs off from grasshoppers and skinning rabbits alive has been around here stirring up my anatomy with a lot stuff from a hardware store. I think he had knives, saws, monkey wrenches, crow bars and two or three other things that I dont [sic] know the names of. Whew! I can taste that cold steel yet.

[Whenever I get rich I am going to hire some fellow with sledge hammer fists and pompadour hair to just go around and lick that fellow handsomely.] But I am getting well by jumps. Have gained ten pounds in two weeks despite surgical operation. They say this is remarkable and that hideous yellow of the jungle fever is giving way to a rational color [Scott printed "a good American color"]. Hope to start home in a week.

[As to the governor business I wish you would get in it and make a try for the nomination if you are pretty sure the party is going to win next fall—otherwise not. Of course you know more about that than I do a hundred times. It took my breath away when I learned that the pops [Populists] carried Kansas

in '96. But Lord Old Man I surely would like to see you governor. I would put my old derby on the ground and kick a hole
through it. You can poll as big a vote as anybody or bigger, but
<u>dont</u> [sic] get the nomination if there is much danger of the
ticket being swamped at the polls.

[I am mighty glad about that little girl. The Egyptians are
good people. Charlie Gleed writes me that he too has another
little girl but I tell you she will have to get up and hustle to be
half as sweet as Cornelia, his other. By the way isnt [sic] it a
little bit rank for you fellows to come around and throw such
things up to me. It makes a bachelor feel sort of useless and
no account in this world.

[As to the lecture business I cant [sic] just make up my
mind about it. I believe I could make money at it + I need
money, but wont [sic] the whole thing look a little bit like trying to make capital out of my wounds—a thought that jars on
my nerves badly. Have had two requests to lecture one from
Kansas City other Ottawa Chataqua [sic].

[It is mighty good of you to offer to loan me money, but I
am going to try getting along for the present as it is. But it
will keep me sailing a bit close to the wind, for a while. I have
a horror of being in debt even to my most intimate friends and
I am a little in debt already, but not much, but I appreciate
your offer just the same.

[Many thanks for the Registers you have sent me and the
good things you have said about me in the paper.

[Lovingly,
[Fred]

P.S. All the letters that I get and I have had 100 address
me as Colonel. Seriously I don't want that military title to
stick to me. Lord knows I earned it if ever a man did, but I
don't want it. I'd a whole lot rather be just plain Fred.[10]

Fred's letter illustrates some of his best qualities: his sense of humor, his independence in his own financial affairs, and his integrity
when he was concerned that a lecture tour might look like he was
trying "to make capital out of [his] wounds," a thought that bothered
him greatly. His lifelong modesty and humility are apparent. Regarding being called Colonel: "I'd a whole lot rather be just plain Fred."
   While in New York City, Fred did do some article writing for
publication—and for pay. He told the story of the cavalry charge at
Desmayo in *Harper's Weekly*. By chance, Fred encountered on a New
York street one day the son of famous engineer, artist, author, and

lecturer F. Hopkinson Smith. Fred mentioned lecturing, and Smith's son encouraged him to talk to his father. Fred did so, but it was a typically laconic conversation on his part about his Cuban war experiences. Question by question, Smith elicited details, and then encouraged Fred to tell his story to the public. When he left Smith, modest Fred, not surprisingly, apologized for talking about himself.[11]

Before leaving New York City, Fred met Theodore Roosevelt, Assistant Secretary of the Navy and former New York Police Commissioner. Likely, Roosevelt was eager to meet the Yankee hero from Cuba and sought him out after reading the news accounts about him. That summer Roosevelt at the head of his Rough Riders was to become the hero of the battle of San Juan Hill in Cuba during the Spanish-American War. The next year, he traveled by train through Kansas and, on arriving in that state, complimented Fred, who had become nationally famous that year for his exploits in the war in the Philippines and who was still there:

> "Kansas!" he exclaimed. "My! This is a fine country. It makes me breathe free. So this is Funston's state, is it? What a man he is! He is my ideal of the American volunteer. I met him in New York after he came back from Cuba, and I saw then that he was every inch a man. I admire him greatly. He is a corker—just think—"
>
> And "he admires you," interrupted [William Allen] White. "He has said so to me and in letters I have received since he went to the Philippines he has repeated it."
>
> "I am grateful to him for his good opinion," said the thoroughly pleased rough rider, "for such an opinion from such a source is worth treasuring. My, what a fighter he is! What a dare-devil! How I would like to be with him with a troop of rough riders. The [Twentieth] Kansas boys and my boys would be invincible."[12]

In early February, Fred left by train for home, stopping on Sunday, February 6, in St. Louis to visit Mary Norris Berry, the former State University of Kansas student who was blessed "with a voice of more than usual power and sweetness..."[13] Mary gave a delightful dinner in honor of "the distinguished military gentleman." This was a significant social event duly reported in the *The St. Louis Republic's* column "Notes Taken In The Polite World." The newspaper also published an extensive interview with Fred about his Cuban experiences.[14]

Fred reached home two days later, getting off the train at the Carlyle station "where he was met by every able bodied man, woman and child within a radius of miles."[15] The joyous reunion of Fred and his family likely exceeded even that on his return from Alaska in October of 1894. *The Iola Register* soon reported to its readers that "[i]n appearance Fred is physically much as he was when he left for Cuba. His face is full and flushed and he weighs about 130 pounds. His face, however, is swollen and red from the effect of the arsenic given him in the New York hospital and he lacks several pounds of his former weight. The principal change in his appearance is caused by a full Vandyke beard which has been flourishing many months. He says he shaved until he lost his razor and then trun'em [sic] loose. He looks a good many years older too, aside from the change made by the beard."[16] Fred had returned home "quite recovered except that he was slightly lame from his crushed hip," according to his mother.[17] This slight limp was to plague Fred even when fighting in the Philippines in the spring of 1899, but surgery that summer in Manila at last restored him to normal functioning.[18]

Now, perhaps heeding F. Hopkinson Smith's advice, it was time to tell his story on the lecture circuit, and time to earn some money for his own support. Charlie Gleed recollected that Fred "did so with decided success, although with no greater pleasure to himself than he had experienced before."[19] With his speaker fees, Fred repaid, with interest as calculated by him, the sum that Charlie had lent him on Fred's departure for Cuba.[20] Fred was determined to make this lecture tour a financial success. Unlike his prior lectures after his two Alaska expeditions, Fred retained a professional to handle booking of lecture engagements and other related matters. On February 16, he hired J. A. Young of Kansas City, Missouri, for the period ending June 1st, 1898.[21] One of his earliest lectures was before a packed house in Topeka on March 3. Among the 500 people in attendance was the governor, John W. Leedy, a Populist who had unseated the incumbent Republican governor in the 1896 election. An orchestra provided music for the occasion. "A slight little man, with a close clipped beard which covers a determined chin and lip; a hand which seems fragile to the grasp; an erect and imperative figure, such is Colonel Frederick K. [sic] Funston..."[22]

Fred's lecture was frequently titled "On the Inside of the Cuban Revolution."[23] Fred used the term "revolutionists" in recognition of what they had done, rather than the commonly used word "insurgents."[24] Reviewers differed in their assessment of Fred's ability as a speaker. *The Kansas City Star* reported that "Colonel Funston is not an orator. His delivery, though not forcible, is strong and his style is distinctively colloquial. His talk last night bore many features of a chat with his hearers..." The *Star* also provided insight into Fred's delivery style: "His mannerisms are all good, he avoids periods, stilted phrases and even the elaborateness that all lecturers lend to their discourses. He is quiet, simple and unassuming in manner, but he tells of sights he saw in Cuba with graphic simplicity."[25] A Newton, Kansas, newspaper, reported that "Mr. Funston is no talker, his whole lecture being delivered in an ordinary conversational tone. He holds his cane in his hand all the time, and all the gestures he made were with this cane, describing something in connection with the artillery."[26] In contrast, a Burlingame, Kansas, newspaper reported that "[t]he Colonel is a very fair talker and his story of the Cubans and their struggle for liberty was interesting and enjoyed by all. Col. Funston is rather small in statue [sic: stature], very modest and gentlemanly and has no brag and blusler [sic: bluster] about his fighting qualities. He made many friends while in Burlingame."[27]

H. J. Allen, editor of *The Evening Herald* in Ottawa, who subsequently investigated in Cuba the charge of desertion against Fred, interviewed him before his lecture. Describing him as having "sober, quiet eyes," Allen wrote bluntly about Fred's modesty: "The only objection to Mr. Funston is that he doesn't talk any about the great part he has played. Instead of telling how he killed the Spaniards, like any other Kansas citizen would, he sits quiet like and you are obliged to draw the information away from him with considerable skill and caution. When anybody starts to praise him about the part he played in the Cuban struggle for eighteen months, a tired look seems to steal in among Mr. Funston's whiskers and settle around the corner of his eye—in fact both eyes."[28] Fred's aversion to speaking about his personal experiences stemmed from his being "foolishly afraid he will be accused of boasting," according to Charlie Scott. "Even his most trusted friends talking the night through with him have wrung out the personal details of those two years in the Cuban army only by the most persistent cross questioning."[29] As for Fred's subject of the Cuban revolution, "[h]e was heart and soul for the cause of Cuban liberty," observed his mother."[30]

Fred's successful lecture tour came to an abrupt end. In late April, he received a telegram from Kansas governor Leedy's secretary asking him to come to Topeka immediately, but not stating a reason. Fred met the next day with Governor Leedy, who offered him the command of the newly-formed Twentieth Kansas Volunteer Infantry, one of the state regiments being raised to provide American troops for the recently-declared war against Spain, which had been precipitated by the mysterious blowing up of the *U.S.S. Maine* in the harbor of Havana, Cuba.[31] Fred had not sought the position, and it was a surprise that the Populist governor would tap a Republican, but Fred was clearly the Kansan most qualified for the job. "Fred Funston has earned his commission," said Leedy. "I appointed him because I regarded him as the right man for the place... Funston is fresh from the field, and knows more about modern war than the others." As to the matter of politics, Leedy stated: "This is not a political fight.... I wanted a fighting man for the job; not a politician."[32]

Fred did not accept the governor's offer quickly. A family meeting was held, and all, except Fred, voted that he should decline the offer, believing that he should continue on the lucrative, and less dangerous, lecture platform.[33] Fred was better suited for fighting than lecturing, and thus accepted the commission of Colonel of the Twentieth Kansas Volunteers.

At thirty-two, Fred Funston had come of age. His assessment on his return to the United States that out of the Cuban war he had gotten "only broken health and wounds" was understandable but wrong. The extraordinary adventures on which he had thrived in Death Valley, in Alaska and the British Northwest Territory, and, particularly, in the crucible of war in Cuba, had helped to mold and complete his personality, and he now knew fully who he was. Independent, self-confident, and modest, he was no longer troubled by his short height. He had the self-confidence to believe that his small physical stature did not matter, and he knew that he could successfully meet challenges that few, if any, other men could. Soon after Fred's return home from New York City, he stayed a night in a Kansas City hotel. There, "in simple language" he quietly told a group of listeners about some of his adventures. One listener "unconsciously" interrupted him with the exclamation, "But you are so much smaller than I had imagined." "Funston smiled and caught up the thread of his story. 'Yes, I'm rather a small man to have gone through some of the experiences I have and come out alive, but I'm here...'"[34]

As part of this new acceptance of his short height, Fred made his shortness a subject of jokes. He enjoyed telling about having been characterized as a "little sawed-off conductor" when he worked at age twenty-two on the Santa Fe Railway.[35] Another story that he frequently told occurred when he was giving testimony at a court-martial in the Philippines. The judge advocate, sitting behind a table, said, "Colonel Funston, I wish to remind you that it is the custom for officers testifying in military courts to stand up." Fred's response? "Sir, I am standing up!" When Fred told this story about himself, he would remark that "he was just about as tall standing up as a 'regular man' sitting down."[36] "Altitude," joked Fred, "has never been one of my charms."[37]

Not only had Fred's short height become irrelevant to his self-image, the man who had described himself five years before as always "damned small potatoes with the girls" was small potatoes no more.[38] After a whirlwind romance in the fall of 1898, the dashing Colonel married the *three inch taller*, 24-year-old Oakland, California, violinist and socialite, Eda Blankart.[39] The awkwardness and "almost illimitable clumsiness" noted in his days as a school and university student and in Death Valley had disappeared.[40] He had honed his physical and mental skills to become an accomplished soldier. He thrived on fighting, fearless all the while. In the spring of 1899, his superior officer, Brigadier General Harrison G. Otis, described Fred as "the greatest daredevil in the army, and [he] would rather fight than eat. I never saw a man who enjoyed fighting so much."[41] He was soon to become a professional soldier, a career that he successfully pursued until his death nineteen years later. "His varied and interesting life of preparation..." had concluded. [42] He had become Frederick Funston, extraordinary man and American hero.

After Fred's capture of Aguinaldo, the leader of the Filipino forces, in March of 1901, an incredible and exhausting physical and mental accomplishment, the famous war correspondent, James Creelman, was interviewed about "Fearless" Fred's actions during the fighting in the Philippines in 1899:

> As we advanced slowly toward the bristling insurgent trenches Colonel Funston seemed to see through the dense fogliae [sic] that hid the enemy. I never saw such an extraordinary demonstration of penetrating eyesight and quick wit. He seemed to instantly understand every movement in the woods before us.
>
> Again and again I accompanied Funston after that. Each time he surprised me by his wonderful gift of understanding the mysteries of guerrilla warfare and his ability to determine the precise moment when personal courage and a sudden dash of his troops would decide the battle.
>
> With all his reputation for fearless charges, Funston has never led his men into a trap. He is the most cautious man in the army until the time for a desperate rush is reached. During the careful advance he is watchful and reticent, keeping his men under cover as much as possible, but when his line is within sure striking distance he leads his men in person shrieking like a devil.
>
> It was my good fortune to be with Colonel Funston when his regiment forded and swam the Tulihan river during the advance of MacArthur's division to Malolos, the insurgent capital. And it was my bad fortune to lie in the mire that day

with my wounded horse on top of me while Funston lay under his horse only ten feet away.

It was a characteristic day in Funston's life. For hours our army had been driving the main insurgent force through a dense bamboo forest; the Kansas regiment was at the center of the line, with Funston dashing about on horseback, cheering, waving, directing, reprimanding.

His slim little figure was the most conspicuous thing in the confusing scene. Wherever the firing was heaviest there his voice was to be heard in command. ["He yelled louder than the bugler could blow." [43]]

Suddenly, the Kansas regiment arose from the forest in sight of a small swift river. There was no sign of the enemy. The truth was that the insurgents had crossed the river and lying silently in the trenches on the opposite bank, waiting for the Kansans to come within three hundred yards before opening fire. It was a well laid trap.

When the Kansans had almost reached the edge of the river volley after volley blazed from the concealed Filipinos. Funston leaped from his horse and lay on his stomach behind the stone foundation of a ruined house. That was the hottest fire I have ever experienced. The insurgent bullets came so thickly that the leaves were cut from the bushes around us and stones were splintered within two or three inches of Funston's head.

"I don't often crawl," said the Colonel as he spread his blue print map of the country on the ground, "but this is terrific. Just hear the whiskers on those bullets! My horse can't conceal himself, poor fellow...."

Then the Colonel thrust his head up above the stone foundation and looked carefully at the ground beyond the river.

"If I had one cannon I would make our position safe," he said. "As it is, we must cross that river if we have to swim. Rivers don't count."

Leaping to his feet the little Colonel walked down to the river bank, leading his horse by the bridle. As he advanced under the fire in plain sight of the enemy he seemed to grow cooler. With a wave of his hat he ordered Company E to enter the water and as his dripping men ascended the other bank he rode into the river himself and crossed, while bullets splashed around him in the rapid current.

And when the bloody charge was over he paid no attention to the corpse strewn field, but went to give a dying Filipino a drink out of his own canteen.

"That was a daisy fight," he said quietly, as he sat down beside me under the shade of a palm tree.

A few days later I saw Funston charge into the insurgent capital at the head of Company E. He waved his hat and yelled, "Give them hell boys!" as he ran at full speed toward the low stone barricade that barred the entrance to the public square where Aguinaldo's palace was on fire. I was one of three correspondents who raced with the Colonel for the honor of being the first man to enter the enemy's capital.

But the moment we leaped over the barricade and found that the enemy had fled, leaving the city in flames, there was a sudden transformation in Funston. He was all caution. His orders were given in a low voice. His eyes searched every street and every nook. He was stealthy, catlike. As he pursued the retiring foe through the city he felt his way slowly and surely.

All this indicates the soldierly qualities of the general whose capture of Aguinaldo has astonished this world.[44]

Fred Funston thrived on adventure—the more dangerous, the better. His voice has guided us through much of the story of the adventurous first thirty-two years of his life, and it is only fitting that his own words conclude our story. On one occasion, Fred was riding his horse through a Philippine jungle when a native came out of the brush and fired his pistol point blank at him. The shots missed their intended target, and Fred's horse bolted. Dropping his pistol, which was tied to his wrist, Fred used both hands to control his horse. Bringing it around, he fired a shot at his assailant, which missed. Swinging his horse around again, Fred fired just as the Filipino reached for another clip of bullets. This shot broke the native's wrist. "That was one of those wild moments," Fred later recalled, "that are worth an ordinary life time."[45]

Frederick Funston in the uniform of the Cuban Liberation Army. His blue baldric bears the two gold stars of a lieutenant colonel. Photograph taken on February 10, 1898, in Iola, Kansas, at the Iola Art Studio, which was located on the northwest corner of the town square. This photograph was likely taken in connection with Lieutenant Colonel Funston's soon-to-be-commenced lecture tour about the Cuban Revolution.

Cuba Libre!

DON'T FAIL TO HEAR

COL. FUNSTON

HERO OF

24–GREAT BATTLES–24

In the War for Cuban Independence. He is the only American who can give authentic account of the conflict.

See the man and hear him discuss the situation on the War-Wasted Island.

HAMILTON HALL

TOPEKA, KANSAS,

Thursday, March 3, 1898

Handbill for Funston's talk.

Colonel Fred Funston of the Twentiethth Kansas Infantry,
United States Volunteers

Eda (Blankart) Funston

Chapter Ten Notes—*Letters XVII, XVIII, XIX, and XX*

Epigraphs: *Emporia Daily Gazette*, March 5, 1898. Editorial by William Allen White. "Funston is Sick And Sore," *The Kansas City Star*, January 11, 1898 (Frederick Funston Papers, hereafter FFP) (Archives Division, Kansas State Historical Society).

1. "Funston Is Back," *The Kansas City Journal*, January 11, 1898.

2. "Funston Is Sick And Sore," *The Kansas City Star*, January 11, 1898 (FFP).

3. "Fred Funston," *The Iola Daily Register*, January 18, 1898.

4. Fred Funston to Charles F. Scott, January 13, 1898. Photocopy of original letter in collection of Frederick Funston's letters from Cuba and New York City at Allen County Historical Society, Inc., Iola, Kansas. Typescript in FFP.

5. Fred Funston to Charles F. Scott, January 18, 1898. Photocopy of original letter in collection of Frederick Funston's letters from Cuba and New York City at Allen County Historical Society, Inc., Iola, Kansas. Typescript in FFP.

6. "To-Day's News," *The Iola Daily Register*, January 24, 1898.

7. "They Know Col. Fred," *The Iola Daily Register*, January 26, 1898.

8. "A Letter From Major Fred Funston," *The Lawrence Daily Journal*, January 17, 1898.

9. For "got an expensive surgeon," see "How Funston Left Cuba," *The Kansas City Star*, no date shown but it is September 4, 1898, at "Camp Merriam, Presidio, San Francisco, Aug. 29 [1898]" (*Wilder Stevens Metcalf and Frederick Funston With the Twentieth Kansas in the Philippines During the Spanish–American War*) (scrapbook of newspaper clippings, Spencer Research Library, University of Kansas). "'Better by Jumps,'" *The Iola Daily Register*, January 27, 1898.

10. Fred Funston to Charles F. Scott, January 24, 1898. Photocopy of original letter in collection of Frederick Funston's letters from Cuba and New York City at Allen County Historical Society, Inc., Iola, Kansas, except the last two paragraphs and the postscript are missing; this problem is corrected in a typescript in FFP.

11. James B. Morrow, "F. Hopkinson Smith. Engineer, Artist, Author, Lecturer—Discoverer," *The Washington Post*, December 8, 1907.

12. "Hero 'Teddy,'" *The Kansas City Journal*, June 24, 1899 (FFP).

13. "Brief Local Items," *The Lawrence Daily Journal*, September 13, 1898.

14. "Notes Taken In The Polite World," *The St. Louis Republic*, February 8, 1898.

15. "Fred Funston Home," *The Iola Daily Register*, February 8, 1898. Two days later Fred spoke about Cuba to the students and teachers of the Iola High School, where he was "cheered lustily" at the conclusion of his talk. "Upon dismissal a line was formed and all shook hands with the Cuban hero as they passed out" ("Fred Funston Talks," *The Iola Daily Register*, February 11, 1898).

16. "Fred Funston," *The Iola Daily Register*, February 11, 1898. A humorous, mostly accurate description of Fred written by Dave Leahy appeared in *The Kansas City Times,* and was reprinted in *The Iola Register*: "The net results of the Cuban war on Fred Funston are as follows: Two lungs penetrated, compound fracture of the left arm, part of his right heel shot off, one ear grazed with a fragment of a shell, indigestion by swallowing his commission as chief of artillery when captured, wound on the right hip from a Mauser bullet, and his beauty marred by 8,842 grains of powper [sic: powder] sticking in his face" ("Local Notes," *The Iola Daily Register*, March 12, 1898).

17. Ode C. Nichols, "Funston, From Babyhood to Present Day as His Mother Knows Him," *The World*, May 21, 1899 (FFP).

18. "His lame leg does not keep him from limping ahead of [his soldiers] when they charged into Coloocan" (William Allen White, "The Hero Of The Philippines," *The St. Louis Republic Magazine Section*, May 21, 1899). Fred's surgery was on July 29, 1899. His hip wound, now a fistula, had two openings, one three inches to the right of the anus and the other two and one-half inches to the left, and they were "communicating with rectum anterior surface." The right side opening was closed by a deep row and one superficial row of catgut, and the left side was "packed" (Reserve Hospital, Manila, P.I., July 28, 1899, Frederick Funston, Ward No. 12. RG94) (Records of Adjutant General Office, pi17 entry 522, Frederick Funston combined military service record, 20th Kansas Volunteer Infantry, Spanish American War, arc 300400) (National Archives and Records Administration).

19. Charles S. Gleed, "Romance and Reality In A Single Life. Gen. Frederick Funston," *The Cosmopolitan Illustrated Monthly Magazine*, July 1899.

20. C.S. Gleed, eulogy, *Report of Select Committee*, Hall of the House of Representatives, Topeka, Kansas, February 26, 1917 (FFP).

21. Agreement between J. A. Young and Frederick Funston dated February 16, 1898 (FFP).

22. "Fred Funston Tells Of Cuba," *The Topeka Daily Capital*, March 4, 1898.

23. "Colonel Funston's Lecture," *The Evening Kansan*, Newton, Kansas, March 25, 1898.

24. "Facts About Cuba," *Osage City* (Kansas) *Free Press*, March 31, 1898.

25. "Cuba As Funston Saw It," *The Kansas City Star*, March 11, 1898.

26. "Col. Funston's Lecture," *The Evening Kansan*, Newton, Kansas, March 29, 1898.

27. "News Notes," *Burlingame* (Kansas) *Enterprise*, March 24, 1898.

28. "Col. Funston Here," *The Evening Herald*, Ottawa, Kansas, April 19, 1898.

29. Chas. F. Scott, "Remarkable Career of a Kansas Boy," *Mail and Breeze* (about March 20, 1898) (FFP).

30. Ode C. Nichols, "Funston, From Babyhood to Present Day."

31. "How Funston Was Appointed," *The Topeka Capital*, February 27, 1917. This account was written by E. C. Little, private secretary to Governor Leedy (FFP).

32. "War News In Topeka," perhaps *The Topeka Capital*, April 28, 1898 (FFP).

33. "Fred Funston's Restless Life of Adventure," *The Chicago Sunday Tribune*, May 7, 1899 (FFP).

34. "Fred Funston's Exploits," *The Kansas City Star,* February 20, 1898.

35. Chas. F. Scott, "Remarkable Career of a Kansas Boy."

36. "Major-General Funston," unidentified newspaper with date of March 10, 1917. This was written by a staff correspondent of *The New York Times* (Frederick Funston Papers on microfilm) (Archives Division, Kansas State Historical Society).

37. *Memories of Two Wars: Cuban and Philippine Experiences* (New York: Charles Scribner's Sons, 1914), 155.

38. Fred Funston to Edward C. Franklin, January 29, 1893 (FFP).

39. "The whole world is yet filled with astonishment at that brave exploit of Funston and his daring followers [crossing the Rio Grande River on rafts with the enemy on the farther bank]... Yet, Mrs. Funston laughingly said: 'Really, he tells me the hardest battle and the longest siege of his life were for my affections. How long? Well, I knew him just five weeks and was engaged to him two days before we were married, and two days after the wedding, Fred had to leave for Manila'" ("Mrs. Funston A Woman As The General Is A Solider," undated and unidentified newspaper; likely a Denver, Colorado, newspaper dated about 1902) (*Wilder Stevens Metcalf and Frederick Funston With the Twentieth Kansas in the Philippines During the Spanish–American War*) (scrapbook of newspaper clippings, Spencer Research Library, University of Kansas).

In leaving two days after his wedding with the American military forces to occupy the Philippines in the aftermath of the Spanish-American War, Fred was like his father, who had left to fight in the Civil War the day after his own wedding. After his marriage, Fred telegrammed his parents to tell them his good news. The messenger delivered the telegram to Lida, who opened it and then called for Ed. She showed him the telegram, and this conversation ensued between them:

> "Well, what did he want to do that for?" exclaimed his father.
> "Even so, we shouldn't be angry with him," she said, seeing the rising anger in the face of the elder Funston.
> "Shouldn't be angry? How should we feel toward a boy that would get married just as he is going off to war?"
> "Well, that's just exactly what you did."
> "Hm, I hadn't thought of that. Well, I guess its [sic] all right" ("Fred Funston's Restless Life of Adventure," *The Chicago Sunday Tribune*, May 7, 1899) (FFP).

In response to Fred's telegram, Ed wrote a "Dear Son" letter which read, in part, as follows:

> Your marriage was a surprise to all of us. You had put the matter off so long that I began to think you had decided to go it alone. You have done the proper thing, however, and I congratulate you. My only regret is that your wife will be com-

pelled to undergo so many hardships in order to be with you [Eda followed Fred to the Philippines on another troop ship.]....

You have acted wisely in marrying. It is the natural condition of man, and to have lived single would have been selfish as well as unnatural.

My experience has been that a great wife is above all other earthly blessings. Your good mother has been the light of my life, and every day makes her more necessary to my happiness (Edward H. Funston to Frederick Funston, November 21, 1898) (FFP).

Fred concurred in his father's assessment about "a great wife." Writing a couple years later to longtime friend Charlie Gleed, Fred made this observation: "My dear wife is as good and handsome as ever... All the things you ever told me about the cussedness of being a bachelor are gospel truth. The best thing I ever did for myself was when I married" (Fred Funston to C. S. Gleed, April 5, 1901) (FFP) .

On November 4, 1898, Fred wrote his mother while on board the steamer *Indiana* en route to the Philippines; the letter was mailed from Honolulu, Hawaii: "I suppose that by this time all of you are pretty much over your surprise at my very hasty and altogether unexpected marriage. In fact I am as yet scarcely over my own surprise. I am very sorry that circumstances are such that I cannot bring my wife east on a wedding trip, and show her off to the folks at home. I think that you would be quite proud of your new daughter and that you would unhesitatingly approve of my choice of a wife." Fred described his bride to his mother: "She is a very handsome girl, tall and dark and has a very vivacious and lively disposition. She is a fine violinist and often plays at concerts in San Francisco and Oakland. But there I go, bragging again" (Fred Funston to Ann E. Funston, November 4, 1898) (FFP).

Fred informed his friend Charlie Scott, editor of *The Iola Daily Register*, by "special telegram" about his marriage, and in reporting this news in the *Register,* Charlie wrote that "the surprise amounted to almost a shock for it had been hardly five months since the gallant Colonel had solemnly assured the proprietor of this paper that marriage was not for him. He got laughed at then, and there would surely be occasion to 'smile' if he were within reach now" ("Fred Funston Married. The Gallant Colonel Has Fought Through His First Engagement and Surrendered at Discretion," *The Iola Daily Register*, October 26, 1898).

40. H. Irving Hancock, "General Frederick Funston," *Leslie's Weekly Illustrated*, October 28, 1899. In 1899, an unidentified Twentieth Kansas soldier "who knew him both at school and at the university, leaned back and laughed heartily as he told me of the student days of the Little Man of War: 'What amused us most of all was his almost illimitable clumsiness. He stumbled over any obstacle that another fellow would step over. To see the easy, dignified General Funston of to-day would give you no conception of the school-boy Funston.'" I suspect the unidentified soldier was Schuyler Brewster, his Iola, Kansas, boyhood and university friend.

41. "Brigadier-General Frederick Funston," *The Literary Digest*, Vol. XVIII, No. 19 (May 13, 1899). Otis also noted that Funston "seemed to bear a charmed life, as he was never touched by a bullet." This changed on May 4, 1899, when Fred received a severe bullet wound in his left hand.

42. Quotation from sermon at Funston's funeral. See the last quotation in Appendix A.

43. "Vivid Memories of Spanish War," *The Kansas City Star*, estimated date of 1964 (Homer M. Limbird Papers, Archives Division, Kansas State Historical Society). Quoted is Homer M. Limbird, who served in Funston's Twentieth Kansas Volunteers in the war in the Philippines.

44. "Creelman On Funston," *The Iola Daily Register*, April 4, 1901 (*Frederick Funston: Adventurer, Explorer and Soldier*) (scrapbook of newspaper clippings, Spencer Research Library, University of Kansas). Creelman (1859-1915) covered the Cuban uprising starting in 1895 and then returned to Cuba for the Spanish-American War in 1898. His work as a reporter was praised. "By his own account, he wanted only to write something interesting, something reflecting the finest elements of human experience" (Benjamin R. Deedee, editor, *The War of 1898 and U.S. Interventions 1898-1934 An Encyclopedia*, New York: Garland Publishing, Inc., 1994), 126.

45. "Random Thoughts," *The Kansas City Star*, April 12, 1942. Story told by Dr. Ernest Robinson of Kansas City, Missouri, a friend of Funston, who had performed a 1902 surgical operation on him in Kansas City, and who had been a military surgeon in the Philippines.

The Miami Herald

MEMBER FLORIDA
STATE PRESS
ASSOCIATION

MEMBER
ASSOCIATED
PRESS

Tuesday, February, 20, 1917.

FUNSTON DEAD

There will be general sadness, this morning, at the news of the death of General Frederick Funston, which occured at San Antonio, last night, without warning.

The affection of the American people for Frederick Funston arose, very largely, because he, himself, sprang from the common people, and without the usual education at West Point made his way to the highest rank of the army, by sheer American grit and ability.

No history of any of the celebrated characters brought out in the course of our national life, reads more like a romance than his. The stories of his bravery and his resourcefulness are innumerable, and while an army officer does not, outside the circle of his immediate friends, always obtain that popularity that men in other walks of life sometimes do, yet Frederick Funston was a national hero and the object of great national affection. His death, in the very fruiting of manhood, will be regretted.

OUR FIGHTERS

(Center) THEODORE ROOSEVELT. President United States.
Born New York, October 27, 1858.

(Upper left) GEORGE DEWEY. Admiral U. S. Navy.
Born Montpelier, Vt., December 26,1837.

(Lower left) HENRY W. LAWTON. Brig. Gen. U. S. Vol.
Born in Ohio,1843. Killed in battle of San Mateo, Dec. 18, 1899.

(Upper right) WINFIELD SCOTT SCHLEY. Rear Admiral U. S. Navy.
Born Maryland, October 9, 1839.

(Lower right) FREDERICK S. [sic] FUNSTON. Brig. Gen. U. S. Army.
Born in Ohio, 1865.

Copyrighted Nov. 1901.

What's Next?

If you are interested in more detail about Frederick Funston's experiences in Cuba, I suggest reading for yourself the first part of his *Memories of Two Wars: Cuban and Philippine Experiences*. It is available in paperback.

If you wish to learn about the next stage in the life of Frederick Funston, I recommend the second part of Funston's *Memories of Two Wars* and Thomas W. Crouch's *A Leader of Volunteers: Frederick Funston and the 20th Kansas in the Philippines, 1898-1899*.

Thoughts On Writing A Biography:

"The ethic of care that goes into telling the story of a man's life when that man can no longer speak for himself, and the responsibility that entails."

In the early 1960s, I started researching and writing a biography of Frederick Funston. I was only a junior high school student who had become fascinated by Funston's adventurous life several years earlier upon visiting his boyhood home north of my hometown of Iola, Kansas. This newly-opened museum had many Funston family artifacts, including Funston's snowshoes that he had walked 1,000 miles on in the Arctic cold.

To learn more about him, I spent much time after school and on summer days reading microfilm of *The Iola Register* on the big microfilm reader at the *Register's* office, the only microfilm reader in town and probably the only business that had a need for one. I read Funston's lengthy published letters from Death Valley and Alaska and carefully copied them by hand into a notebook (this was the only way to copy them; microfilm readers were not yet designed to print copies). Sometime later, I had the opportunity to spend a summer day at the Kansas State Historical Society in Topeka, Kansas, researching their many original materials about Fred's life (I have been on a first-name basis with him for many years now).

Perhaps surprisingly, my early attempt as a child to write a biography of Fred's life was heavily centered on the use of primary sources, instead of secondary ones, since I used largely his letters published in the *Register* from Death Valley and Alaska. This early attempt was a limited, handwritten affair reflective of the young age of the author. Fast forward to 1995 to the opening of the Funston Home as a museum after its move to the Iola town square and its restoration to look as it did in the late 19th century/early 20th century. I believed that our Allen County Historical Society, Inc., the owner of the museum, and of which I was president, needed a biography of Fred in book form which we could sell to museum visitors. This goal became more pressing with the opening in 1997 of the adjoining Funston Museum and Visitors' Center. In the center's movie theatre, the Society shows a nearly-half-hour video of Fred's life, the script for which I researched and wrote.

By this time, I was a trained historian, having earned both a BA and MA in history and completed nearly all of a doctorate in the same subject. My graduate work was done at the University of Wisconsin-Madison whose history graduate program was ranked third or fourth in the nation when I was there in the early 1970s. The number of graduate students in history was an astonishing 650. Today there are around 130, as I understand it.

It was a real challenge to write the script for the video biography of Fred's entire jam-packed life. Because of time constraints, I was forced to rely heavily on secondary sources rather than researching primary ones. One fact that I struggled with involved Fred's attempt to qualify for West Point when he was eighteen. Secondary sources did not agree on the facts but most stated that he was too short and failed the entrance examination. Thus, I went with these allegations for the video. They were not true. This experience leads to my observations here on writing a quality biography. I should note that since 1975 I have been a practicing attorney. My skills as an attorney have reinforced and enhanced my training as an historian.

My thoughts on writing a quality biography are in no order of priority and are not comprehensive. They are simply what I regard as major points. Other biographers and historians may not agree and may have written quality works by successfully employing a different approach. That is fine. These are simply my thoughts based on my experiences.

A prospective author should not have preconceived notions about his or her subject, and thus fall into the trap of seeking only facts that support them (confirmation bias). That does not mean, however, that one cannot have a general idea or thesis about the subject to be researched. In my case, I had no preconceived notions as to whether Fred had particular flaws or particular virtues in his personality and no general thesis about him. My initial interest in Fred stemmed from Fred's adventurous life, and I wanted to learn more about what kind of person he was. I simply followed the evidence that I located in my efforts to understand who Fred was and how he became the person that he ultimately was at age thirty-two. I learned both positive and negative information about him. With no preconceived ideas or thesis, I merely followed one clue to the next in order to find more information. The more facts, the closer I came to the truth about his life. In contrast, a preconceived notion may cloud both the research and the analysis of the facts discovered.

Not only did I not approach my research with a pre-determined interpretation of what kind of person he was, I had no ideas as to his motivations for the actions he took. I was the proverbial tabula rasa. In the late 1990s, I visited the Museum of the City of San Francisco, which has information about Fred because of his prominent role in connection with the great earthquake and fire of 1906. In discussing

201

a particular book about that horrific event with one of the staff members, she told me that years before the two authors of that book came in with the intention of finding only information that would support their thesis in connection with the book that they were writing. Included in their thesis was a negative portrayal of Fred and his role in the 1906 calamity. Everything else was ignored, according to this staff member. Not the way to approach writing a biography and not the way to approach analyzing an historical event.

Obviously, the importance of relying on primary sources is paramount. Whenever possible, each original document should be examined, not a purported copy or typescript of the same. In doing so, one has the opportunity to see exactly what was written rather than relying on its being quoted or paraphrased in a secondary source.

I love jokes and this favorite one is applicable here. A young monk named Bartholomew joined a monastery. This monastery was the largest and most important monastery in the entire world and at the monastery they copied documents by hand and then these documents were transmitted throughout the world to all the other monasteries.

When Bartholomew got there, he was placed in the charge of Brother Peter. Peter showed Bartholomew the documents that he wanted to have copied and Bartholomew went to work. Later that day he said to Peter that he believed that it would be better if he were copying from the original documents because the documents he was copying from were only copies.

Peter agreed and said that all the original documents are stored in the basement. Peter disappeared and never came back. Bartholomew became worried, and with other monks they descended into the basement. Arriving there, they could hear loud cries. When they got to the room where the documents were stored and where Brother Peter was, Peter was gnashing his teeth and rending his clothes. Peter was holding in his hand a document and screaming, "The word is celebrate!"

Of course, one must have a healthy skepticism for each primary source in terms of evaluating it for potential bias or inaccuracy or lack of completeness. This is difficult to do, particularly if sources are many decades old, but one must at least attempt to do so. In Volume One of this trilogy on Fred's early life, I accept most of what his sister, Ella (Funston) Eckdall, wrote about him but on the issue of his drinking alcohol, I stated that I do not agree with her conclusion and why I did not agree. My conclusion was based on my broader knowledge about his life at that point as a result of all of my study and review of other sources which allowed me then to draw the conclusion that I did.

In locating primary sources, frequently the lead for such a source comes from an endnote or footnote in a secondary source. The note is meant to document and support the allegation or statement made by the secondary author in the text. Unfortunately, one should not assume that the source cited in the note actually supports the allegation. A classic example of how not to do this occurred in connection with an alleged incident during the war in the Philippines.

Both Stuart Creighton Miller, author of *"Benevolent Assimilation": The American Conquest of the Philippines, 1899-1903*, and David Haward Bain, author of *Sitting in Darkness: Americans in the Philippines*, in their respective works accused Fred of summarily executing twenty-four Filipino prisoners of war in retaliation for the ambush of an American patrol. Brian McAllister Linn, author of the monumental *The Philippine War 1899-1902*, analyzed their accusation. He noted that both authors cite the same source, an article appearing on page 485 in *Public Opinion*, when it actually appears on pages 486-487. How could they both make the same mistake? Did Bain in his 1987 work copy the incorrect citation from Miller's 1982 work? I don't know. And did Miller copy the incorrect citation from an unidentified secondary source? I don't know. Or did both Bain and Miller copy directly the incorrect citation from the same unidentified secondary source? I don't know.

But the most astounding part of this is that, according to Linn, "the *Public Opinion* source cited makes no reference to the killing of twenty-four prisoners. Instead it refers to Funston's summary execution of two guerrillas caught in the act of killing U. S. native scouts.... Funston summarily executed these two [guerrilla] officers, basing his action upon General Orders 100, an internationally recognized code of conduct for armies in the field." Linn concluded that "[t]here is no documentary material which suggests Funston ever killed twenty-four prisoners nor was he threatened with a court-martial for killing prisoners. Indeed, barring the execution of the two Filipino guerrillas, which Funston could justifiably claim was based on international law, there is no evidence that Funston executed anyone without trial."[1] I checked *Public Opinion*, and Linn is correct. The cited source appears on pages 486-487 and the subject is the execution of two, not twenty-four, Filipino guerrillas.

Returning now to the issue of Fred's attempt at age eighteen to become a West Point cadet, my research in primary sources gave me the answer as to whether he was too short to qualify and whether he failed the entrance examination. I contacted West Point which provided me with the rules and regulations at the time that Fred applied. The minimum height requirement was stated to be 5 feet and Fred was 5 feet, 4 inches. He was not too short. As for purportedly failing the entrance examination, which was taken after the physical examination, West Point had no record of the examination results. *The Iola Register* and other Kansas newspapers, however, carried news stories about the results of the competitive examination which showed that Fred was not the successful applicant, but some of these news reports did indicate that he placed third in the examination and was only slightly more than two points below the winning applicant's score. All of this is a lot different, obviously, than the commonly repeated story about Fred and his unsuccessful attempt to become a West Point cadet—too short and failed the entrance exam. I believe that, at times, one secondary author simply copies from another secondary author's work and that helps to both transmit and perpetuate false statements. There certainly are many of those with reference to Fred's life and career.

As for secondary sources, they deserve, in my opinion, an even healthier skepticism. The user of the secondary source is at the mercy of the potential bias of the author just as is the case with primary sources. With the use of secondary sources, however, there is the additional problem of how skilled is the author as a researcher and as an analyst of the materials reviewed. Is he careful? Does he follow all leads? Does he have a breadth of understanding of his subject? Et cetera. All hinges upon the quality of the research and of the analysis. Additionally, if the research results in the secondary author relying on other secondary sources, then there is the compound effect of the potential bias of these further secondary sources as well as the skill or lack thereof of these other authors in research and analysis.

Another concern in dealing with any secondary source is the integrity of the author. When my family and I visited the Kit Carson home, which is now a museum in Taos, New Mexico, a good number of years ago, I visited with a staff member who told me about an author who at times would omit in a quotation the word "not" if necessary in order to prove his point. That type of perfidy by an historian is appalling. Rarely are what I regard as dishonest historians caught, but certainly there is the notorious case of Professor Michael A. Bellesiles who received the prestigious Bancroft Prize in American History in 2001. This was rescinded the next year.

As a lawyer, I have the required academic training in the law and I had to pass a bar examination before becoming a lawyer. Thereafter, I am always subject to discipline, including disbarment, for such offenses as lying to the court or misrepresenting the facts. In contrast, anyone can call himself or herself an historian and there is no one to discipline them if they misbehave. I do not believe there should be a disciplinary organization for historians comparable to that which lawyers are subject to, but it is certainly frustrating to see misrepresentation, whether done ignorantly or deliberately, of the facts from time to time in various writings. Unfortunately, at times some self-described historians are enabled by others to publicize their factually inaccurate writings, which an unsuspecting public accepts as gospel when it is anything but.

British historian Felipe Fernández-Armesto describes history as the "people's discipline" since it is "the only academic subject that demands no special professional training." After correctly acknowledging that a Ph.D. in history is not required to write well about history, he lists the "rare but accessible qualities" needed: "insatiable curiosity, critical intellect, disciplined imagination, indefatigability in the pursuit of truth" and getting to know the dead by studying the sources they left behind. An additional part of writing well about history is to write about what you know. He also observes: "History's accessibility to non-specialists makes it seem dangerously, delusively easy."[2]

On the subject of having a preconceived notion, I believe there are times that some authors decide that a certain historical subject was a bad person, and having already come to that conclusion, interpret all of the evidence that the authors locate in that negative light even if some of it might provide a different point of view. The analysis is thus clouded. Most human beings have complexities unique to them in their personalities and in their actions, and the role of a biographer is to attempt to sort out, to the extent possible, those various aspects, recognizing that some may not be reconcilable with each other. A person's flaws, however, should not negate recognition of his or her achievements just as the achievements should not be allowed to obscure the flaws.

Another important aspect is that when one is using a secondary source, one should not dip into the book without understanding the purpose of the book. The classic example is Stuart Creighton Miller who, as discussed in Chapter One of Volume One of this triology, created the poisonous tree which has damaged posthumously Fred's reputation. In his *"Benevolent Assimilation": The American Conquest of the Philippines, 1899-1903*, Miller does not attempt to provide an account of the history of the Philippine War. Instead, his purpose, as he stated in 2000, was to show the climate of opinion "based on both fact and fiction..." He further wrote: "I should have made it clear that I did not check the veracity of such [stories of less than civilized behavior on both sides]."

The result of Miller's lack of clarity in his book on his policy of non-verification of the truthfulness of sources is that users of this book rely that the accusations against Fred, such as his summarily executing twenty-four prisoners, are true, and they repeat them without qualification. The now deceased Professor Miller was in his fifties and a longtime historian when he published this book in 1982, and thus it is surprising that he lacked the acumen to clearly state his non-verification policy, which nearly twenty years later he clearly admitted. His *"Benevolent Assimilation"* has not only damaged Fred's reputation posthumously but damaged Miller's own as a credible historian. His account of the execution of twenty-four prisoners discussed above raises serious questions about his skill and integrity as a researcher. The damage to Miller's own reputation is a self-inflicted wound. In my eyes, his legacy as an historian is as the creator of the poisonous tree.

My practice, whenever possible, has been to obtain a copy, usually through inter-library loan, of each article and book so that I may read the original myself and form my own judgment about it in all respects. To do less makes me not only uncomfortable but I feel that I am not fulfilling my obligation as biographer. Unfortunately, it is not always possible to obtain the desired copy.

All of this discussion leads to the subject of the use of endnotes, footnotes, or none at all. Richard Taylor published his biography of Fred and Eda Funston in 2015: *Pain and Passion: The Lives and Times of Frederick Funston and Eda Blankhart*. The title alone is enough to give the reader pause because of the misspelling of Eda's maiden name, Blankart. It is not Blankhart as consistently spelled by Taylor. Then, on the first page of chapter One, Fred is described as having "twinkling grey eyes" yet three lines later as having "eyes dark brown." No need to read any farther in *Pain and Passion*.

There are no endnotes or footnotes in Taylor's book. Taylor justifies this in his "Notes on Sources": "This story is intended to make it readable and believable, unburdened from the format of a Ph.D. dissertation or academic exercise." I do not believe that providing the reader with notes that support the author's facts and statements is a "burden" nor do they burden a book from being "readable and believable." Readers who are not interested in sources can ignore the unobtrusive small-size note numbers in the text and skip the notes themselves, whether they are endnotes or footnotes. I personally have no confidence in a biography that lacks notes. Frequently, in reading a biographical study, I want to know where the author obtained certain facts and I check the notes accordingly. This becomes particularly important if what I am reading is relevant to a subject that I am working on.

Notes make an author accountable. In the current terminology, the author's work is transparent when it includes notes. This assumes, of course, that the content of each note is accurate and not fudged by the author. I do not deny that having a note to support each fact and for every assertion is a *lot of work* but it keeps an author honest to the benefit of the reader. If the author cannot find appropriate supporting material, then the alleged fact or assertion should not be included in the text.

In Chapter Two, Volume One, I criticize Mark Carnes for his 1998 article "Little Colonel Funston" where he asserted that Fred had a "stark lust for martial glory." There are so many errors in this article that I wrote to the editor of *American Heritage Magazine,* which had published Carnes's article in its September 1998 issue. One question I asked was why footnotes are not included in the magazine's articles. In response, the editor, Richard S. Snow, stated that from the beginning the editors "envisioned *American Heritage* as being directed at a lay audience, and thus thought it was inappropriate to include the scholarship apparatus of footnotes." I find this attitude condescending to the "layman" since it would appear that a layman would accept unquestionably whatever is in print in the magazine. Editor Snow did go on to note that the founders of the magazine "established rigorous fact-checking procedures" and enclosed a copy of an editor's note from 1993 to explain the procedure. According to this, the system "mandates that each word in each article be checked against the author's source and, should any conflict arise, against other sources." Naturally, in response to this letter with its enclosure, I wrote again to Editor Snow asking about six specific points in Carnes's article and what the source was for each one. I never received a response.

In the short author bio at the end of the article, Carnes is described as a Professor of History at Barnard College, Columbia University. It further notes that a version of the same essay appears in *Forgotten Heroes*, which consists of biographies of "notable but often overlooked Americans." This book was written by members of the Society of American Historians and edited by Susan Ware. It was published that same month of September 1998. I assumed that *Forgotten Heroes* would contain notes in each separate biography, including the one about Fred. Instead, not at all. There are no notes to support any alleged facts and conclusions. Thus, all of the errors in Carnes's biography of Fred are perpetuated in both magazine and book form.

Context is important with reference to a person's life. To the extent of available material, the world in which he or she grew up should be detailed. For Volume One of this trilogy, I was able, with much digging, to describe precisely much of the local world of Fred Funston's youth. This world was in Allen County, Kansas, and more specifically, in his part of it. At times, authors of biographies or histories might describe, say, life in rural eastern Kansas but since the actual facts of each part of eastern Kansas are not identical, this can lead to the wrong impression of what the actual environment was in the area in which the biographical subject grew up. The details of life even in adjoining towns such as Iola and Humboldt are not necessarily, and automatically, identical. Each is a unique creation.

I do all of my own research. After my "fluke" stroke in 2010 (a blood clot in a clear artery) which left me with only one functioning hand and mobility challenges, I hired a good friend, Rick Danley, to obtain copies of various materials locally, and a long time out-of-town good friend, Bill Crowe, did the same at the Kansas State Historical Society. Bill made many trips. All of this was done under my direction as to precisely what I wanted. Some authors use research assistants. In my opinion, likely even the best of such assistants undoubtedly do not know as much as the author does (or else they likely would be the one writing the book), and thus they may not recognize the importance of certain points or words in a primary source that the author would immediately recognize with the author's greater knowledge. Many a time I have recognized something significant in an article or document only because of my broad knowledge about Fred, and I could see immediately a clue that would lead me to new material or to new insight about Fred.

I should note here that Rick Danley, a highly learned person, is the source of the quotation in the title of this chapter. He not only helped on research but read and critiqued the original manuscript which covered all three trilogy volumes. Rick told me that he had learned many things in working with me, and the quotation in the title was one of them. He also noted that "you're absolutely succeeded in telling a STORY (a feat harder than it sounds).... [Y]ou were right in your decision to include so much of his primary work—his letters, his articles, etc. The union between your two voices—yours and Fred's, two sons of Allen County—contributes mightily to the vigor of the book."

Don't embellish the facts. A 2008 book review of a biography contained this compliment: "Also, Swift's book is mostly free of the kind of scriptwriter's parentheticals—*He strolled through the doorway, pausing to light a cigarette*—that some authors of historical nonfiction feel compelled to include, even though they are writing perhaps 100 years after the fact and didn't actually see the guy light the cigarette."[3] Bain in *Sitting in Darkness* described a United States Senate committee hearing chaired by Senator Henry Cabot Lodge. The witness leveled charges against Fred of committing atrocities in the Philippines. Bain wrote: "Lodge hustled the witness away as soon as he could manage."[4] The verb "hustled" has stuck with me ever since I read that book more than twenty years ago. I wondered what occurred factually to justify Bain's use of the word "hustled." As far as I can tell, there is no endnote on that point. My late good friend, John E. Miller, historian and author, read the first draft of the trilogy as far as it had been written at that time. He commented: "You can certainly see the lawyer in there. You don't say anything that you cannot support." This compliment has meant much to me, and I regret deeply that he is not alive to see the completion and publication of the trilogy.

Recently a friend asked me how I know when I am finished writing. There are two parts to my answer. First, I read the entire manuscript looking for any weaknesses in my arguments and for any essential topics not fully discussed or not discussed at all. Any I find I rework either by rewriting or by adding additional information or both. Then I read the complete manuscript one more time looking for any such weaknesses or inadequacies that I may have missed. Once I am satisfied that I have done the best that I can to support my narrative, I am ready for the second part. I read the manuscript straight through again, this time looking for continuous narrative flow. My prose should flow easily for the reader and thus without the reader stumbling over any words or sentences. If I get sidetracked by how I have worded a sentence, other readers most certainly will have the same problem. If a sentence simply does not work, I scrap it and start over with a new one. Once I am satisfied that my narrative flows "like an ever-rolling stream," and after a final reading of the complete manuscript, I call it quits. I have done the best that I can.

My final point is Time. The research and writing of this trilogy occurred over twenty-four years from 1995-2019, and in the three years since then I have refined and tweaked my work. My thinking about Fred has evolved during this period of time as I found more and more information and as I had the luxury of time to think about and evaluate its meaning as to who Fred Funston was. I was never under a deadline and thus my work was never rushed.

That was an unexpected benefit of my 2010 stroke since I was forced to give up much of the fabric of my life, including community service, local historical work, and public speaking on various subjects, including historical ones. My suddenly restricted world provided the opportunity to bring to fruition a project that matters greatly

209

to me. The progress of one's life is not pre-ordained. It is marked with unexpected twists and turns—some good, some not. I have always tried to do the best that I can in meeting both with grace, dignity, and a sense of humor.

In closing, I emphasize that the foregoing are simply my thoughts. Undoubtedly there are biographers and historians of integrity and skill who successfully follow different guidelines in creating their quality work. I commend them for it.

Researching and writing this trilogy has been a wonderful and fun experience. Thank you for spending part of your time with Fred and me.

Clyde W. Toland
Iola, Kansas
28th March 2022

Notes—Thoughts On Writing A Biography

1. Brian M. Linn, "Guerrilla Fighter: Frederick Funston in the Philippines, 1900-1901," *Kansas History*, Spring 1987.

2. Felipe Fernández-Armesto, "Faulty Navigators: Seeking to revolutionize views of the Age of Exploration, four books reveal more about the state of popular history," *The Wall Street Journal*, September 17-18, 2011.

3. Brian Burnes, "Before Jim Thorpe...," *The Kansas City Star*, August 10, 2008. Review of *Chief Bendex's Burden: The Silent Struggle of a Baseball Star* by Tom Swift.

4. David Haward Bain, *Sitting in Darkness: Americans in the Philippines* (Boston: Houghton Mifflin Co., 1984), 391.

APPENDIX A
Select Comments About Frederick Funston

In 1899, Charlie Scott described to a reporter his good friend: "'Although Gen. Funston is only 5 feet and 3 [sic] inches in height,' Mr. Scott said to me, 'his big head, sturdy shoulders and erect carriage do not leave the impression of a small man. He is modest. He is a ready and pleasing talker and a graphic writer. He knows Kipling by heart. He has the gift of the most delightful humor. He is a good judge of men and is a good business man. He is quick witted and resourceful. He does what he sets out to do, with an inflexible purpose; but he is not stubborn. And finally he loves his friends and his friends love him'" (R. M. Ruggles, "Leaves From The Diary of Gen. Funston's Eventful Life," unknown newspaper, May 11 [1899]) (FFP).

* * *

In 1904, Brigadier General Funston assumed command of the Army's Department of the Lakes. A Chicago newspaper described him thusly: "A small man in stature is Fred Funston—his name is Fred, not Frederick—his manners are most mild, his voice low, his face bearded, and when he looks at a caller with eyes that are clear and steady the soldier is not suggested so much as the shrewd, capable business man who has confidence in himself and is satisfied that he can successfully cope with an emergency. The effect is heightened because the general wears no uniform" ("General Funston Undecided," *The Iola Daily Register*, October 3, 1904, reprint from *The Chicago Record Herald*).

* * *

In Lawrence, Kansas, in 1908:

When seen by a Journal reporter General Funston, was just on his way to catch his train out of here. He is very genial and seemed to be feeling especially happy, it may have been because he just had finished breakfast. He looks much older than when he was last here and is considerable [sic] fleshier. He is the same old Fred Funston though without affectation and bears no outward sign that he is conscious of his place and power and of the distinction that is attached to his name.

"I think I was here five years ago," said General Funston, "But the last time that I remember distinctly about was when the Twentieth Kansas returned and I rode in the procession. I remember that especially because I kept thinking about how I was just a K. U. student a little before, and it seemed so queer to be riding in the procession...."

"You see I have been so far away, and I am really very glad to come back to Kansas for it means a great deal to me."

There is perhaps no other person in the United States army who occupies the same position as Fred Funston does, for he is still plain "Fred Funston" to many Kansans ("Funston Here," *Lawrence Daily Journal*, August 14, 1908).

* * *

Charles F. Scott in 1914: "There are a few more interesting men in the world with whom to spend an evening in friendly, personal conversation than Gen. Funston, for few men have had so varied and unusual and exciting a range of experience, and still fewer have so vivid and picturesque a style of narration. The old adage fails in his case, for nowhere is he more honored than here in his own country and among his own people, and nowhere is he more welcome when his public duties permit him to return" ("Not An Interview With Gen. Funston," *The Iola Daily Register,* December 11, 1914).

* * *

In 1941, at the dedication of a Kansas historical marker to be erected at the Funston homestead, William Allen White described Fred: "Fred Funston was kind and gay, but not carefree. Small in stature, but a giant in moral and physical courage, Fred Funston was extremely fond of telling jokes on himself. He was an inveterate self-deflationist." White concluded: "I can imagine that if Fred Funston were looking down on this gathering [of more than 1,000 people] today he would say to me, 'Billy, who would have thought that the state would erect a memorial marker to me, and that they'd think your worthy of making a speech dedicating it—what a laugh!'" ("Famous Family Honored," *The Iola Register*, October 27, 1941).

* * *

"You know your father lived a very strenuous life, and I wonder he survived as long as he did....

I have never forgotten your father's kindness to me, for he was always interested in my welfare. So anything I can do for you, I am glad to do" (Ella (Funston) Eckdall to her niece, Elizabeth "Betsy" Funston, December 23, 1953).

* * *

"Frederick Funston always, always was proud to tell people that he was a citizen of Iola and a citizen of Allen County, Kansas." Frank Funston Eckdall about his uncle on June 17, 1995, at the dedication of the restored Funston Home on the west side of the Iola town square.

Frank Funston Eckdall (1907-2000) and I enjoyed a warm friendship despite the forty-year difference in our ages. His mother, Ella (Funston) Eckdall, after Fred's death lit the torch of preserving and publicizing the story of her famous brother's life. When Ella became too old, her son Frank took the torch, and, in turn, when he became too old, the torch passed to me in the 1990s. Mr. Eckdall, as I always called him, was a pleasure to visit with. He told me that, as far as he was concerned, "The Toland family is a branch of the Funston family." I regard this as a high honor. I regret deeply that he did not live to see the completion of my Frederick Funston Trilogy. He did, however, know that I was writing a book on his uncle's early life and was pleased. In a 1998 interview with *The Iola Register*, the following conversation occurred:

> "I've always felt my uncle was a great man," Eckdall said. "To find someone like Clyde, who appreciated him like I do, was very special."
>
> Eckdall's daughter, Deborah Helmken, who accompanied her father to Iola, said Toland's knowledge of their relative was impressive and motivational when the museum project got under way.
>
> "He finally met his match," she said of her father's impression of Toland ("Funston's nephew is cheerleader for history," *The Iola Register,* June 1, 1998).

* * *

An Army nurse stationed at Fort Sam Houston, Texas, had the "privilege to have enjoyed [the Funstons'] hospitality in a delightfully informal way." In a lengthy letter to her mother, the nurse wrote about the General and Mrs. Funston:

"General Funston, the soldier, or "Fighting Fred," as he is called by his many admirers in the army is, in appearance, straight and soldierly, wears a closely trimmed beard and has iron-gray hair; his eyes are blue and can be stern, but usually have a merry twinkle in them as he has a keen sense of humor. He is a very approachable man; never forgets an old friend, and is very cordial to persons whom he meets for the first time, and yet carries himself with a great deal of dignity.

Mrs. Funston is young and beautiful, has dark hair and eyes and very brilliant coloring. Her carriage is queenly and she is greatly beloved by all of her friends....

The Funstons are devoted parents and their home life is delightful. They are both very simple and natural, caring not at all for the pomp and ceremony of their position. They entertain a great deal in a very informal way....

General Funston adores his family and daddy's home-coming is a joyful event and means playtime as the General can refuse them nothing, and Mrs. Funston has all the discipline in charge and she says the General is just another boy when with the children....

It was a very trying spring and summer [1916] for everybody at Fort Sam Houston, but the burden of responsibility rested upon the shoulders of our Commanding General. He never left the post without giving his exact location and telephone number, as there were times when the situation might have changed in an hour's time. His recreation and exercise was taken in his garden which he planted and weeded himself. Barbara shared her father's love for farming and being of an artistic nature, painted some of the General's white chickens blue. I had a garden too, and the General and I had many good laughs about our gardens, especially as the cut worms attacked both at the same time. The General made a determined campaign against them and he finally decided that the only way to exterminate cut worms was to get out at night with a lantern and meet and slaughter each worm.

He has a keen sense of humor and tells many amusing yarns at his own expense. He said upon landing in San Francisco from the Philippine Islands, he went into a barber shop to have his hair and beard trimmed. The barber eyed him rather sharply and after a time he said, "Do you know who I thought you were at first?" The General said, "No, who?" and the barber said, "That damned little false alarm Funston."...

His personality calls out great loyalty and support from the officers and men who surround him, and if the time comes when we cross the border and he leads the way, he will be cheerfully followed by the little army of men who have been the border patrol now for five long years....

Fort Sam Houston, March 1, 1917.

Since writing this letter our "Little General" has been called to a higher command and there are many sad hearts throughout the army. He was on duty to the last hour and cheerful and happy as usual.... His death was due to angina sclerosis or hardening of the muscles of the heart.

From the highest ranking officer to the humblest private the "Little General" was beloved by all. The solder telephone operator who gave the news of his death over the telephone sobbed as he repeated the message, "The General is dead" (Army nurse's letter to her mother dated February 2, 1917, with March 1, 1917, postscript, Frederick Funston Papers, Archives Division, Kansas State Historical Society).

* * *

"He had that American trinity of virtues—pluck, push and perseverance. Courage, endurance, energy, initiative, ambition, industry, good-cheer, sympathy—these were his attributes" ("Fighting Fred Funston" article).

* * *

"In every place he was sent, in every place where duty called him, he proved equal to any and every emergency that arose, and his rare tact and ability many times carried him and his command through dangers that would have overcome one less brave and resourceful.

He was absolutely self-made. No store of wealth was his, no sponsor stood for him, no godfather helped him to go to the front. He went there by his indomitable pluck, ability and perseverance, unaided and alone, and against difficulties that daunted other men[,] he made his way to the highest place in the military world" ("Funston," *Lawrence Daily Gazette*, February 20, 1917).

* * *

"But when the sun is setting low in the life of a parent, nothing brings such deep and unmixed joy to the heart as honor to one's child" (Edward H. Funston about his son, Fred Funston, on March 28, 1901, after receiving news about Fred's capture of Emilio Aguinaldo).

* * *

And, finally, in 1917, the Reverend William Kirk Guthrie, pastor of the First Presbyterian Church in San Francisco where the Funston family worshipped, observed at Funston's funeral: "His varied and interesting life of preparation, his career in the army, is known to you all; and while no man goes forward in this world of so many little jealousies, without being criticized by those he leaves behind, yet I think the final verdict must be that the honors he received, he deserved, and the high position he achieved, he earned" ("Body Is Buried In National Cemetery," *The San Francisco Examiner*, February 25, 1917).

215

APPENDIX B

The Letters of Winchester Dana Osgood and William Henry Cox

Other American *expedicionarios* wrote letters home from Cuba. Those written by Winchester Dana Osgood and William Henry Cox have survived through magazine and newspaper publications, respectively. They provide additional and interesting contemporary perspective on fighting for *Cuba Libre* and thus are printed here.

Biographical information about Osgood appears at the beginning of the Introduction in this book, and is repeated here. The most famous, at that time, of the *expedicionarios* was 25-year-old Winchester Dana Osgood, an outstanding amateur athlete. The son of an army officer, "Win" Osgood was a student at Cornell University first, and then at the University of Pennsylvania where he received bachelor's and master's degrees in civil engineering. He was "also a good French and Spanish scholar and was well versed in English literature." Osgood was a star football player, oarsman, bicyclist, tennis player, boxer, wrestler, and all-round gymnast. Known as the "American Firebrand," Osgood was the object of devotion by the Pennsylvania student body, whose cheer was "Who's good, Osgood, the whole damn team's good." This was shouted by the students even in the Chapel "under the Provost's nose." He belonged to a church and was greatly interested in the work of the Young Men's Christian Association.

Built like an Achilles, when Osgood stripped, he revealed almost perfect muscular development that rivaled that of his slightly older contemporary, Eugen Sandow, the famous German bodybuilder and showman, who today is considered the father of modern bodybuilding. Although Osgood possessed tremendous physical strength, he was a gentle and bashful soul. He neither smoked nor drank nor swore. He joined the Cuban Liberation Army primarily from a sense of fairness, a desire for adventure, and a liking for army life. He may also have sought to forget a failed romance. In joining the Cuban Liberation Army, football-great Osgood stated that he wanted to "get into the game." He was five feet, eight inches tall and weighed 160 pounds.

Win Osgood's father, Captain, later Brigadier General Henry B. Osgood (1843-1909), permitted publication of two of his deceased son's letters in the January 1897 issue of *The Red and Blue*, a publication of Win's alma mater, the University of Pennsylvania. In doing so, Captain Osgood wrote: "He died for human liberty, as some of his ancestors did, and while we mourn, we too rejoice that he had enough of the heroic in him to lead him to battle for the rights of an oppressed people whom he believed and I believe to be whole souled and heroic too. We trust that God will grant that his death be not in vain."

In publishing these letters in the February 1897 issue, there first appeared an introduction by George W. Orton, who had been Win's college friend before he left to fight for Cuban independence. Orton's introduction follows:

WINCHESTER DANA OSGOOD

Three times did the report come from Cuba that Osgood, Penn's old half-back and celebrated athlete, had been killed.

The first two proved unfounded, but, alas, his many sorrowing friends and admirers all over America are now convinced that this last report is only too true. Now, his fellow athletes and students, hundreds of whom are still in the University, look back with regret upon his many stirring deeds upon the gridiron and athletic field and are truly sorrowful that such a man has been cut off in the very flower of his youth. "Dear old Win," are the terms in which his fellow athletes speak of him; "Poor Osgood," those in which the general mass of students recall him. Yes, he was dear to all. And why? Because, not only was he an athlete of ideal calibre, and one unsurpassed in almost every branch of athletics, but his personal qualities were such as to command the respect and esteem of his many fellow students and the love and sympathy of his many friends. Osgood was in the first place and above all an earnest man. This was the mainspring of his nature. On the football field he bent all his energies to his task. As a student, he was thorough and well read, not only obtaining his M. S. in the Civil Engineering Department, but being also a good French and Spanish scholar and well versed in English Literature. In society, his earnestness gained him many friends, for that is a quality which appeals to all and which is only too rare in this *fin de siècle* age. To us, his brothers in Phi Gamma Delta, he was ever true. It seems so sad and sorrowful that he, of all persons, should be dead. Always so full of animal spirits and fun, his every motion and look prophesied long life and robust health. This he would doubtless have attained had not a treacherous Spanish bullet crushed out his life and thus cut short a career which promised so much.

For me, his room-mate in his final year at college and his fellow athlete, it is hard to believe him dead. I held out the contrary to the last. I did not attend the Fraternity meeting in which resolutions were drawn up over his death, copies of which were sent to his parents. I could not do so, as I then firmly believed that I should see his kindly face again. But later reports in confirmation of the earlier ones have left no room for doubt. He is indeed dead and lost beyond recall.

Kind readers and fellow students, think not of him as buried in Cuban soil or rotting in some marshy grave. Such thoughts were sacrilege. That Apollo form, those muscles fit to vie with those of Sandow or Hercules, that kindly beaming face and graceful carriage may indeed have gone the way of all flesh. But let us remember him as we all have seen him, flashing down the field for a touchdown or tackling as none other could, crossing the line a winner in the bicycle race, or a victor with the gloves or in a wrestling bout. Or again let him be remembered as the perfect gentleman, pure in word and deed, faithful to friends, gallant to ladies and courteous to all.

Thus shall I remember him in general, but in particular he shall be to me as at our last meeting.

I was opposed to his going to Cuba and thus was not taken into his confidence. The evening before his departure, he came up to my room to see me. I asked him for his photograph which he had promised me. He went down stairs and did not return for over half an hour. He then came back. "I have found you a photograph," said he. "I had to look through all my belongings to find it. You see, your old chum would still do a lot for you." He then said "Good bye" with much more affection than ordinarily, as I afterward remembered, and the next day he had set out for Cuba and was seen by me no more. To me, he shall always be as when he said that last farewell. The memory of that last hand clasp, the vision of that noble form, will remain with me forever.

George W. Orton

* * *

In Battle For The Freedom Of Cuba
Extracts from letters of Major Winchester Dana Osgood

At last it seems a proper time to write and tell you what we have been doing, for to-day, April 11, 1896, I receive my commission as Commandante in the Cuban army—the grade next above "Captain" and next to Colonel and corresponding to our Major. It has been hard and anxious work since I wrote you, "ashore Cuba" on the fly-leaf of that Spanish book, which, I suppose, you received in due time.

We landed on the north coast, coming ashore in broad daylight, having failed in the darkness to find the inlet which we intended to enter. The old Captain had the true spirit, for when we missed the break in the reef, he stood off until daybreak, and then ran the ship up to within half a mile of the shore and lay there until we had taken two boatloads ashore and gone back for the rest. It was nearly noon when we saw the ship vanish in the northern sky-line. I was the first man ashore and had to race and beat X. [probably William Henry Cox] to reach it first. He is the other young American who has come with the expedition to work the cannon, and together we are assigned to the cannon and hope to give a good account of it.

It is a latest pattern gun, and part of our ammunition for it is canister and part shell. In the total cargo, we had a good many rounds of rifle cartridges, part of them forty-three calibre, Spanish (instead of "Mauser," as I at first supposed), the rest Winchester, forty-four. The cannon, however, is the cynosure of admiration and has to be displayed at least a dozen times a day to the various visitors (many of them fair), who pay their compliments at camp. After we had safely *cached* all the arms and ammunition in the woods ashore we started inland, finding at last a deserted house surrounded by cocoanut trees, ripe fruit all ready for us. Marching further south, we came to an impassable "mangle" swamp and after suffering a day for water, we had to return at last to the house. Here we had to leave X. and B. exhausted, already having left S. sick at the beach with nothing but salt water. Then, marching to the west to avoid the mangle swamp, which I had reconnoitred [sic] from a tree top at the crest of a hill, our trail at last brought us out on the beach at a deserted hut of a fisherman, filled, however, with good barrels of rain water. We began to believe that the island was deserted and the loneliness seemed to the imagination such as would prevail on a plague-stricken derelict ship. These same lonely shores, however, were fairly alive with people four days later, when we found friends far inland.

It was fast growing dark and we had been marching since daylight, but here with so much good water we had to remember poor S., far down the beach sick and alone, with nothing but salt-water to drink, and so I found an old two gallon oil can with no top; half filling it, we slung it by a rope on our rifles and started on a two league march in the faint, new moonlight. Found the poor fellow asleep in the bottom of one of the boats, and very grateful for some water. Next morning we turned one of the boats and caulking with a shirt a hole we had chopped in the other, we sailed around into the inlet I had discovered, and up the seven miles to its extreme end without seeing a soul. In fact, every inch of the shore was lined with tangled "mangle," in which we hauled up and concealed the boat; slept in the swamps among the mosquitos [sic], each man building a fire in the circle; marched all the morning through the rain, and at last approached a house at which a party of horsemen were halted.

Our old commander shouted out *"Qui Vive?"* and I plumped a cartridge into my Winchester ready for a fight in case it should be *"Espana,"* but it was *"Cuba Libre,"* and we were soon in the arms of friends, hugging in the true Cuban fashion with a little pat on the back. And how they have treated us since then! —like lords; and it culminated last night at a grand camp banquet. President Cisneros at the head of the table; next General Roloff, General Rodrigues,

General Catillo (whom I sat opposite) Brigadier Santanna, Surgeon General Sanchez, and so on, twenty more. We "Expeditioners" had been called over in the afternoon and been formally thanked for distinguished services in a very pleasant speech by the President, and I had answered (they all speak English) that it was very pleasant to be so kindly appreciated, and we hoped this was but the beginning of greater and better services. And so they have made me a major —the consideration that I am a civil engineer, which always commands a captaincy, and that I am an American, has made it major.

We have a thousand men and more here, with two cannon and the determination, and, I pray God, the ability, to begin to roll back the Spaniards toward Havana, to tear them out root and branch and cast them into the sea. How earnestly belligerency is desired here I cannot describe to you, and it must ere this have passed, although we have as yet no definite news. I sleep in a hammock, with my revolver always round my waist and the stars of heaven overhead.

The other night I dreamed of home and went to church with mother, and dreaming that, as in the Catholic church, the minister was sprinkling us with holy water, awoke and found the dew drops falling on my face.

It is a very happy, free and lovely life, and we soon hope to get some fighting. I bought a horse the other day for $2.25. Have you heard the Spanish report that they had captured and killed us and thrown our bodies in the water? Of course it is a lie like all their reports. They are just as Sherman said of the South—a "shell," and soon it will hatch and Cuba Libre will emerge. We have adapted "Vive, vive Cuba Libre" "Dios and Libertad" to the tune of "John Brown," and it has captured the camp "hang General Weyler on a wassima tree" (Cuban elm). That our army is "bandits and niggers" is another cursed Spanish lie. They are the most whole-souled and generous lot of gentlemen that I have ever met. That they may be tattered may be true, but that is no one's fault but Spain's, and the fact is history that Washington's troops were tattered too. We are just on the verge of the rainy season, but that it will not extinguish the bright, fierce glow of Cuban liberty, but, on the reverse, the last Spanish spark of hope that she may ever reshackle the glorious "Queen of the Antilles."

* * *

[July 5, 1896] Again comes a red letter day. They assure us at the government that they have sure and speedy communication with the States. Just here our chief of artillery came over to tell me that there were letters for me, and I flew over to headquarters and was overjoyed, almost overcome, by receiving eight. Indeed, they were a very great joy, and I feel that the only way I can answer all their love and affection is by returning home some happy day instead of living out here the rest of my life, as I have sometimes contemplated. Have been waiting these two days to find out where I am to be sent in the general shuffle about to ensue. I have been temporarily attached to the artillery, but am accounted an engineer (my own great preference), and by latest inside information from General Roloff, Secretary of War, am to be placed in command and in position to permanently organize an efficient engineer corps, which we found to be a fatal fault at the last battle.

Yes, I have been in action at last and five times under fire already. Pity 'tis, 'tis true, and that we did not take the fort, but we could and would have with any but the commander we had. He told us American artillerists that we were "*loco*" (mad) when we wanted to storm the place with dynamite after two days' shelling but we were not *cowards*, as we proved at the guns within seven hundred yards of the fort, when with three of our men shot down we silenced their fire, and only retired after firing our last cartridge.

L. [Latrobe?] and I on the second day circled round the fort within four hundred yards, not a shot fired at us so cowed were the Spaniards; entered their wharf storehouse on the edge of the canal 200 yards from fort, sacked it of a great boat load of stores and provisions and set it afire.

You need not worry a particle about the yellow fever for the Cubans do not have it at all. It never appears in their camps which are in the open country, only in the cities and camps of the Spaniards near the salt water. The rainy season is upon us and I was soaked to the skin for two hours the other day on the march. It doesn't hurt me though, the climate is so mild. The rain only comes in the afternoon when it is a blessed relief and the nights are very calm and serene, just made for pleasant sleep. I have learned Spanish with what I consider a very creditable swiftness and can always get the gist of what is said to me and can speak better still for my college work stands me in good stead, being able to read anything.

Tell the boys that they are missing the chance of their lives not helping to fight for Cuban freedom. This makes the twelfth successful expedition, not a single one having been stopped by the Spaniards. I must hurry, for we march in another hour. We all do hope and pray you will soon pass "Belligerency" and then give us more substantial aid—that we wanderers may get home again. We are hoping that the next opening season will end the war, for [filibustering] expeditions are landing every ten days or so. Do give us "Belligerency" and let us finish the work and get home...."

My tender love to all at home and hope to soon be with you there...

WIN D. OSGOOD.

July fifth, the last line written before the fatal fight.

* * *

Win Osgood was killed on October 18, 1896, during the siege of Guaimaro. In the spring of 1897, the University of Pennsylvania placed a brass tablet above the fireplace in the Trophy Room of Houston Hall. The tablet was in memory of Winchester Dana Osgood, noting that he is "One of Freedom's Heroes" and then stating "Truth, purity, justice and honor have need of just such examples to win for them all the world as willing followers." Nearby was hung a large picture of Osgood in his baseball suit. In describing this in the college booklet, *The Red and Blue*, the writer, after noting the bravery of the man who fights for his own country, observed that "still braver is the man who lays down his life that a country, other than his own, may have freedom from the tyrant. Osgood was great as a scholar, athlete and soldier, and is a worthy example for college men" (*The Red and Blue*, June 1897). All information from *The Red and Blue*, except for this concluding paragraph, which is courtesy of the Hathi Trust.

WILLIAM HENRY COX

William Henry Cox went to Cuba with Win Osgood on the filibuster ship *Commodore*, which left Philadelphia on March 6, 1896. He wrote several letters home, which were published in Philadelphia newspapers.

* * *

On March 19, "Will" Cox wrote his mother while still on board ship. This letter was published in an article in *The Philadelphia Inquirer* on April 18, 1896:

There is no longer any doubt where the absent Sergeant William H. Cox and several of his comrades of Battery A. National Guards, of this city, have gone. They are in Cuba helping to fight the battle for liberty. Included in the party is the former half-back of the University of Pennsylvania football team, W. D. Osgood. They left here on the 6th of last month, going first to Charleston, S.C. Some of them had been shadowed by Spanish spies but they succeeded in eluding them at the last and most important movement.

"We left here on last Friday week," says her son, "going to Charleston, where we stopped for several days. We went on board the steamer Commodore on Monday last [March 9]. Tuesday morning steamed out into the harbor and cast anchor. On Wednesday had such a storm that we expected we would go to pieces.

222

HOPEFUL OF VICTORY

"Left Thursday night and put to sea. Part of the voyage the waves seemed as high as a house. I was not sick. There are nine in our party—not including myself. Osgood, of the Pennsylvania University, is with us. Expect to land to-night (the 19ᵗʰ). It has been an eventful trip thus far and I cannot tell you all as I have not a minute to spare. Had to write this in the galley and can't keep it as clean as I would like to. Remember me to all my friends and when Cuba is free will once more see you again. With my best regards to all. From your son, Will."

The newspaper included at the end of the article "Young Cox's Record":

Young Cox is 23 years of age, is of athletic build, stands 5 feet 11 inches, and weighs about 140 pounds. He has always been of the strictest temperate habits, cool headed, considering well all he did. He is a member of the Church of the Covenant, at Twenty-seventh and Girard avenue, and was one of the foot ball team composed of young men of that congregation. He was a fast runner and had won medals at athletic sports attending excursions of the church.

This was his first enlistment in Battery A, and his second year. He went to camp at Gettysburg as a private and was soon made a corporal. He was promoted to the sergeancy without an examination being required of him. He is said to be a skillful marksman.

* * *

The next letter published by *The Philadelphia Inquirer* was on April 22, 1896. The letter was "dated in the field, about twenty-four miles southwest from Nuevitas, Puerto Principe":

"At last," he says, "I have the opportunity of writing you. We landed on the coast about three miles east of the town of Neuvitas. We had to transport the ammunition in two small boats from the ship and then the nearest to the shore we could get was a square and a half. The eight of us worked hard all day and by evening had unloaded eleven tons of ammunition and one Hochkiss [sic] mountain cannon. We had to wade through the water up to our shoulders. It took all day to unload all the boats and at night we were very tired.

"We hid the ammunition in the woods and went to sleep. The next morning we started out to find the Cuban army. We marched for three miles along a dry, sandy beach and every time we would step our feet would sink at least six inches. Further on we had to go through the swamps, sometimes crawling and then climbing over trunks of trees. Finally we reached a farm-house on the side of a mountain. Here one of our party gave out, for we had no water all day and the sun was

223

scorching hot. We lived on sweet potatoes for five days.

"Later on we marched to the beach to take the ammunition to the troops. All night we loaded horses. The next day we marched fifteen miles and that night fifteen miles more. Our party are special guests of Brigadier-General Santana, Commanders Sanchez and Rodriguez. They have treated us like princes. We sleep in hammocks under large palm and mangoes [sic] trees. This is the greatest expedition yet. Eight men landing eleven tons of ammunition. The greatest before was the Roloff expedition, landing 150 men and eight tons of war material [sic]. The people here almost worship us. They have made me a teniente, or lieutenant, with two horses and an assistant, or servant. We are now camping here awaiting the arrival of the President—Ciseneros—and the Lieutenant-General and Governor-General.

"Word was received this morning that the United States had recognized the belligerency. My goodness, how the men hugged each other! A Spanish paper has just reached us from Havana. It says that the Commodore expedition party had been captured and all hands killed. So, according to it, I am dead. The Spaniards are awful liars. They do not go over the country trying to find the Cubans. They remain in the forts and wait for us to come along. About fifteen of our men attacked a Spanish column of cavalry the other day and they—200 of them—turned their horses and made for the fort. The meat we eat is killed right in our sight.

"Osgood, the football player of the University, tells me I am getting fat. He is all right. Every day we ride to the creek to take a bath. Everywhere we go we ride. Our horses are saddled all the time. They are very small, about the size of our mustangs, but they can go all day long and not get tired. I cannot go on describing these things any more, except to say that this is the ideal spot on earth."

* * *

Cox next wrote from Las Tunas on April 10, 1896 (published in *The Philadelphia Inquirer* on March 19, 1897):

"It has been a little over a month since we left Charleston. I think we left on the 8th of March, and landed on the 19th. I have become entirely Cuban in color and manner, except I am not an expert with a machette [sic]. I wish you could see one of these fellows swing them. I have seen them cut a head clean off of a bull or steer running wild in a field. Trees that we would take an axe to they cut down with the machette [sic], but they are matched by the Spaniards with the Mauser rifle, the bullets from which will go clear through a man. We have quite a number of men who have bullet wounds completely through them.

224

"Cuba they pronounce as if it was Kooba. The streams here are filled with fish, a species of bass, and you can catch any amount of them."

* * *

An extract of Cox's letter of May 2, 1896, was published on July 11, 1896, in *The Philadelphia Times:*

"We are having hard times in this section of the country. There is very little to eat, and necessitates our riding out of camp for something to eat. Sometimes we have a ride of thirty or forty miles to obtain a breakfast from some poor farmer in the country. Then we get a few borneatoes (sweet potatoes), yukas (a root something like our white potatoes), and some meat that has been dried in the sun. For supper to-night we had two bananas baked in the ashes of our campfire. We are waiting in this wretched district for General Garcia, who landed here with an expedition from New York, and will probably be here in a couple of days.

"It rains here every day so hard that you can hardly distinguish objects 100 yards away. Just think of it, rain for four months every day. I will at least have the satisfaction of having a good shower bath.

"Yesterday, on our way out of camp, we had some trouble with the guards, and when we arrived back in camp we were all ordered under arrest for intimidating the guards. We were going to shoot the guards for insubordination, and they reported that we had refused to surrender our passes. When we had explained the case at headquarters we were released. We expect to have a hard fight in a few days. There is a column of Spaniards moving this way, and we expect to meet them. If we are successful and defeat them we will move on and try to take the town of Puerte [sic] Principe. We have reports of General Maceo taking the town of Pin del Rio (in the western part of Cuba) and capturing 1,100 rifles and two cannon, and putting the Spaniards to fight. From present indications the war will last a year yet. I have made many friends here among rich tobacco planters and cane-raisers and can obtain almost anything I desire if I only ask for it. They are very nice people and look upon an American as a supreme being."

* * *

On May 26, 1896, Cox wrote a further letter, an extract of which appeared in *The Philadelphia Inquirer* of March 19, 1897:

"We have been having some very hard marches, having marched to Baracoa, the easternmost end of the island, and are now on our way back to civilization. We shall have rain now every day until October, and the rains are so dense that you cannot see thirty feet from you. Words fail to express the condition of our roads, with mud up to our horses' shoulders.

"I have seen as many as 500 dead horses, and I walked my horse on their dead bodies in order to save my own horse. I have three horses at present, all good ones. My favorite is a black stallion, which I caught wild and have tamed just enough to ride him. He is a corker and can jump like a breeze. We have some very high mountains here in the East, and many times have I been above the clouds. Descending on horseback is something that ordinary mortals do not take pleasure in. Before the rainy season we used to march about twenty leagues a day, but now we can only march about ten. We saddle up about 3 A. M. and march until sunset."

* * *

In his letter dated August 11, 1896 (extract published in *The Philadelphia Inquirer* of March 19, 1897), Cox wrote:

"We have just reached Laiaga, on the Cauto River, after a month's march in the mountains of Santiago de Cuba, but, thank God, we are in the open country again, where there is more to eat. I am feeling miserable, having been quite sick, but now I am better and ready to fight. General Gomez is here with us, and we expect to enter some town near here in a few days. I have received a number of letters and I hear there are others for me, but they have not been able to reach me. Tell my friends to write as often as they can. Osgood had a letter a few days ago, and he was disappointed because there were no more. I had a very narrow escape the other day. We were coming down a steep hill, and at the bottom was a mountain stream with a swift current. The path was slippery and my horse went down, dragging me into the stream. The current turned us over and over. My leg was caught in the stirrup, and there we were, sometimes the horse on top of the water and sometimes myself. But at last I managed to loosen the stirrup and crawl to the bank, exhausted and feeling half-dead. I want to give you a pointer—stake all you can on the next issue of Cuban bonds. This is a dead sure thing for the insurgents, it only being a matter of time.

SPANIARDS DESERT

"The Spanish soldiers are continually deserting and coming to our ranks, not out of sympathy, but to get something to eat. In the larger towns the soldiers have scarcely anything to eat, and have not been paid for six or eight months. Their clothes are ragged and they need shoes badly. I wish you would go out to the battery and see the boys and tell the captain I will write to him at the next opportunity."

* * *

An extract of a letter written in November 1896 by Cox appeared in the *St. Louis Globe-Democrat* on February 8, 1897:

"You complain of hard times in the United States, but you should see the people of Cuba, and then you would not complain. Even the armies are in a bad state. I do not know which one is the worse off, although the Spanish soldiers beg in many of the towns. We take what we want. Personally, I have suffered much for lack of food, or rather a lack of the proper kinds. It is hard to be well and live happy on three principal things, meat, fruit and sugar cane. Meat is the main food, and I hope when I leave here never to see any more of it."

* * *

Cox celebrated Christmas Day of 1896 at "Bayoms [sic: probably Bayoma], province Santiago de Cuba" by writing to friends in the Pennsylvania National Guard Battery A that he had belonged to before departing for Cuba. *The Philadelphia Inquirer* appears to have published the entire letter in its issue of February 8, 1897. Since Cox and Fred Funston fought together as artillerymen starting in October 1896, Funston would likely have been involved in the events Cox described, including the machete charge:

"With me in my battery, I have had three Americans, but one is now in the hospital suffering from serious wounds. My dear, brave friend, Osgood, was killed in a furious fight we had more than two months since. He carried himself like the true American soldier he was and fell in the thickest of battle. Poor fellow, we mourn him sadly, for in him we lost a staunch friend and the most fearless, dashing spirit in our midst. And his taking off was felt keenly by the insurgents, too, for they idolized him.

MULES AS GUN-BEARERS
"Of the twelve Aericans who came here with us three have been severely wounded and one was killed. Our artillery is something quite different from anything you fellows have been accustomed to handle. All we have here are three twelve-pound Briggs-Schroeder guns and three Hotchkiss two-pounders, all of them breech-loaders. We do not move them on the regular gun carriages, but carry them fastened on the backs of little mules, the piece being on one, the trail on another and the wheels on a third mule. We have no caissons, but carry our ammunition carefully strapped to the backs of mules.

"In all our experience here the fighting has been one-sided. You cannot imagine anything like these dare-devil Cubans. Often I have seen eighteen or twenty insurgent cavalrymen dash into a body of from 800 to 900 Spaniards and cut them down like grass.

DARE-DEVIL FIGHTING

"One fight I remember particularly. A party of perhaps six or seven hundred Spanish troops were quietly resting in a small valley when only sixteen insurgents dashed into their midst, taking them completely by surprise. In an incredibly short time the Cubans killed over one hundred Spaniards, wounded as many more and the rest of the cowardly skulks scattered and made their escape as best they could. The Cubans captured a great quantity of arms, ammunition and provisions, which they carefully stored away in the hills.

"The wounded Spanish soldiers, after surrendering, received proper attention and afterward were given their liberty. Not a single Cuban was killed in this wild charge, yet when the official statement of the fight was made public by the Spanish they had the nerve to give the insurgent loss as 168, while the Spanish had seven wounded and one mule killed. When the paper was read and interpreted to us we roared with laughter over the report, for it seemed ridiculously funny to us after we had been eye-witnesses to the occurrence.

THE COWARDLY SPANIARDS

"I have been near enough to the Spanish troops on several occasions to see the color of their eyes, and I can assure you they are a sorry, half-starved-looking lot. One day when our guns had been delayed I took part in a machete charge and had my horse shot from under me within fifteen yards of the enemy. I unsaddled and went to the rear, but by the time I had secured another horse the cavalry charge was over.

"While I am writing this letter we are lying in wait for a Spanish column that is skirmishing about in this vicinity, so we are likely to have some fighting before I finish writing. We had a rattling hot engagement day before yesterday and, as usual, came out on top. Those Spanish ducks are all at sea over our artillery and get beside themselves when our birds commence to sing. They can stand for ordinary rifles or machetes, but they dread a sight of the field pieces and the 'Los Americanos' who handle them.

"Kindly give my regards to all the boys of the Battery and tell them that Battery A will never be dishonored by William H. Cox, for up to this time I have had no fear of a Spanish bullet and I don't think I ever will."

Cox has since been promoted to major, vice Osgood.

* * *

An extract of a letter written by Cox on January 30, 1897, appeared in the *St. Louis Globe-Democrat* of February 8, 1897:

"There is a vast improvement in our condition, and the army is certainly in pretty good form just now. We are receiving more arms and other munitions of war, although just how they get there no one seems to know. The higher officers are, of course, aware of the expeditions that bring us such substantial re-enforcements, but I understand an order was given by Gomez some time ago that there should be as much care exercised in the matter of information at this end of the line as at the other. Of course, there are traitors here, but they are not known. Occasionally one is given away, and you do not need to be told what the treatment is.

Everybody in the ranks feels better this month than ever before, and the spirit of fight is becoming stronger daily. You would be surprised at the number of recruits who offer themselves every day, and in all parts of the country. The Spanish army is in a fearful condition. The men are losing heart each day. Some of the battalions which are favorites are well treated in comparison with the others, but as an army I am sure there is much discontent and suffering."

* * *

As to Will Cox's future after fighting in Cuba, Fred Funston wrote in 1910 that he understood that Cox was running a truck farm near Kansas City. I know nothing further about him.

UPDATED ACKNOWLEDGMENTS
for *Becoming Frederick Funston Trilogy*

My great thanks to the following:

Members of the Funston family: first and foremost for their invaluable assistance and friendship, the late Frank Funston Eckdall and his daughter, Deborah (Eckdall) Helmken. Also, Martine Funston, Ellen (Lees) Stolte, the late Don Funston, Dale Funston, and the late Greta Funston. Each of these assisted me in one or more essential ways. Although she died long before I started work on this trilogy in 1995, I am grateful to Fred Funston's sister, Ella (Funston) Eckdall, whose writings and scrapbooks on her brother's life provided much important material and, at times, information that otherwise would have been lost forever.

Mitchell family: Burt Bowlus, grandnephew of Lida (Mitchell) Funston, mother of Fred Funston.

Brenda Cash, Resource Sharing Head, Southeast Kansas Library System, performed great work obtaining through interlibrary loan numerous essential materials. Also, Roger Carswell, then-Director of Iola Public Library, for an essential item that he obtained.

In 2010, a "fluke" stroke left me with only one functioning hand and mobility challenges. My longtime friend, Bill Crowe, made innumerable trips to the Kansas State Historical Society, Topeka, Kansas, to review various collections and to obtain copies of needed materials for this trilogy.

Rick Danley worked for me part-time from 2016-2019. He helped me organize and use my ever-growing collection of materials; checked microfilm at the Iola Public Library; and read and helpfully critiqued the entire trilogy manuscript after its completion.

John E. Miller, historian, professor, and author, who died unexpectedly in 2020, my friend since graduate school days in history at the University of Wisconsin-Madison. John read several years ago the manuscript as completed to that date and validated the worthwhileness of this work.

Jarrett Robinson, my comrade in arms for more than twenty-five years in our belief in the importance of preserving and publicizing the details of the life of a worthy man, Fred Funston. Among other help, Jarrett shared with me helpful "finds" on the early years of Funston's life. Jarrett also was a great sounding board on certain chapters of volume three.

Members of my family helped in various ways: Nancy, my wife, in multiple ways, including proposing the title of *Heat and Ice* for Volume 2; David Toland, our son, and his wife, Beth Toland; Elizabeth (Toland) Smith, our daughter, and her husband, Bart Smith; and our grandchildren, Caroline Toland and William Toland.

Bob Hawk prepared the excellent map showing Fred Funston's route through Alaska and British Northwest Territory and the map of Cuba, and assisted with the technical aspects of numerous photographs. Bob, long an admirer of Fred Funston, played an essential role in the creation of the Funston Home Museum and the Funston Museum and Visitors' Center.

American Hero, Kansas Heritage was made possible in part by the Center for Kansas Studies, Washburn University, Topeka, Kansas, which funded formatting and design costs. Carol Yoho used her valuable computer and design skills on this book, including its cover. And special thanks to Thomas Fox Averill, noted Kansas author and emeritus professor of English at Washburn University, whose belief in this book made its publication a reality and who provided great editorial assistance.

As to *Heat and Ice*, the Center for Kansas Studies provided additional financial support; Tom Averill continued his support and editorial role; and Carol Yoho again did the formatting. In their respective roles, they all hung in there for the long haul with "*Yankee Hero.*"

Amy Albright, professional graphics designer, was responsible for the covers for volumes two and three.

Thea Rademacher, JD, owner of Flint Hills Publishing, Topeka, Kansas, enthusiastically published volumes one, two, and three.

Andres Rabinovich translated Prats-Lerma's crucial account about Funston's Cuban military experiences.

Barbara Diehl faithfully typed nearly all of my manuscript from my handwritten draft, and made changes and corrections in the typed draft, and Terri Jackman faithfully typed the balance and made needed changes and corrections throughout the typed draft.

For their help: Sally Huskey, Richard Zahn, Ed Fitzpatrick, Margaret Robb, the late Dorothy (Carnine) Scott, the late Emerson and Mickey Lynn, the late Winifred Bicknell, Scott Jordan, the late Ed Kelly, William Berry, Donna and the late Ray Houser, and Don Kubler. Also, Katherine Crowe, Curator of Special Collections & Archives at University of Denver Libraries; Gary LaValley, Archivist for the United

States Naval Academy; Kurtis Russell, Executive Director of Allen County Historical Society, Inc.; and Allen County Register of Deeds Jacque Webb and her successor, Cara Barkdoll.

The excellent staff at Kenneth Spencer Research Library, including Becky Schulte, Sherry Williams, the late Mary Hawkins, and Kathy Lafferty; Barry Bunch of University Archives; Kevin L. Smith, Director of Libraries; Brian D. Moss, Head Reference Librarian, all at the University of Kansas.

Tim Horning of University Archives, University of Pennsylvania.

The excellent staffs at Manuscript Division, Library of Congress; Kansas State Historical Society; Special Collections and Archives, Emporia State University; Lyon County History Center & Historical Society; Elwyn B. Robinson Department of Special Collections, Chester Fritz Library, University of North Dakota; Government Documents, North Dakota State University; Department of Rare Books and Special Collections, Princeton University Library; The Rutherford B. Hayes Presidential Library and Museum; American History Center, University of Wyoming; Smithsonian Institution Archives; U. S. Army Heritage & Education Center, Carlisle, Pennsylvania; Special Collection, Sheridan Libraries, Johns Hopkins University; and the Kansas Supreme Court Law Library.

My parents, the late June and Stanley Toland, encouraged and supported my interest in history starting in my childhood. I am definitely a product of that influence, and I shall always be grateful to them.

Funston Museum Complex, Iola, Kansas

Lifesize statue of Major General Frederick Funston stands in front of the Funston Museum and Visitors' Center. A semi-circle of five flags frames the statue. The five flags are of four states of importance in Funston's life: Ohio, California, Alaska (then a territory), and Texas, and the fifth is the revolutionary flag of Cuba.

To the right is the Funston Home Museum and, not visible, the United States flag and the Kansas flag.

5'4" Major General Frederick Funston and his biographer, 6' Clyde Toland wearing a Funston Museum cap, and bowing in salute. Taken after the dedication at the Funston museum complex on a cold, rainy October day in 2006 of the statue of Frederick Funston as Colonel of the Twentieth Kansas Volunteers.

BIBLIOGRAPHY

Collections

Allen County Historical Society, Inc., Iola, Kansas
Collection of Frederick Funston's letters from Cuba and New York City (photocopy)

Emporia State University, Emporia, Kansas
William Allen White Collection

Kansas State Historical Society
Charles A. Arand Papers
Joseph L. Bristow Papers
Frederick Funston Papers (Manuscript Collection 33, and Microfilm: MS75 – MS77)
Homer M. Limbird Papers

Library of Congress, Manuscript Division
Osmun Latrobe Papers
Frank Ross McCoy Papers
Leonard Wood Papers

National Archives and Records Administration
Frederick Funston combined military service record, 20th Kansas Infantry, Spanish-American War

Scrapbooks

Allen County Historical Society, Inc., Iola, Kansas
Eckdall Scrapbook III (photocopy)

Spencer Research Library, University of Kansas
Wilder Stevens Metcalf and Frederick Funston With the Twentieth Kansas in the Philippines During the Spanish-American War

Manuscript

Potter, David, *Frederick Funston: A First Class Fighting Man: A Biography* (Department of Rare Books and Special Collections, Princeton University Library)

Select Books and Articles

"A Kansas Cuban Soldier," *The Iola Register*, December 25, 1896 (reprint from *The Kansas City Star*, December 13, 1896).

Auxier, George W., "The Propaganda Activities Of The Cuban *Junta* In Precipitating The Spanish-American War, 1895-1898," *The Hispanic American Historical Review*, August 1939.

"Brigadier-General Frederick Funston," *The Literary Digest*, Vol. XVIII, No. 19 (May 13, 1899).

"Colonel Frederick Funston Gives Some Facts About Cuba," *The St. Louis Republic*, February 7, 1898.

"Colonel Funston's Cuban Record," *The Evening Herald*, Ottawa, Kansas, August 23, 1898.

"Creelman On Funston," *The Iola Daily Register*, April 4, 1901.

Crouch, Thomas W., *A Yankee Guerrillero: Frederick Funston and the Cuban Insurrection, 1896-1897* (Memphis State University Press, 1975).

"Daring Little Col. Funston," *The New York Times,* April 30, 1899.

Fenn, Emory W., "Ten Months With The Cuban Insurgents," *Century Magazine*, June 1898.

Flint, Grover, *Marching with Gomez: A War Correspondent's Field Note–Book Kept During Four Months With The Cuban Army* (Honolulu, Hawaii: University Press of the Pacific, 2004, reprinted from 1898 edition).

"Fred Funston, Darling of the Gods," *The Kansas City Star*, March 19, 1916.

"Fred Funston's Restless Life of Adventure," *The Chicago Sunday Tribune*, May 7, 1899.

"Frederick Funston," *Harper's Weekly*, March 5, 1898.

"Funston, Brig. Gen., U.S.V.," *The Kansas City Star*, May 7, 1899.

"Funston, Fearless Fighter and Tactful Chief, Seen at Close Range," *The New York Times Magazine Section*, Section Five, February 25, 1917.

Funston, Frederick, "Desmayo—The Cuban Balaklava," *Harper's Weekly,* March 5, 1898.

Funston, Frederick, *Memories of Two Wars: Cuban and Philippine Experiences* (New York: Charles Scribner's Sons, 1914).

Gleed, C. S., eulogy, "Report of Select Committee," *Journal of the House*, Hall of the House of Representatives, Topeka, Kansas, February 26, 1917.

Gleed, Charles S., "Romance And Reality In A Single Life. Gen. Frederick Funston," *The Cosmopolitan Illustrated Monthly Magazine*, July 1899.

Gonzales, N.G., *In Darkest Cuba: Two Months' Service Under Gomez Along The Trocha From The Caribbean To The Bahama Channel* (Columbia, S.C.: The State Company, 1922; reprint by Forgotten Books, 2015).

Hancock, H. Irving, "General Frederick Funston," *Leslie's Weekly Illustrated*, October 28, 1899.

"How Funston Left Cuba," *The Kansas City Star,* September 4, 1898.

Joyce, Arthur Royal, "New Stories of Funston's Exploits In Cuba," *The Kansas City Times*, October 29, 1899.

Latrobe, Osmun, "The Fight at Guaimaro and the Death of Winchester Dana Osgood," *The General Magazine and Historical Chronicle*, Vol. XXXIV, number 4, July 1932 (University of Pennsylvania alumni publication).

Merchan, Rafael M., Gonzalo de Quesada, F. G. Pierra, and Ricardo J. Navarro, *Free Cuba: Her Oppression, Struggle for Liberty, History, And Present Condition* (Publisher's Union, 1897).

Musgrave, George Clarke, *Under Three Flags In Cuba: A Personal Account of the Cuban Insurrection and Spanish-American War* (Boston: Little, Brown, and Company, 1899; reprint by Forgotten Books, 2012).

Nichols, Ode C., "Funston, From Babyhood to Present Day as His Mother Knows Him," *The World*, May 21, 1899.

O'Brien, John, and Horace Smith, *A Captain Unafraid: The Strange Adventures of Dynamite Johnny O'Brien* (New York and London: Harper & Brothers Publishers, MCMXII) (Biblio Life Reproduction Service).

Oswald, Felix, "A Guerilla Eden," *The North American Review*, March 1896.

Prats-Lerma, Armando, "La Actuación del Teniente Coronel Frederick Funston, (Norteamericano) en la Guerra de Independencia de 1895-1898," *Boletin del Ejercito* (Habana, Cuba, Noviembre y Diciembre de 1931).

Quesada, Gonzalo de, and Henry Davenport Northrop, *The War In Cuba: Being A Full Account Of Her Great Struggle For Freedom* (Chicago: Monarch Book Company, 1896).

Reno, George, "Operating An 'Underground' Route To Cuba," *The Cosmopolitan Illustrated Monthly Magazine*, August 1899.

Rickenbach , Richard V., "Filibustering with the 'Dauntless,'" *The Florida Historical Quarterly,* Vol. XXVIII, Number 4, April 1950.

Roberts, Andrew, *Churchill: Walking with Destiny* (Viking, 2018).

Rubens, Horatio S., *Liberty: The Story of Cuba* (New York: Brewer, Warren & Putnam Inc., 1932).

Rubens, Horatio S., "The Insurgent Government of Cuba," *The North American Review*, May 1896.

Ruggles, R. M., "Leaves From The Diary of Gen. Funston's Eventful Life" (unknown newspaper), datelined May 11 [1899].

Scott, Charles F., "Frederick Funston," *The Independent*, April 11, 1901.

Scott, Chas. F., "Remarkable Career of a Kansas Boy," *Mail and Breeze* (about March 20, 1898).

Steep, Thomas White, "Funston's Comrade Tells Of Fighter's Days in Rags," *New York Tribune,* February 20, 1917.

Tone, John Lawrence, *War and Genocide in Cuba, 1895-1898* (Chapel Hill, The University of North Carolina, 2006).

Webster, Frank Lundy, "Mexican Coffee Bean Was Lucky Stone That Carried Funston On Road To Fame," *The Denver Post*, February 25, 1917.

White, William Allen, *The Autobiography of William Allen White* (New York: The Macmillan Company, 1946).

White, William Allen, "The Hero Of The Philippines*," The St. Louis Republic Magazine Section*, May 21, 1899.

Wright, Marcus F. (General), *The Official and Pictorial Record of the Story of American Expansion Portraying the Crowning Achievements of the McKinley – Roosevelt Administrations* (War Records Office, Washington, D.C., 1904).

Young, Louis Stanley, and Henry Davenport Northrop, *Life and Heroic Deeds of Admiral Dewey* (Philadelphia: Globe Publishing Co., 1899).